Acclaim for DONO

Aftermath: The Remnants of War

"This powerful book describes how today's wars inflict horrifying scars on the landscapes and people of countries for generations. The soldiers go home, the guns are silenced, the tanks are rolled back, but the killing and maiming goes on from the millions of unexploded bombs, shells and landmines that lie hidden in fields and woods until some unsuspecting footstep or plow's blade triggers them. Donovan Webster takes us to these battlegrounds to confront the aftermath of war in all its terrifying forms, a reality of life today for people in scores of countries. He reminds us that just as we have too often laid waste to the Earth in pursuit of some short-term political gain, we also have a responsibility to save it." —Senator Patrick Leahy

"Engrossing. . . . Webster describes the sites he visited in prose that is measured and never overwrought, suffused with more sadness than anger. He is not a crusader, but one who has seen firsthand something that is both intractable and deadly." —*Cleveland Plain-Dealer*

"In his vividly reported, dismaying book, Donovan Webster charts the growing horror of the 'aftermath' of his title." —*Los Angeles Times*

"A powerful and troubling piece of reporting, starkly detailing five of this century's battlefields whereupon the pollution of warfare, much of it still murderous, is appallingly apparent. Webster is an astute witness." —*Toronto Globe and Mail*

DONOVAN WEBSTER

Aftermath: The Remnants of War

Donovan Webster has written for *The New Yorker*, *Smithsonian Magazine*, and *National Geographic*. He lives in Charlottesville, Virginia. This is his first book.

AFTERMATH

The Remnants of War

DONOVAN WEBSTER

Vintage Books
A Division of Random House, Inc.
New York

For Janet

FIRST VINTAGE BOOKS EDITION, MAY 1998

Copyright © 1996 by Donovan Webster

All rights reserved under International and Pan-American Copyright Conventions.
Published in the United States by Vintage Books, a division of Random House, Inc.,
New York, and simultaneously in Canada by Random House of Canada Limited,
Toronto. Originally published in hardcover in the United States by Pantheon Books,
a division of Random House, Inc., New York, in 1996.

A portion of this work was originally published, in a slightly different form, in
Smithsonian Magazine, February 1994.

The Library of Congress has cataloged the Pantheon edition as follows:
Webster, Donovan.
Aftermath: the remnants of war/Donovan Webster.
p. cm.
Inclused bibliographical references.
ISBN 0-679-43195-0
1. War.   2. War—Psychological aspects.   3. War and society.
I. Title.
U21.2.W392   1996
355.02'8—dc20
96-7649
CIP
Vintage ISBN: 0-679-75153-X

Author photograph © Dick Kane
Book design by Jo Metsch

Random House Web address: www.randomhouse.com

Printed in the United States of America
10   9   8

CONTENTS

AFTERMATH

Prometheus

BEGINNING OF THE CENTURY

ON APRIL 13, 1888, when Alfred B. Nobel—a Swedish chemist living in Paris—awoke to read the morning newspaper, he found his own obituary. Mistakenly run in place of one for his older brother, Ludwig (who'd died the day before in Russia), the item left Nobel stunned.

The obituary vilified him as the man responsible for Europe's recently dizzying arms race, singling him out not as a wonder scientist and industrialist without peer but for being, literally, the Merchant of Death. The reclusive Nobel—who had become enormously wealthy as the inventor of dynamite, blasting caps, smokeless gunpowder, and blasting gelatin—was deeply shaken to learn his life's work had produced such a reaction against him: his own view of his achievements was quite different.

Today it is inconceivable that Nobel could have considered himself anything but a modern-day Prometheus. Despite nine centuries of gunpowder — beginning when Chinese miners discovered its central element, potassium nitrate, around the year 900 — weaponry had not really changed until Nobel's discoveries boosted the bloody art of war from bullets and bayonets to long-range high explosives in less than twenty-four years, forever altering the way armies killed one another.

A NATIVE OF Stockholm, Nobel was born into a family of inventors. In 1851, at eighteen, he began his travels to Russia and the United States as an apprentice to established inventors and engineers. One of these was John Ericcson, an American naval engineer and creator of the *Monitor*, used in the U.S. Civil War and famous as the first armored warship. After four years of study, the young Nobel returned home, immediately joining his father, Immanuel, in his engineering business. (The elder Nobel's most famous ideas were probably the first viable sea mines, which he produced for the Russians, and the first household hot water heater.)

At home, Alfred became fascinated by nitroglycerine. A clear liquid concocted in 1847 by the Italian chemist Ascanio Sobrero, nitroglycerine was extremely unpredictable at room temperatures, often exploding ferociously when shaken. In 1862, Nobel set himself the task of making nitroglycerine safer. Within a month he had invented the blasting cap: a small gunpowder charge topped by a length of fuse. When a blasting cap was attached to a sealed tube of nitroglycerine and its fuse was lit, miners and engineers had time to leave a blast zone before the blasting cap's smaller, "primary" explosion set off the more powerful nitroglycerine. The invention earned the thirty-year-old Nobel his first explosives patent. Millions of "Nobel's Igniters" would be sold to mining and construction firms worldwide.

Yet nitroglycerine remained touchy to handle and transport. So Nobel kept working to make it safer. Unfortunately, his tests were not without tragedy. One morning in 1864, while Nobel and his father were away, the Nobel factory was destroyed in an explosion that killed all its workers, including Nobel's twenty-one-year-old brother, Emil. The senior Nobel was heartbroken; he suffered a stroke and never recovered. Alfred only hardened his resolve to puzzle away nitroglycerine's dangers.

Forbidden by the Swedish government to rebuild his factory, Nobel decided to leave solid land behind and took to the water, creating a floating factory on a harbor barge outside Stockholm, where he began experimenting once again. Two years later—and completely by accident—Nobel discovered some spilled nitroglycerine inside a shipping box. The liquid had been absorbed by a claylike packing material called *kieselguhr*, and the result could be handled safely without losing any of its rage. After testing his findings—using blasting caps to detonate a few piles of it—Nobel began packaging his discovery in paper-wrapped sticks he called dynamite (from the Greek *dynamis*, meaning power). It was a product that changed the world. Harnessing the force of dynamite, men mined ores and coal quickly and safely, carved out harbors and the Panama Canal, blew stumps effortlessly from farmers' fields, and punched highways and railroads through mountains. New jobs and whole industries were created, and the global monetary order expanded in explosive bounds. Thanks to dynamite, an industrial world where raw materials were converted to salable goods sprouted overnight, and nations with natural resources to exploit became instantly—and appreciably—richer.

So on that morning in 1888 when Nobel read of his own death, the obituary reviled him not so much for dynamite but for his variations on dynamite's theme. He had invented blasting gelatin in 1876, a more powerful semi-solid explosive that withstood storage without decomposing as dynamite did. It had become the payload of choice in artillery shells. He developed the world's first low-smoke gunpowder, ballastite, in 1884. It was nearly as strong as dynamite yet far less expensive, making it —and its British variation, cordite—perfect for small-bore artillery shells, an advance that further hurried the European arms race. He had also invented colloided—or smokeless— gunpowder in 1887. Revisiting one of his failed dynamite theories, Nobel tried soaking bits of cotton in nitroglycerine ("colloiding" it). Then he dried the cotton and mixed it into gunpowder. The result was far more explosive than either ballastite or common black powder, and it produced far less smoke. Inside of a year, Nobel's smokeless powder not only had artillery shells and bullets traveling farther when shot, it had a simultaneous effect on battlefield dress as well. Coming from an age when thick clouds of cannon and rifle smoke obscured vision, soldier's uniforms had been designed for visibility. They were red or bright blue—often with white diagonal accents and brass buttons—to be better seen on cloud-draped battlefields.

With smokeless powder, the opposition was suddenly visible across a battlefield's reach, making whole armies easy targets for the more efficient weapons, inspiring the drab greens and browns of today's military dress.

The obituary plunged Nobel into a depression that did not lift for months. Out of this despondency came a plan to rescue his name for eternity. In the years following his death, his estate would give annual cash awards to outstanding men of science, literature, and peace. These, he decided, would be called the Nobel Prizes. In the last years of his life, embittered by the way his inventions had destroyed his happiness even as they made him among the wealthiest men on earth, Nobel renounced all explosive experiments and many of his 350 patents. In their place, he became obsessed with the study of a newly discovered piece of the universe. A tiny, mysterious thing, Nobel felt it was a building block whose power could only elevate life for everyone on earth. He had become fascinated by the atom.

ALFRED B. NOBEL died on December 10, 1896, spiritually broken and completely alone. A life-long bachelor, he had no wives, lovers, or children. No one was at his side—neither siblings nor servants—when a heart attack killed him as he waited for breakfast in his villa outside San Remo, Italy.

Even in his last days, Nobel called war "the horror of all horrors, and the greatest of all crimes." Until the moment he died, he remained convinced his creations could save the world from war, not make killing more efficient. "My factories may make an end of war sooner than your Congresses," he wrote to peace crusader Bertha Von Suttner in 1892, "because the day that two armies have the capacity to annihilate each other within a few seconds, it is likely that all civilized nations will turn their backs on warfare."

One hundred years after his death, if blaming Nobel for today's instruments of war is something like cursing Henry Ford for air pollution, it is important to remember that although refinements have been made to most of Nobel's creations, none has ever been discarded. Variations on dynamite, cordite, and blasting gelatin, for example, are still used in field artillery shells, land and sea mines, and bombs dropped from aircraft. As for the blasting cap, although the charge inside its cylinder has been upgraded (to hotter-burning lead azide), the impact fuzes in most modern bombs and artillery shells still resemble what Nobel invented in 1862. Today's smokeless powder—despite modern nitro-compounds and manufactured flakes instead of crumbly potassium nitrate—still rests on Nobel's idea of adding nitroglycerine to common gunpowder. Fifty years after his death, when the searing breath of nuclear weapons was first unleashed at Trinity Site, New Mexico, in 1945, even *those* roots were in Nobel: the atomic chain reaction blast took its model from the two-stage explosion first exhibited by a Nobel's Igniter in 1862. And in unwitting homage to the igniter's creator, when the time came to detonate the first nuclear bomb, cordite was its primary-explosion trigger.

Regardless of his end-of-life renunciations, the work of Alfred Nobel, a solitary man laboring alone on a barge outside Stockholm's harbor, altered the world. The chain of technology Nobel initiated has led to more than 100 million deaths by war since he died, making this—by hundreds of times—the bloodiest century in the history of the world.

The remnants of these wars exist as unexploded artillery shells and swaths of buried land mines. They drift as sea mines in oceans and molder as dead soldiers left unburied beneath forest leaves. They even lace the soil with invisible death: dirt made poison by radioactivity from nuclear tests, blasts that render land uninhabitable for millennia. The weapons we have warred with, and their effects on the world's landscape and cultures, have become our century's most prevalent history. Only now, at century's end, can we begin to sift through the past and discern a trajectory that begins with Alfred Nobel, arcs through the nuclear age, and ends in the stockpiles we have labored to create for wars still unfought.

1

A Forbidden Forest

FRANCE, 1914-1918

SIX OF US are walking through a dense forest just outside the French city of Verdun, 160 miles east of Paris. Scattered across the uneven ground, in and among the still existent bomb craters and trench lines, unexploded artillery shells from World War I are everywhere. A 170-millimeter shell (long as a man's leg, big around as his thigh) rests like a leaf-swaddled child at the edge of a bomb crater.

A few steps away, at the top of a trench, sits a stockpile of 75-millimeter shells, the most widely used artillery pieces of the war. From today's perspective — seventy-five years after the war's end — they resemble nothing so much as a stack of corroded hairspray cans. One by one, the rusted, moss-blanketed shells are lifted from their sleep and transferred to our trucks.

In a nearby foxhole are a dozen German grenades: the "rac-

11

quet type," which means their baseball-size explosive charges are lashed to foot-long (now rotted) throwing sticks of wood. They look like potato mashers, which is what American soldiers came to nickname them. One by one, their remains are scooped up and carried to the trucks.

All around me, the *démineurs*—or "deminers," as France's weapons disposal experts are called—are clearing the forest of explosives, carrying them to the cargo beds of four-wheel-drive Land Rover trucks we've driven into this forest. Each man wears the uniform of France's Département du Déminage: blue coveralls made from special antistatic flannel, their pant legs tucked into the tops of high rubber boots. Each *démineur's* hands are covered by thick rubber gloves, as protection against any toxic substances—mustard gas or phosgene or chlorine— that might seep through the rusted shells to blister or kill them instantly.

The *démineurs* work steadily and efficiently. They lift the shells from their long sleep on the forest floor and, careful not to trip over tree roots or rusty trench wires as they walk to the vehicles, they gently lower each shell into the wooden transport racks at the backs of the Land Rovers. After three hours, I survey the area they've been clearing. There are still shells everywhere: they seem no fewer than when the *démineurs* started this morning. I walk off, beneath the limbs of the beech trees, moving into a section of forest said to have already been cleared.

These forests were home to some of World War I's worst fighting. In November 1918, in fact, just after the Armistice, the hills above Verdun were so thick with unexploded shells and

grenades (plus the uncollected dead) that the French government simply closed them off. When the fencing was over,
nearly 16 million acres across France were off limits, including
the almost 2 million acres we are in today. The French call
these boundaries the Cordon Rouge, the "Red Line," and the
land inside has been closed ever since. Today, fences posted
with big, red-lettered TERRAIN INTERDIT ("forbidden ground")
signs still ring this Zone Rouge. We are, literally, inside a forbidden forest. After the war, not even local farmers could return to collect whatever belongings might have survived—not
that there would have been much.

The sector of the Zone Rouge we're in today is called the
Vaux Forest, named for Fort Vaux, a French stronghold that
once stood nearby. The "forest" part of this name is new, however, since back in 1918 there were no trees here. In fact, on
November 11, 1918, the day of the Armistice agreement, this
part of France had endured two years of almost nonstop
shelling and flame-thrower attacks; there wasn't a tree for
miles. The tall beeches I stand under today were paid for by
the Germans after the war, as one of the terms of the truce.

Today, three-quarters of a century later, the trees are strong
and old. They've grown up among the trenches and unexploded shells, and sixty feet overhead the day's breeze has autumn's leaves fluttering in the canopy. At my feet, a trench
winds across the earth, a remnant of the 12,000 linear miles of
trenches that twisted across northern France during World
War I. It is deeper than a man is tall, and its path is gnarled
and kinked so that, if a German machine gunner somehow
made it inside, he couldn't wipe out whole French divisions by

its exposed nose, seeing if it budges beneath the tree's grip. When it doesn't move, their faces lengthen. They look one another in the eye, talking in quick bursts. "Do we blow it up here?" one of them wonders aloud.

"No," Bélot says. "We can get it out."

Bélot dispatches one of the *démineurs*, a twenty-fivish thickset blond named Christian Cleret, to the Land Rovers for a shovel. As Cleret disappears, Bélot tells me a little about the shell. The paint on the outside has been corroded off, so it is impossible to know whether it contains cordite, explosive powder, or toxic chemicals. "If a toxic shell is exploded in this forest," he says, smiling, "the poison gas becomes hard to control." Bélot also tells me that even if the shell is the standard variety the caustic explosive inside has spent the past half-century melding with the shell's iron skin, a circumstance that makes it far more volatile than normal. "You scratch this one with a shovel," he says, "and maybe *boom*."

Also, as with all fired but unexploded ordnance, something is amiss. Or, as Bélot puts it, "This shell has a secret." For some reason, it didn't go off after being fired in 1916 or 1918. There is likely a problem somewhere along the pathway between the shell's detonator and its blasting cap. "It could be a big malfunction," Bélot says, "so this is completely dead. Or it could be a small problem, and moving this shell will revive its memory." He shrugs. "Usually, it's a big problem, but you never know."

A minute later, Cleret returns through the woods, carrying the shovel. He begins to spade—slowly, gingerly—around the tree's roots. A minute passes and the roots are eased back.

Clods of rust-streaked dirt fall to the forest floor. In a few more seconds, Cleret drops the shovel and, slipping on his rubber gloves, begins to ease the shell from the home it has had since the age of horse-drawn carriages. He's lifting the shell now, straining, breathing heavily. Another of the *démineurs* tells Cleret that he's coming to help; he wants to be sure there's no miscommunication beforehand. They lift and steady the shell, which weighs about a hundred pounds. Finally, the shell is free of the roots, and the two *démineurs* slowly lower its base to the ground.

"C'est le *Minenwerfer*," Cleret says, "explosif." This is a 250-millimeter shell from a German *Minenwerfer* cannon. It contains no toxic gas; instead, it carries ninety pounds of high explosive. The shell's flaking, corroded skin meets sunlight for the first time since 1918, and the air fills with its scent. It smells old and damp, like the darkest corner of an unused basement. Cobwebs come to mind. Cleret rests for a moment, then—on the count of three—he and the other *démineur* hoist the shell and slowly, being sure not to stumble, begin walking toward the trucks.

It is almost lunch time, so the other *démineurs* head toward the trucks, too, picking up shells as they go. There is a shell at the edge of an explosion crater. And another over there, in the trench, next to that rusted canteen. As I follow Bélot through this forest, World War I seems more recent—and far more real—than Neil Armstrong's stroll across the moon. We come across a damp, slick-looking 105-millimeter shell, big as a mackerel, among the downed leaves. Bélot slips on his rubber gloves and lifts it, carrying it against his body like a newborn child. We continue on, headed across the fallen leaves and explosion craters toward the truck.

As we follow the edge of a trench, I spot a bronzy-looking flat spot on the ground: a 155-millimeter artillery shell. A third larger than the 105 Bélot carries, it is flush with the leaf-paved forest floor. Bélot stares at the shell's skin for a moment, assessing it. He nods a few times. "Impact must have driven this one deep into the soil," he says. "Now, like stones that pop up in a farmer's field each spring, it has worked back to the surface."

I kneel and start to claw the earth away from the shell.

"No, no," Bélot says. "Leave that one. It could be dangerous. We'll get to it sooner or later. We have plenty of time."

THE FRENCH INTERIOR Ministry estimates that, more than seventy-five years after the close of World War I, 12 million unexploded shells from that conflict still sleep in the soil near Verdun. Millions more await discovery in the World War I battle zones along the rivers Marne and Somme, southwest and northwest of Verdun. Millions of undiscovered shells from World War II remain embedded in the beaches of Normandy and Brittany. As do long-forgotten sea mines in waters surrounding France. As do unexploded remnants of World War II's Allied campaign from the Normandy beaches and into Germany. Everywhere in France—in potato fields and orchards, under town squares and back porches—the fallout from two world wars has turned the soil into an enormous booby trap.

After World War I, France was so nationally decimated it

could conjure no workers to clear its land, so the unexploded weapons and artillery shells simply lay where they had fallen. It was not until after the close of World War II, in 1946, that the nation again was strong enough to establish its Département du Déminage. Since that time, more than 630 *démineurs* have died in the line of duty, and the department has collected and destroyed more than 18 million artillery shells, 10 million grenades, 600,000 bombs dropped from aircraft, and 600,000 underwater mines. Through these efforts, more than 2 million acres of France have now been reclaimed from the explosive and toxic tools of war. Still, many more acres remain littered with unexploded weapons and are cordoned off. The Déminage also warns that, because not all explosives are found during the ground-clearing process, even places considered safe may spit up unexploded ordnance. Thirty-six farmers died in 1991 alone when their machinery hit uncollected shells. That same year, the only recent one in which a tally was kept, fifty-one other civilians were injured when they happened on a bomb or shell unexpectedly. Consequently, the *démineurs*—123 men in eighteen districts stretching the length and breadth of France—continue to clean the place up.

We are now at lunch, six *démineurs* and myself, in a little Alsatian restaurant in the village of Eix-Abaucort, a wide spot in the road between Verdun and Metz. The mustard yellow building looks more German than French, like a life-sized cuckoo clock. Outside, it has a high-peaked roof and gingerbread balcony. Inside, the decor leans to thick wooden beams and pastoral murals, which have been painted directly onto the plaster walls. Everything about this place says: Germany. Which is understandable, considering that, in the past 200 years, this part of what is now France's Alsace-Lorraine has been warred over, captured, and rechristened as Germany or France no fewer than four times. The salad has arrived: all the *démineurs* sit around one table; they are all having herring soaked in white wine, along with a beer aperitif.

I've been driven directly to the restaurant by Bélot. The other *démineurs* arrived a few minutes later. They had to drop off the morning's collection of shells at the depot, where they also changed into street clothes. Bélot changed out of his coveralls while we were back in the forest, explaining to me in shouts from behind a tree that the Département du Déminage wishes not to alarm citizens, so *démineurs* always wear casual clothes in public. "It is unwise to imply we're working so close to civilian homes," he said. "It makes people nervous to know so many explosives are nearby."

In 1991 and 1992, one of the *démineurs* says, as the French national railway began to dig a new bed for its TGV bullet train—for a line that one day would connect Paris and London via the Channel Tunnel—the *démineurs* of that district, home to the battlefields of the Somme, were on constant duty, with daily collections of five tons of shells and bombs being the norm. Miraculously, no *démineur* was injured on this project. The same record cannot be claimed by the project's excavation machinery, however. Four front-end loaders were destroyed by buried ordnance, as were a number of earth movers.

Bélot then tells of another explosion last winter. Five lumberjacks were working in the steep hills of the Argonne Forest, not far from Verdun, and another site of fierce fighting in the

Great War, and it began to snow, so the lumberjacks built a fire
to warm up. "They set their fire over a shell that was just beneath the dirt's surface," he says. "*Boom.* All of the lumberjacks
were killed."

Just a few months ago, another *démineur* chimes in, in
Caen, near the Normandy beaches, an English-made airplane
bomb from World War II—500 pounds and the size of a bath-
tub—was unearthed by a construction crew. That type of bomb
has two detonators: a primary one, which didn't work in this
case but is designed to explode on impact; and a secondary
one, which was still operative and which explodes if the fallen
bomb is moved after hitting the ground. For the people of
Caen, the find provided some excitement, since the bomb had
to be destroyed on the spot. A local farmer donated a few hundred bales of hay, which the *démineurs* used to build a tall enclosure around the site. Then, after clearing the area, the
démineurs attached plastic explosives to the shell and piled a
ton of sand on top of it to muffle the noise. Then they blew it
up. The concussion shook the town, cracking windows and
loosening red clay roof tiles for blocks. When it was over, as the
démineurs dismantled the straw enclosure—bits of steaming
shell fragments embedded in the bales—they also distributed
damage claim forms.

Baskets of bread arrive, as do bottles of red wine. Bélot tells
me the eighteen Déminage zones across France reach from
northernmost Dunkirk, on the English Channel, to the
beaches of the Mediterranean. About 80 percent of the bombs
and shells, however, come from northeastern France, in a crescent that extends from the English Channel to Nancy, just

south of Metz. Not surprisingly, that crescent follows the curve of the French–German border. Bélot pauses for a moment to sip his wine, then says, "The shells don't just come from the two world wars. Once in a while, we find one from the Franco-Prussian War."

From the War of 1870? I ask.

"Oh, sure," another *démineur* says. "In that war, both armies used observation balloons tied behind the battle lines. That way, military tacticians could ascend and gain a vantage, which helped planning for future offensives. Both armies had phosphorous artillery shells as well, which could burn up the balloons. About a month ago, Christian and I found a phosphorous shell in the forest, and we were taking it back to the depot with the rest of our load when we hit a bump in the road and everything shifted. Something banged a hole in the phosphorous shell, and it lit up the back of the truck with flames, spraying fire everywhere."

Everyone around the table begins smiling and chuckling.

"We were driving down the road," he continues, his wine-glass waving casually in the air, "with more than a ton of bombs in the back of the truck—and one of the shells spitting fire. So Christian pulled out a fire extinguisher, and he started spraying. There was enough explosive in that truck to level any village we were driving through. We had to keep going. But it was very dangerous."

What's the *démineurs'* least-favorite type of shell? I ask.

"The toxic ones," they all say.

I ask why.

"Two reasons," Bélot says. He lifts his right hand into the air, holding it as if he's gripping something loosely. "First, you never know how solid their skins are. They are often very rusty, so they may leak gas and kill you as you lift them. Also, they are harder to destroy."

To destroy the usual explosive shells, I am told, deep pits are dug, which the *démineurs* then fill partway with the bombs and shells they've collected. After that, they attach plastic explosives to the top of the pile and blow the whole thing up. "The blast is directed straight into the air," another of the *démineurs* says. "No one gets hurt—"

"—but with the toxic ones," Bélot adds, "we have to take very special precautions. It is very difficult. Very secret. It happens at Le Crotoy. It is something you'll be shown. You'll see."

We eat. A few minutes pass. From outside, the hardened gold of late September sunshine streams through the windows. The chicken is tender and delicate; the wine tastes firm and tart against the cream sauce. As we clean our plates, I ask how many *démineurs* were killed or injured last year. Bélot says that five were killed and another eleven were hurt. "It was a good year," he says. "We didn't lose too many."

Then Bélot takes a final bite of his chicken and after swallowing it says, "Every day, you can die. It's something you remember each morning. You never know when. You can't anticipate it. Out there is a shell with your name on it. Today, if you lift it, you are in the past." (Shortly after our time together, Bélot was gravely injured when poison gas from a rusted shell leaked beneath his gas mask. Though he survived and returned to work, he has never recovered completely.)

Christian Cleret puts down his silverware. He lifts a piece of bread, takes a bite, and points the remainder of the slice at me. "It's very sad when one of us dies," he says, "since all the other *démineurs* know him. There are so few of us, we've all become friends. We see each other at briefings and official meetings. We sometimes see each other at the detonating depots, where we blow up the shells we've collected. We come to know each other's families. When one of us dies, we have lost a member of our family."

Then, for a long minute, no one says anything more. I look around the table; everyone has finished eating. All of the men are staring down at their plates.

AFTER LUNCH, BACK in the forest, the *démineurs* have returned to their coveralls; everyone is working. As Bélot walks beneath the tree limbs, lifting shells and carrying them back to the Land Rovers, I follow. He hoists a German 105-millimeter shell the size of a fireplace log and cradles it in both hands as he heads for the truck. As we approach the Land Rover, he stops walking and tells me to put my ear close to the shell. He tilts it up and back in the air, and from inside comes a sloshy, *swish-swish* noise.

"That's the mustard gas," he says. He tells me that although the poison in each toxic shell is called "gas," it is generally a liquid inside the shell that becomes vaporized at the moment of explosion. Bélot places the shell into the truck's rack, then slips a wooden shim beneath it, securing it solidly. "We find 900 tons of shells a year," he says. "About 30 tons of those are toxic." With his gloved hand, Bélot scrubs the shell's dirty, rusty skin. Its gritty patina falls away, and three stripes of white paint become faintly visible on the shell's body. He points at the rings. "These mean toxic," he says.

As we return to the woods, Bélot explains the philosophy of toxic artillery. Intended as a strategic, area-denial tool, the Germans used it first: near Ypres, Belgium, in 1915. They would "toxic-barrage" a strategic area—such as a crossroad or rail junction—not in hopes of killing vast numbers of troops, but to keep the enemy out. Then, after the poison dissolved and became inert, which took about a month, the Germans would move in and control the zone.

Bélot bends to lift another 105 shell from the earth. "But like much in World War I," he says, his voice wavering as he lifts the shell, "things grew perverted. The Germans started shelling French troops with gas. And, of course, the French retaliated. Which is how infantries on both sides learned of hell on earth."

Before the war was over, Bélot says, 100,000 tons of toxic materiel were deployed, killing 91,000 soldiers and permanently wounding more than a million others. As we begin walking back to the truck, Bélot is shaking his head. "Every day, I thank God the war didn't last longer," he says. "If the Americans hadn't driven the Germans back and forced the Armistice, General Pershing's army had twice the toxic weapons of all other nations combined. He planned to use them."

We deliver another shell to the Land Rover, and before we return to the woods again, Bélot stops and leans against the truck. He smiles and stares into the trees. "I doubt we'll ever clear these forests completely," he says. "We haven't even got-

ten to the big shells yet. They're still deep in the ground."
Then he tells me of the Paris Guns, train-mounted German
cannons that fired 2,200–pound shells. The Train Guns, as
they were also called, required 100 soldiers to operate. Once
fired, their shells returned to earth at twice the speed of sound,
and the Département du Déminage estimates that unexploded
shells from the Paris Guns are still sixty feet underground —
scattered across the Zone Rouge and beyond. "They're slowly
working to the surface," Bélot says. He turns and looks at the afternoon's growing pile of shells inside the truck. He shrugs and
smiles. "Any dreams France has of farming this land in the next
century," he says, "they are just that: dreams."

As we head into the woods again, Bélot says that while the
task of clearing these long uninhabited forests is interesting, it
is more controlled than most of the Déminage's cleanups
around France. To get a more accurate picture of how history
intersects with today, he says, I should visit a place where civilians and weapons coexist. For that, I should visit the Marne.

IN BOTH WORLD wars, the German plan of attack into
France was the same: strike fast and hard, slamming down out
of Belgium in the north while bleeding the French with a second front along the Alsace-Lorraine provinces to the east. It
was a strategy that had been around since 1905, when a German general named Schlieffen invented it to spur an increasingly imperialist Kaiser Wilhelm. As everyone knows, after
receiving Schlieffen's plan, the Kaiser meditated on it for more
than a decade before — in a terrorist attack — his cousin Arch-

duke Franz Ferdinand was assassinated in Sarajevo, setting off an elaborate series of alliances that culminated in the First World War.

In World War I, the Schlieffen Plan didn't work. Thanks to massive sacrifices by French and British forces, the Germans were staved off at Amiens and Reims in the north, and at Verdun to the east. The result was a war of attrition. Two armed and opposing forces—each millions of men strong—dug in with trenches, then launched themselves at one another to see who would sacrifice more lives before surrendering. In World War II, however, the German attack worked so well—and so quickly—that France surrendered unconditionally within a month.

In both wars, the northern battlefront met its eastern counterpart at the deep, wide valley of the Marne River. The brown and furrowed earth in this part of France is nearly shaved of trees, and in every direction I can see the horizon as it bends against the dark, stormy-looking sky. It is harvest time, and the fields are full of large pieces of farm machinery, threshers and diggers. The farmers in this region serve up much of France's food; its potatoes, sugar beets, and wheat come from here, as do its apples, cheese, and chocolate. Its wars come from here as well. In this century alone, battlefronts have moved through the area four different times. And the remnants are everywhere.

I am with another Département du Déminage Land Rover, rolling through the flat farmland just north of the Marne, ninety miles northeast of Paris. We are on a straight, empty two-lane right now, moving along a low ridge between sugar beet fields. We are heading toward a tiny village called

Chevry/Val, but it is taking us longer to get there than planned, since we have to keep making stops. Every mile or so, a bomb or artillery shell stands along the road like a miniature, dirt-crusted obelisk. Each shell has been uncovered by a farmer, who has to climb down from his harvester, lift the thing from his furrow lines, and lug it to the roadside. The *démineurs* call these finds "incidentals."

A *démineur* named Rémy Deleuze is telling me the history of this road between the fields. It is called the Chemin des Dames—the "Ladies' Way"—and it got its name from King Louis XV's daughters, who once used it for carriage rides through the countryside. It was also the site of two major battles in World War I. The first was in February 1917, when, after nearly three years of fighting, the northern-tier German attack progressed this far—about thirty miles—into France. It was here, along the Chemin des Dames, that the French and British troops finally halted the German advance. By the morning of February 15, 1917, the Allies had stabilized battle enough for a counteroffensive. To repel the Germans, the French and British rained an estimated 11 million artillery shells on their enemy in a single day. The bombardment did little damage. The Germans were well fortified (one of their trenches even had a small-gauge railroad built into it), so as the shelling ended and French and British infantries advanced across the muddy farmland on foot, the entrenched Germans cut them to pieces with machine-gun fire. When the sun set on February 16—and despite the largest single-day artillery barrage of the war so far—more than 118,000 Allied casualties lay among the craters.

Still, Deleuze is saying, although the failed counterattack was a disaster for Britain and France, it was equally no victory for Germany. The Kaiser's army remained stymied by the deeply entrenched Allied forces. It was a deadlock, plain and simple, and it lasted for another year. Then, on May 27, 1918— with their army weakening after nearly four years of offensives—the Germans made a last-ditch lunge toward Paris. On that day, beginning at one o'clock in the morning, 3,719 German cannons opened fire on the six French and British battalions spread along the Chemin des Dames. In the three hours of shelling that followed, more than 700,000 German missiles fell, and when the bombardment was over, fifteen German battalions blew through the dead and dazed Allied troops like floodwaters through a picket fence. By nightfall, the Germans had leapt thirteen miles closer to Paris: the largest one-day movement of the war.

Within another month, Deleuze says, the Germans would be turned back by overwhelming British and American force at Château-Thierry and Belleau Wood, the two most critical battles of the northern-tier war. But on that spring day in 1918, the Germans owned the field of battle. After more than three years of nonstop shelling and fighting, the Germans seemed on their way to Paris.

Rémy Deleuze is second in command of this squadron: the *démineurs* of the Marne, one of the eighteen districts of Déminage. He is twenty-seven years old and has short auburn hair, light brown eyes, and a long, slim nose, which lends his face a distinctly foxlike appearance. Because of the two counterpunch offensives in 1917 and 1918, this district's team of thirteen *démineurs* has the distinction of finding more artillery shells each year than any other squadron. As we roll down the Chemin des Dames, Deleuze sits on the passenger side of the Land Rover's bench seat. Driving the truck is another *démineur*, Patrice Delannoy, who is short and solid, with intense gray eyes. His hair is cropped and dark, and he has a thick, graying mustache. For the past half-hour, Deleuze has done all the talking while Delannoy—who is hard at work, scanning the road for more shells or bombs—has yet to say a word.

Up ahead, Delannoy spots something in the roadside grass. As the Land Rover brakes to a stop, Deleuze gets out. When he sees what it is, he clasps his hands. "Ah," he says, "a *crapouillot*." The weapon doesn't resemble the aerodynamic artillery shells we've been lifting for days. Instead, four pinwheel fins extend from its sides, and a shaft sticks from its base. It looks like a large spear. As Deleuze bends to lift it, his gloved hands grasping the projectile's nose and tailward shaft, he tells me *crapouillots* are French-made cousins to the modern mortar. Their shafts fit into smooth-bore cannon barrels; when the cannons were fired, the *crapouillots* were spit out to fly short distances. The fins, he says, helped it to spin, stabilizing it gyroscopically to improve accuracy. He lifts the shell from the dirt, and we walk to the rear doors of the Land Rover, which Delannoy has swung open. With a deep breath, Deleuze sets the *crapouillot* gently into the transport rack. Then we keep rolling.

While fields around the Chemin des Dames have long ago been "officially cleared" by the *démineurs*, Deleuze says, each year the earth spits up bits of more deeply buried ordnance. "The soil around a buried shell is never quiet," he says. "Rainwater seeps around it, eroding openings beneath. After that, the soil at the top of the shell crumbles into the cavity below. That pushes the shell slightly to the surface. This happens year after year. Eventually, the shell pops up."

Patrice Delannoy gears the Land Rover to a stop once again, and Deleuze and I step out. This time, we find a British 155-millimeter shell—longer than a man's forearm—from World War I. It is sitting next to a house-size pile of sugar beets, which have been recently dumped here by a harvesting machine. The beets await a collection truck, which will take them to a sugar refinery in Soissons; the shell awaits us. Before lifting the shell, Deleuze pulls a knife from his pocket and slices a chunk from one of the sugar beets. He hands it to me, and I taste it.

"It's sweet, yes?" he asks.

I nod.

"This is the time of year most farmers die from accidents," Deleuze says, reaching now for the shell. "Their harvesters can't distinguish a hand grenade from a potato, a mortar from a beet. The machines scoop up everything solid they encounter. Each time a farmer dumps his harvester, he may get blown up." He lifts the shell and carries it to the rear of the Land Rover, where Delannoy again mans the tailgate. As Deleuze places the shell into the transport rack, he says, "Like so many things in life, sugar beets can taste sweet—or they can go boom." He shrugs and grins. "It happens all the time."

We climb back in the Land Rover and continue down the road. We pass a German graveyard on the left. It has row upon row of black steel crosses, which is how it can be distinguished from the French or American cemeteries, even at a distance. French memorial crosses are made of white marble, and the arms and headpiece of each cross are pointed. The American crosses are white marble with squared-off ends. As we pass the cemetery, Deleuze tells me the earth in the German memorial belongs to the German nation. If a shell pops up among the crosses, the Département du Déminage is not allowed to remove it. "We have given foreign nations little bits of France to commemorate the First War, a great tragedy," he says. "After that, the memorials are theirs to maintain. The Germans must care for their own graves."

Ahead is a side road. Delannoy brakes and turns onto it from the Chemin des Dames, heading south now. We crest the ridge, then drop into a valley on the hill's far side. A small, reed-lined creek runs through a fenced pasture. Inside the steel fencing, a few black and white milk cows and a shaggy brown Shetland pony stand in the mist. We cross a bridge and ahead see a white, rectangular sign that reads CHEVRY/VAL.

Beyond the sign are the prim stone houses of a traditional French village; each seems to have two rooms downstairs and two up. Many of the houses still have their windows shingled against the morning's weather. We pass a grove of trees and beyond that a graveyard of French crosses from World War I. Then we follow the pavement through an opening between two buildings and we are inside the village walls.

"We are looking for No. 1 Place St. Georges," Deleuze says. "It's the home of Madame Painvin. She has something in her garden."

The village is small, and as we follow its main street, it happens we are driving along Place St. Georges. As the addresses ascend, however, we realize we are going in the wrong direction, so Delannoy turns the truck around, steering it past a hedgerow gate and into the gravel courtyard of one of the houses. The truck crunches across the gravel, scattering the owner's flock of gray geese. Then, as Delannoy begins to back from the courtyard, the geese turn in unison and attack—summoning what menace they can with honks and flaps of their wings. For the first time this morning, Patrice Delannoy smiles and speaks. "They are brave, eh?"

A minute later, we drive through the gate of No. 1 Place St. Georges, cross its gravel courtyard, and stop the truck. This house is larger than the others in town. It is also not mortared stone but a golden stucco with a slate mansard roof and large windows across its ground floor. Deleuze gets out of the Land Rover and goes to the door. He knocks, and Madame Painvin opens it. She appears to be about thirty years old and is wearing a ruby-colored bathrobe; her dark, shoulder-length hair (still wet from her bath) is shiny and combed straight back on her head.

"I'm from the Département du Déminage," Deleuze says.

Madame Painvin opens the door and steps outside. "Ah," she says, "the bomb is across the road. I'll show you. Let me get my shoes."

A minute later, Madame Painvin is leading us across the narrow street to her walled garden. She swings open an ornate metal gate and leads us through. Because it is the last week of September, many of the plants are already dead and brown. In the garden's far corner, a thick shrub is growing against the garden wall, and Madame Painvin stops walking and points to the bush.

"There," she says. "Get it out of here."

Rémy Deleuze slips on his gloves. He drops to one knee and, reaching between the shrub's base and the wall, finds an unfired artillery shell with its propellant cartridge still attached. He lifts the shell from behind the bush and sets it gently on the dirt. It looks like a two-foot-long bullet. "Well, what's this?" he says. "An unfired American 75. It is probably a round from one of their tanks. From the Second World War."

"Get it away," Madame Painvin says. She is almost shouting. "Get it out of my garden. My children found it yesterday. I looked out the kitchen window, and they were playing with it."

"Certainly, certainly," Deleuze says, "but I think there are more surprises here." He reaches through the shrub branches—into a deep cavity between two rocks in the wall—and extracts another shell, identical to the first. He lays it gently on the dirt, examining it for danger signs. Then, still kneeling, he hands both shells to his partner. As Deleuze stands, slapping the grit from the knees of his coveralls, he says, "Voilà! No more bombs in the garden today."

As we return to the truck, Deleuze tells Madame Painvin the probable scenario. Back in World War II—most likely during the Allied push from the Normandy beaches toward Germany in late 1944—an American soldier set these shells into the wall's crevice during a skirmish, then forgot to retrieve them. As we leave the garden, with Madame Painvin shutting the gate behind us, Deleuze smiles and shrugs. "It's nothing strange," he says. "Only the usual story. The soldiers moved on. The war moved on. The bombs stayed."

WE LEAVE CHEVRY/VAL and head for another village, Pont-St.-Mard, which is only a few miles away. In this town, we are looking for the house of a farmer named Coorevits; he has some shells and grenades near his barn.

The road connecting the two villages crosses a wheat field, and as the Land Rover rumbles along, Deleuze is telling me why unfired American shells are such surprises. He says that 80 percent of the shells they find each year are from World War I, mainly because that war's battlefront was static. "It was opposing armies, with their infantries at the battle lines," he says. "The heavy artillery was set far behind the fighting, and those guns kept shelling and shelling and shelling for four years. That left many unexploded shells in the soil."

Things were different in World War II. In that war, the Germans captured France in a month, then occupied it almost peacefully for nearly four years. In the second war, it wasn't until the Allied armies swept through and liberated France in 1944 that any more fighting took place, and then the conflict was short-lived: the Allies drove the Germans out in about four months. "The second war was very fast and mobile," Deleuze says. "In the second war, the fighting wasn't conducted along entrenched battle lines, but was moving combat."

Also, Deleuze adds, the detonators on World War II shells were better designed than their World War I counterparts, making for fewer duds. "In the first war," he says, "about 15 percent of the shells didn't go off. In the second, where far fewer total shells were fired, detonator failure dropped to only 6 percent. So, as I say, France has many more shells in its soil from the first war than the second."

We pass the white, rectangular sign for Pont-St.-Mard. At the edge of the village, Deleuze tells of something that happened here last week. "A Belgian's car broke down on this road," he says, "and the guy couldn't find anything to loosen a wing-nut under the hood. Then he saw a 75-millimeter shell a farmer had laid at the roadside a few days before. He made a bad decision. He used the shell to tap the wing nut. *Crack!* The Belgian lost an eye."

As our Land Rover snakes through the narrow, bricked streets of Pont-St.-Mard, I ask Deleuze how he knows where to collect these shells.

"When a farmer or homeowner finds a bomb," he says, "they call the mayor of their town, and the mayor calls the Déminage. It's simple. An everyday thing." We pass through the town square, and Deleuze pauses for a minute, staring at the rows of parked cars there. Then he says, "Each year, among the *démineurs* around France, we have more than two million pickups telephoned by citizens. People do the craziest things with old shells and grenades. They keep them in their closets. One man, a shoemaker, used one as an anvil for forty years. He pounded shoes into shape on its nose cone. In his forty-first year of making shoes with that anvil, he hit the shell wrong and—*bang*—it blew up. Killed him."

At the far end of town, Patrice Delannoy gears the Land Rover to a stop in front of a square house of red brick. Across the road is a weathered wooden barn with a wheat crop beyond. As we get out of the truck, Monsieur Coorevits comes out through the house's front door. He is about seventy years old, bowlegged, and dressed in traditional French farmer's clothes: dark blue trousers, a blue rib-knit sweater, and tall rubber boots. As he hustles down the house's sidewalk, he is waving a fist in the air. "They're across the street," he is saying. "Three of them, plus grenades."

Coorevits brushes past us, pointing toward a heap of rags piled between his barn and a fenced pen where he keeps his foie gras ducks and geese. He lifts a large white rag, and beneath it are three 105-millimeter shells from World War I. Nestled between the shells are egg-sized lumps of rust: they're a pair of "pineapple-type" hand grenades from World War II. "I found the grenades," Coorevits says, "but my crazy neighbor found the shells. He's been sick in the head for years. He found these while digging in his yard. He started throwing them at his house. *He was trying to blow his house up!* He said he'd had enough of this house, this world. The doctor took him away."

Deleuze lifts one of the shells from its rag bed. Its nose is flat; the cone-shaped detonator has been removed. In the space where the nose cone used to be, a small, slim blasting cap sits in the open air, awaiting explosion. "Look here," Deleuze says, pointing at the cap, which looks like a silver-plated penlight battery embedded in dry clay. "This is what sets the whole thing off," he says. "It's very sensitive."

Deleuze tells me that blasting caps can be detonated by electricity, friction, or even temperature extremes. In artillery shells like this one, he adds, impact is what usually initiates explosion. When a fired shell hits the earth, a lever inside the nose slams into the blasting cap. "The cap makes a *pop*," he says, "like a firecracker. And that small explosion sets off the big, secondary charge, which is that brown material deeper in the shell. The secondary charge is what blows the buildings down. Still, the cap explosion is critical."

Deleuze points at the little silver cylinder again. "You tap this with your finger, and boom," he says. He chuckles, then turns to Coorevits and says, "Your neighbor is lucky. He could be dead. Instead he is only crazy."

We collect the shells and grenades, placing them alongside the thirty or so other shells in the truck's cargo bed. As we shut the Land Rover's rear cargo doors and prepare to leave, Coorevits stops Deleuze by raising a hand to his chest. "Are you interested in collecting more shells?" Coorevits asks. "I have many in my orchard. I would like you to take them. I'll show you."

Coorevits recrosses the road to his house and goes inside. Seconds later, he is backing an ancient Citroen pickup truck from the driveway, pointing it back toward town on the road we have just driven. We follow. A mile later, Coorevits turns up a two-track road so overgrown with leggy grass and sedge it is invisible. He bumps up the trail for a quarter mile, entering an orchard of skeletal apple and nectarine trees, their leaves already fallen. We park the Land Rover and get out as Coorevits strolls into the orchard. "Over here," he says, pointing at the ground. "I have collected them over the last few years. They stick from the ground. I find them in summer, when I am tending my orchard."

Like a refuse pile at a construction site, a thigh-high mound of damp, rusting artillery shells waits in the tall grass. Every bore of field artillery seems represented. There are 75s, 105s, 155s, plus the 77s and 170s exclusive to Germany. "In summer I have trouble mowing the orchard around these," Coorevits says, still pointing at the pile. "I am always afraid one of them will have been moved by a child playing here. I fear the blade of my mower will hit one, blowing me up. Take them away, please. If you will."

Deleuze and Dellanoy grin and shake their heads. "See what I mean about these shells being everywhere," Deleuze says to me. "They're all over this part of France, if you take time to look." The two démineurs return to the Land Rover for their gloves; then they begin making collection round-trips as Coorevits stares. There are some corroded World War II hand grenades in the pile, too, plus knobby, tubular lengths of the German shells World War I Allies called "pigeon mortars," for the undulating, pigeonlike whistle they made as they returned to earth.

Deleuze gestures open-handedly toward the pile. "Most of these are German, from the First War," he says, bending down to touch the base of one of the shells. "I'll show you how to tell the German shells from others. You look here, at the shell's foot." He points, and I understand: Where the Allied shells have smooth bases into which the cannon barrel's rifling has pressed grooves, the German shells were pre-rifled. Each German shell looks as if it has a ring of checkerboard squares around its base. "The Germans wanted every shell to fly just so," Deleuze says. "They made them all like this, even though the force of the propellant explosion and the rifling of the cannon's barrel cut grooves into the shell's exterior anyway, which is why the Allies didn't spend time pre-rifling. Many of these shells come from the German 170-millimeter guns. They were formidable field pieces."

The *démineurs* go back to work, and in another ten minutes the pile is cleared. Saying goodbye to Monsieur Coorevits, we get back into the Land Rover and drive off. It is almost lunchtime, Deleuze says. Time to go back to the depot.

DELANNOY STEERS THE truck down a series of farm roads, and near Soissons he turns it inside a fenced gate. A sign is wired to the fence. Written in French, it says:

KEEP OUT
THIS AREA IS BOOBY-TRAPPED

Deleuze jerks a thumb at the sign. "This keeps the curious away," he says.

Inside the gate, a grassy berm blocks out whatever is at the end of a long driveway. As the truck rolls beyond the hill, I see the arched stone doorway of an ancient fort. At the top of the arch's door, carved in the capstone, is the date 1880.

"This is Fort Montberault," Deleuze says. "Our depot."

Delannoy drives through the arched entrance and inside the fort's walls. Just past the main gate is a fortified yard the size of a basketball court stacked with row after row of shells, mostly the 155-millimeter size. It looks as if someone has taken thousands of rusting, industrial-size fire extinguishers and stockpiled them one atop another.

We drive beneath a few more arches, passing through still more bomb yards. Then Delannoy stops the truck near a series of arched doorways leading inside an earthen revetment. He gets out and finds a wheeled cart in one of the doors. As he and Deleuze unload the truck, rolling and stacking each size of shell in its respective area, I look at the fort itself. Inside the arched chambers, the ceilings are arched, too. They are all made of unmortared limestone blocks, each piece perfectly squared. The hatchings of quarrier's tools are still in the stones. Also carved into the stones are the names and dates of soldiers who must have been stationed at Fort Montberault. In beautiful, looping script dated 1880, twenty or thirty names are etched there.

Deleuze sees me looking at the roll call. "This used to be a barracks," he says. "Those are the men who lived here." He smiles. He finishes unloading the hand truck, then turns to me and says, "Want to see more? Follow me."

Deleuze walks into the tunnel and its shadows. We turn right, down another passage. "This fort is forty-eight acres large," he says, walking now in nearly pitch blackness. "There is a tall wall around the fort, but much of its interior passages are beneath the earth. The French Army used to keep its gunpowder here. In the First War, a German artillery shell hit the gunpowder store perfectly."

We keep moving along the passage, and darkness dissolves toward daylit gray. A few steps later, there is enough light that I can see again. We are in a large, rounded chamber where a number of tunnels intersect. There was once an arched ceiling in the room. Now, a huge hole has been ripped in the top of the fort—an opening the size of a backyard swimming pool.

Grass and small trees line the hole above our heads. The day's mist and gray sunlight drip inside. "This is where the shell hit," Deleuze says. "A direct hit. Many Frenchmen died here that day." He shrugs. "The blind luck of war."

We start into another dark passage, and I ask Deleuze how he got started in the Déminage.

"Most people in this work know someone who does it," he says. "You have to know someone who invites you in. It's a fraternity, which helps to protect our selectiveness and secrecy. Myself? I had an uncle who was a *démineur*. I was getting out of school, and one day he said, 'I have a job for you, if you want it.' That's how I learned of the Déminage."

We exit an arched doorway into a large, triangular courtyard. This one is stacked with rows of 105-millimeter shells. "This is the area of 105s," Deleuze says, looking across the thousands—maybe tens of thousands—of rusting shells.

I ask Deleuze if he has a family. After letting the question settle for a minute, he nods. "I have a wife and a three-year-old son. We have a new baby coming. This time, I hope for a girl." He smiles.

How does his wife feel about the Déminage?

"We don't talk about my work," he says. "My wife? She knows about my job, but we keep it quiet. Most of my family and friends only know I work for the Interior Ministry. It's that way with all *démineurs*. The secrecy is easier. Otherwise, people would bother us all the time—and we have enough worries without that. *Boom!*" He makes an explosion gesture, his hands fly in the air.

He flashes a smile. "I guess we are brothers to the shells and bombs," he says. "Like them, *démineurs* are happiest when left alone."

Deleuze surveys the shell-filled yard for a minute. Then he says, "Come along, I'll show you some old, old souvenirs."

We thread through rows of shells, and atop a chest-high wall at the courtyard's far side, nine cannonballs rest like bowling balls in a rack. "These are from Napoleon," he says. "From about 1800. We keep them around as mascots. They're fun."

Deleuze lifts a hand; he rubs the rounded top of one of the iron balls, as if it were the head of a child. He smiles. "It sounds funny," he says, "but we sometimes get attached to the shells we find. For eleven months a year, we collect shells from 10,000 villages in this district. Then, one month a year, we go to a military camp near Sissons and blow up what we've collected. As we prepare them for demolition, we recognize some of the ones we've picked up over the year. They remind us of things. We reminisce about the day we found this shell, or that one. It's a very fun time. But a little sad, too."

He looks out across the stacks of shells, then says, "To this day, the First War is a nightmare for France. It killed a generation of our men. But that wasn't all. As you wipe those men away, you also destroy our farms and fields, you destroy our homes. Everything. Back when there was no Déminage, the shells only sat in the fields and towns. My grandfather says the people were so poor, if they found one, they would often get blown up trying to strip the copper off it. That was the stakes of the gamble. We were poor and there was copper, which we could sell to the rebuilding effort."

He removes a pack of Marlboros and a blue plastic lighter

from the breast pocket of his coveralls. He lights one, takes a long puff, and exhales. The smoke drifts up through the mist, rising along Fort Montberault's tall, earthen walls. "Twenty years later," he finally says, "when the Second War came along, we were still recovering from the First War. We had nothing — no men, no resources — to fight with. We had to surrender to the Germans." He takes another puff. "We had no choice though, you know? Having no choice is what surrender means."

Deleuze shrugs. With the cigarette clenched between his index and middle fingers, he reaches up and strokes the cannonball one last time. His thick fingers move slowly across the rough, black iron. "Decades of rebuilding," he finally says. "Years and years of hardship. That is what happens when you have wars on your land, not on the land of your enemies."

THE TECHNICAL CENTER for the Département du Déminage is at Marly-le-Roi, in a closed off forest thirty minutes east of Paris by car. The forest was once the hunting grounds for King Louis XIII, and that king's son, Louis XIV, built his mirror-festooned palace there in the seventeenth century. Nowadays, the Palace of Versailles sits a few miles through the trees from the Technical Center, which houses every type of weapon ever used against modern France — while also testing new weapons and explosives for today's French military. As you drive through these closed off meadows and forests, where French presidents still hunt for pheasant, you cannot help but ponder what odd neighbors history makes: cast iron artillery shells and manicured gardens; bloody battles and endless, gold-leaf salons.

It is a sunny Wednesday, and René Teller, head of the Technical Center, is giving me a tour. Short and solid, Teller is about fifty years old and balding. Unlike the other *démineurs*, he wears a businessman's shirt and necktie. He is a rarity in the Déminage for another reason as well: He speaks English. When we meet, Teller explains he was a guest of the U.S. CIA and FBI in Virginia. "I learned English," he says, "so I could brief your agents."

We are standing in the sunny courtyard of the Technical Center, which is another 1880s fort, this one built to protect Versailles. The fort—an enormous dish with six doorways radiating around its interior—sits at the end of a long, fenced off road. Before the fort was decommissioned, large cannons on swivels had been implanted high on the dish's sides. That way, French soldiers could fire at attackers coming from any direction.

Teller is standing near one of the stone portals, which has a steel door covering its threshold. Sunlight drenches the stones, and a dozen dark, eight-inch lizards are clinging to the rock wall, warming themselves. Teller points the lizards out to me. Then, oddly, he points them out a second time, speaking directly to a pair of uniformed gentlemen who—a few minutes ago—materialized behind us. Teller seems familiar with them, but he has not introduced them to me. Each of their uniforms is tan and military-looking; both have been taking notes and knitting their brows each time I ask Teller a question. They are from the DST (Direction de la Surveillance du Territoire) and the DGSE (Direction Générale de la Securité Extrême), the French versions of the FBI and CIA. They're here on a first-time mission. No journalist has been allowed into the Technical Center before, so these snoops are tagging along, obviously concerned that Teller may slip critical national secrets to an American spy.

On the ground near the steel door is a sea mine, round and metal, bigger than a large beach ball. "Let's start here," Teller says, pointing. "This a a magnetic German water mine from the Second World War. Two years ago, we found 220 of these anchored in the Atlantic. They were a minimum of twelve feet under water, off the coast of Bordeaux, chained to the sea floor. Our divers had to deactivate them under water. It is amazing that, in all the years since World War II, no one ran a deep-draft ship through the mine field. A miracle."

Teller lifts his hands in the air as if holding an invisible soft-ball. "Here's how these work," he says. "Inside each mine is a thick lining of explosive, like TNT. At the center of the ball, a magnetic detonator sits on a small trampoline. If a boat strikes the mine, or if the metal of a ship's hull gets close enough to attract the detonator's magnetic charge, the detonator is thrown against the explosive—*kaboom!*" Teller smiles. "It's a very simple idea. And since these mines are generally deep beneath the sea, there's no worry about waves—sea action—jostling the detonator. These mines stay hidden and are very effective."

We move along the fort's curving interior wall, toward a display of different projectiles. First we come to a large, yellow shell about seven feet tall. Its body is like a fifty-five-gallon drum; its nose is a long, steep peak. "This is a 420-millimeter shell from a German Train Gun," Teller says. "It could travel seventeen kilometers—about nine miles—after being fired."

The next weapon we arrive at is large and squared off, like a telephone booth laid on its side. Before Teller begins explaining he says: "No doubt you know of the Maginot Line." A string of forts built along the French border with Germany after World War I, the line was named for André Maginot, a French war minister and their inventor. The line of strongholds was intended to repel future advances into France from Germany, forcing attacks to come from Belgium and cross the plains north of Paris, where it would be easier for France to defend herself. In World War II, however, the Germans swung even wider, through Holland and the Ardennes, outflanking the Maginot Line and pushing the French Army's own back against its line of forts, rendering them useless. Teller slaps the rusty, green-streaked copper of the bomb's skin. "Anyway," he says, "this is what the Luftwaffe, the German Air Force, dropped on Maginot forts. The irony is that these bombs didn't work. They blew up fifteen feet beneath the soil, and the forts of the Maginot Line went down for forty feet. Still"—Teller frowns and shrugs—"the Germans got through."

Teller points to another bomb. This one is about three feet long and fat in girth. It is made of concrete. "This is a German concrete bomb from the Second War," he says. "Initially, Hitler used these to train Luftwaffe dive bomber pilots in target practice. But when the Reich ran out of copper, they fitted these with explosives. Just dropping one of these on a building would shatter the structure, and that was before the explosion."

Next is a 1,000-pound American specimen, a four-foot-tall shell fired from World War II battleship cannons. "These were used in great numbers in the Second War," Teller says. "And they're still found all through the north of France, in villages along the ocean." He smiles. "My favorite story of these is that a farmer in the north once used them as fence posts. He nailed barbed wire into them, and they worked for years. The Déminage finally helped him to abandon his explosive fences. We collected the shells, then paid for some regular fence posts."

We step beyond these shells and bombs then, toward a steel door at another stone fortification. As we walk, I say that, so far, most of the shells we have seen are from World War II. Teller nods. "So far," he says, "that's true." He unbolts the door and swings it open. Inside the passage, a cobbled floor drops slowly into the darkness. Teller steps in and flips on a light. It is a catacomb that works deeper into the earth. Its walls, floors, and curved ceiling are laid with uneven, hand-fitted stones. For a hundred yards, the tunnel goes deeper, tiering flat every fifteen yards before diving deeper again. Along the tunnel's left wall, on shelves three levels tall, are layer upon layer of weapons. Bullets. Grenades. Mortars. Artillery shells. "These are the ones used in the First War," Teller says, smiling.

My jaw drops, and Teller laughs. "Yes," he says, "France has felt explosions in her time."

It is dizzying. Teller starts talking, and the weapons blur together from the sheer torrent of his descriptions. Twenty-seven different types of large-caliber machine-gun bullets were used in World War I: all of them are between 37 and 47 millimeters, all of them are as long (though chubbier) than a Bic pen. There are artillery shells in dozens of permutations—75-millimeter, 83-millimeter, 90-millimeter, 105-millimeter, 150-millimeter, 170s, 210s, 240s, 250s—and all of them come in toxic, incendiary, and standard explosive varieties. All of them have a score of variations inside their calibers, Teller says, pointing out the white stripes ringing the toxic shells. Alongside the toxic weapons are fragmentation shells, which are nearly as large as the beer-keg *Minenwerfer* I found near Verdun, except their skins are like fat, tightened-down coils. When detonated, the brittle iron of each coil shatters into thousands of tiny, razor-sharp pieces. On the next shelf sits a cross-sectioned shrapnel shell, named for Henry Shrapnel, the British Army officer who birthed the idea in 1784. Inside the shell's cutaway, mixed in with the explosive powder, are dozens of metal balls, each ready to be impelled into whatever might be nearby when the shell explodes.

On another tier of shelves are forty-two different styles of trench mortar. All are about eighteen inches long and have aerodynamic shapes and tail-stabilizer fins. "These were meant to be fired across short distances," Teller says. "They fly only a half-mile or so—and in a high arc, so they come down on their noses. They were shot from mobile, smooth-bore cannons about three feet long. The whole apparatus can be operated by a single soldier."

Teller tells me that, in most of the wars of this century, mortar systems were the front-line form of artillery, with different bores of heavier mobile cannons—firing 75-, 105-, 155-, and 205-millimeter rounds—ballasting the second or "field artillery" line of battle, meaning they were positioned a mile or two behind the fronts. Behind the field artillery, Teller says, were the "guns," which were difficult to move and which shot huge-caliber projectiles like 405s. This way, many waves of artillery could be brought to bear on enemy positions simultaneously, the front lines reacting with mobility while the rear-guard artillery pounded away once the enemy was discovered or, in military parlance, "fixed."

Teller turns his eyes back to the shelves. He lifts an especially sleek mortar. Its bulbous front tapers to a wasplike waist before opening into tail-fin stabilizers. He tosses the mortar up and down in his hand. "These days," he says, "these mortars are made by many manufacturers. But in the First War, they were made only in France, by Brandt, which offered its patent to the world after the war." Teller pauses and chuckles. "Now Brandt makes kitchen appliances: refrigerators and dishwashing machines. Their slogan is 'Brandt: Built to Last.'"

There are more shells to be explained. After thirty minutes, we're only halfway down the tunnel; there remain hundreds of explanations to go. On another shelf are some German racquet-type grenades, their stony-looking charges wired to throwing sticks. They are better preserved versions of the grenades we found in the Verdun foxhole. "A year or two ago," Teller says, "we found more than a million of these in a lake in Alsace. During the First War, the Germans must have built a makeshift factory along the lakeshore. When their army was driven back, they dumped the grenades into the lake. Millions of them. It took a whole summer for the *démineurs* to clean it up."

On the next shelf are toxic grenades: canisters of poison without the three-ringed warning. Teller lifts one from the shelf. It looks like a soup can. "These were big favorites in the First War offensives," he says. "Unlike the liquid toxic artillery, these were filled with chlorine gas. They weren't persistent agents, like the oily liquids, which stayed on the ground for long periods. Chlorine gas was nonpersistent. It was used during assaults and offensives. These grenades fell on the enemy, and the gas drifted across him. It made lungs and mouths bleed. Eyes and noses bleed, too. Then, in an hour or so, the wind blows the chlorine away, and your opponent has retreated to tend his wounds. *Voilà*, another trench is taken."

At the next shelf down, we come to some 105-millimeter artillery shells. "These are more shrapnel shells," he says. "They are filled with bullets and loose steel pieces. Ball bearings and screws." He lifts the unscrewed nose from one of the shells, saying that it is not a standard impact fuze but a timed detonator instead. "Projectiles with these fell, and an hour or two later they'd blow up. The delay meant many more casualties."

He hands the detonator to me. It is basically a single piece of inches-long metal with a narrow passageway bored down its length. "It works like a regular impact detonator," Teller says, "except between the detonator and the blasting cap is something called a 'timer pathway.' In some of these timers, acid has to eat through this passage to reach the primary charge. Others have a smoldering fire that must burn the length of this passage."

As Teller is talking, I slide the nose cone back into the shell. The fuses of field artillery shells have come a long way in the past century. Little more than one hundred years ago, exploding shells were cannonballs hollowed out, filled with black powder, and plugged with a cork threaded by a gunpowder-impregnated string, or "fuse." When ready for use, cannonballs were like outsize cherry bombs, and on the field of battle each cannonball was inserted into a cannon's barrel so the fuse faced the cannon's propellant load. When fired, the cannon's blast was to ignite the projectile's string, a less-than-consistent occurrence that made quality gunners extremely valuable. The technology changed, however, in the 1870s, when the British arms maker Armstrong refined the rifled cannon barrel and invented an elongated artillery shell that was virtually guaranteed to return to earth on its nose. Because of this, a mechanical impact "fuze" was invented—and its simple design has changed little since then. Even today, at the end of the century, computerized "smart" weapons and laser-guided missiles often rely on impact fuzes for detonation, since impact remains the surest sign that a rocket, bomb, or artillery round has found a target.

As I lift my hand from the shell, Teller points at the delay fuze. "If you find one of these unexploded in the forest," he continues, "you may not be able to distinguish it from the standard, impact-fuzed shells. You must be very careful. These timed fuzes are far more dangerous, since moving them even slightly can restore the reaction in the timer pathway. These take the lives of *démineurs* every year."

On the worst battlefields of World War I, Teller says, the Déminage estimates 1,000 artillery shells fell per square meter of battleground. Fitting with the general rule that 15 percent of the projectiles fired in that war didn't blow up, that means 150 of those 1,000 shells can still exist in a square meter. In some places, unexploded artillery shells are thicker in the ground than pebbles. "Of course, more often one shell would fall and explode on top of many unexploded ones, destroying them all," he says. "Still, until you visit one of the demolition centers, as you will tomorrow, you can have no idea how many unexploded shells are collected in France each month."

We keep moving. In another hour, we are near the bottom of the tunnel. Now, deep beneath the earth, a small cul-de-sac terminates the passage. Around the cul-de-sac's wall, an array of large-caliber, heavy artillery shells have been arranged. I ask Teller how many varieties of weapon are in this tunnel.

He smiles and lifts his hands. "I've never counted, exactly," he says. "But there must be at least 600 different types. And with variations of construction, many more than that."

What was the worst weapon of the war? I ask.

"That's a hard question," Teller says. "I think it's either these"—he points to a toxic shell on the floor nearby—"or those." He points in the other direction, to a large, cross-sectioned shrapnel bomb, which sits on the far side of the shadowed cul-de-sac. "No matter what terrors came afterward," he says, "nothing could be worse. Atomic bombs or whatever, nothing could be as horrible as these. They brought with them an idea."

Teller pauses for another moment. "You see," he finally says, "with these two weapons, whole armies could be killed without their opponents ever seeing them. When the power to destroy faceless men came into our hands, men learned that God can abandon them. With these weapons, a religion without God had arrived."

IN THE NORTHERNMOST part of France, where the River Somme empties into the English Channel, the unexploded shells and bombs of France's former wars finally meet their end. They are destroyed on a fenced off spit of land a few miles beyond the seaside village of Le Crotoy. Although the Département du Déminage is guarded about how many shells and bombs are actually destroyed there each year, they acknowledge that their Le Crotoy facility is the biggest destroyer of ordnance in France, with more than 300 tons of unexploded shells and bombs "passing through" annually.

Like everything else about the Déminage, the placement of the Le Crotoy demolition center has been painstakingly disguised. Only a few miles from the site, the quaint, brick-built village of Le Crotoy bustles along as it has for centuries. These days, it is mainly a tourist town for the British, who blithely hop the Channel during summers for a taste of French culture. By the time I arrive there, though, on a misty, autumnal Friday, the tourist's Le Crotoy has been shuttered for winter.

As I drive through town, looking for the road leading toward the demolition center, the cafés and puddled sidewalks along Le Crotoy's seawall are empty. Even the sea, which usually washes right against the brick quay, is missing. It is still early in the morning, and the tide is out, leaving a gray flatness of clay sea floor exposed. Even through the car's closed windows, the bay's underside smells of fish and muck, and there is very little vegetation—owing to the fifty-foot tidal swings. As it is later explained to me, the tides immerse anything on the sea floor in total darkness half the day, leaving it exposed to withering sunlight the other half—a tough climate for a plant to survive in.

At the edge of the village square is the road I need. A dozen miles along this two-lane, I have been told, is the gate to the demolition center. I know I am closing in when a ten-foot, chain-link fence suddenly rises from the pasture land. Wired to the fence are the now familiar red and white warning signs of the Département du Déminage. Here they read: "Do Not Enter/Private Hunting Preserve."

Another few miles down the road is a gate, inside of which a white Land Rover sits idling. A man in blue coveralls is idling near the gate, too, slouching against the Rover's far side. As my car approaches, he sees me coming, waves a hello, and opens the gate. Once inside the fence, the *démineur* strolls to my car's windows to check my identification.

The *démineur's* name is Dominique Berlet, and he is the squadron leader for the Déminage, Amiens Division. Short and solid in his coveralls, he has short brown hair and wears aviator-style eyeglasses with gold frames. He also has a shaggy brown beard and a brusque manner. When my identification checks out, he extracts a walkie-talkie from a thigh pocket on his coveralls and radios ahead. He says, "After my truck," then walks to his Land Rover and drives off.

I follow. The road inside the demolition center is not paved; it is a rutted two-track left muddy by a week of daily rains and bounded on both sides by thickets of goldenrod. We splash a mile further, our tires throwing up walls of mud. Finally, rounding one more turn, I see the center. A small guardhouse sits outside the gates. Behind it are a pair of fences like those of a maximum security prison. The outer fence is chain-link, ten feet tall, and topped with layers of barbed wire. The inside fence is five feet taller and electrified. Inside these is a long, low cinderblock barracks, and a few hundred yards away, at the back of the yard, a large steel shed. Arranged everywhere else on the yard's puddled mud—between the houses and all along the fences—are tens of thousands of rusting artillery shells.

Dominique Berlet stops outside the gate and its fences. He rolls down the window of his Land Rover and, sticking his blue-clad arm outside, points forcibly at the mud. "You park here, then walk inside," he says.

I comply. In a minute, I am inside the bomb yard. Every shell I have seen until now is represented here—by the thousands. Just inside the gate (as a decorative element, it appears) dozens of man-sized shells have been jammed into the earth at odd angles. Their skins have been painted blue or red or yellow. They look like a garden against the dark morning, and they add a cheery, vaguely unsettling touch.

Berlet has parked his truck now and is walking across the yard. "Welcome to our home," he says, gesturing across the compound with a sweep of his arm. "This is where old shells come to die." He is smiling. "Come on, I'll show you around."

Inside the bomb yard, the *démineur's* brusqueness has disappeared. Surrounded by all these explosives, Berlet is happy, almost giddy. Our tour begins at two long rows of walled warehouse pallets stacked with artillery shells. As we pass the pallets—each of which is at a slightly different level of fullness—Berlet begins talking about the business of this demolition center. For one week out of each month, he says, the Le Crotoy *démineurs* do nothing but blow up these "parcels" on the tidal flats of the English Channel, which is a few hundred yards away—just beyond the steel shed at the yard's back. "We destroy at least six tons of bombs a day," he says, "for five days each week. One week each month."

Berlet grins and turns in a tight, slow pirouette, taking inventory of this weapon-filled yard. As he looks over the shells, I do the math. That's more than 360 tons a year: at least 60 tons more than I was told, and better than one-third of the 900 tons the Déminage destroys annually.

We stop at one pallet, and Berlet reaches inside, pulling up a 75-millimeter shell to show me the layer below, which is made of more 75s. The shells on this lower layer all have white rings painted on them. He tells me that the démineurs arrange the shells inside each pallet in this same, very specific way: the toxic weapons go on the bottom, with layers of explosive or incendiary shells and mortars placed on top of them. Then, when the packing is finished, the démineurs put a final, hot-burning stratum of either anti-tank mines or plastic explosive on top. When all is ready, Berlet says, the pallets are delivered onto the tidal flat, where their detonators are wired back to shore. When the tide returns, covering the pallets with forty or fifty feet of sea water, the démineurs blow the whole thing up. At the moment of demolition, the layer on top explodes the older weapons beneath, which, in turn, blow up the toxic bombs under them. By the time the explosion reaches these toxic shells, Berlet says, a great deal of heat has been released, and the toxic gas is incinerated under water.

"We destroy most of France's toxic shells here," Berlet says, "because it is safer. The poison gas is consumed before it reaches the atmosphere. Also, we can make explosions hotter if the pallets are blown up under the sea." Berlet pauses and smiles. "We call this layered explosion the 'sympathetic effect,' " he says.

Berlet plucks one of the toxic shells from the bottom of the pallet. He tilts it up and back in the air, and from inside comes the *swish-swish* noise. Remembering Henry Bélot in the forests of Verdun, I ask how the toxic shells from around France are transported to Le Crotoy.

Berlet smiles and pauses for a long time. "That," he says, "is one of the biggest secrets we have. We bring them here in sealed trucks, driving the roads late at night, to minimize the danger from other traffic. With each delivery, the trucks are routed differently. It's a quiet operation, with big security attached, since we don't want to alarm citizens."

We begin walking again, moving between the rows of pallets toward the steel shed at the yard's rear. Inside each pallet, just as Berlet has said, the shells are arranged in the prescribed way. Thousands and thousands (and thousands) of them. Most are 75-millimeter shells, smoothly rounded and big as quarts of milk.

Halfway back in the yard, an orange-painted forklift the size of a dump truck is moving pallets of bombs toward the shed. The forklift—which also has a backhoe attached behind the driver's cab—is what the *démineurs* use to transport the filled pallets onto the tidal flats. I ask Berlet whether the forklift's five-foot-tall, heavily treaded wheels ever get bogged down in the soft clay of the flats.

He shakes his head. "No. One reason we use this place is because the clay is very firm. The sea bottom can support heavy machinery. Also, there's not much animal life in the tidal zone. There are a few clams and shellfish, but the sea here holds very few fish or plants. And anyway"—he shrugs—"a safer France is worth the lives of a few razor clams."

We keep making our way through the pallets as the morning's mist turns to rain. When we near the shed—its barn door entrance opened for the forklift—Berlet stops and points to a stack of five blackened shells sitting in the mud. As tall as my knees, they are covered with sandy sludge and a few barnacles. They are British, and were fired from battleships during World War II. "We found these on the beach this morning," Berlet says.

The rain begins to fall harder, and Berlet and I run for cover inside the steel shed, where four men are preparing pallets for next week's destruction. A dozen pallets are stacked two-high against the shed's back wall, and three more are sitting on the shed's work area, in varying states of preparation. With the rain drumming on the shed's roof, the *démineurs* describe the pre-demolition process. When a pallet is delivered inside the shack, the *démineurs* arrange the shells solidly against one another inside the box, so they will not shift in transit. Then, once the load is secured, they top the old shells, mortars, and bombs with a layer of nine anti-tank mines. Each mine is fourteen pounds of molded, solid TNT; orange and the size of a large frisbee.

After the explosions, I ask, what's left of the shells and pallets?

Berlet smiles. "Nothing," he says. "Sea water blows a half-mile into the sky. The explosion makes a hole fifteen feet deep in the sea bottom. The next day, when the tide is out, you could go looking for the pallet if you wanted, but there would only be a hole."

Berlet walks around to the shed's giant doorway and stares outside. It is raining hard now, and the building echoes with the pounding of raindrops. "We begin blowing up these pallets on Monday," Berlet says. "Come back then. You'll see."

THERE IS A two-day hole in my itinerary. So on Friday night I get back into the car and drive east through the mist, heading back to Verdun. The next morning, in the hushed light of pre-dawn, I have left my hotel to drive into the World War I battle-fields in the hills above town. The road I am following runs north along the River Meuse, whose smooth water slides past in the growing daylight. The landscape is hilly, and poplars line both sides of the road at intervals: a French travel poster. In a few more miles, in the little village of Bras, the road turns away from the river. A large white arrow points up a side road:

LOUVEMONT

VILLAGE DETRUIT

Louvemont is one of the area's nine obliterated villages, one of the places scraped from the earth by a single day of war. At 7:15 on the snow-bright morning of February 21, 1916, after an eight-month buildup, German shells began to fall in the hills around Verdun—and Louvemont was in the way. By noon of that day, no habitable structures were left in the village, and the heat from exploding shells had melted the snow that had coated the fields and rooftops of town only hours before. The result was icy mud.

Through the day, the German attack went on for ten hours. It was the most fearful offensive of World War I. Trees were shattered. Explosions cratered the landscape, then cratered the craters. The barrage continued through the afternoon, and in the long strings of trenches across the hills above Verdun, the French forces waited—hunched over and praying—for the shelling to end. Thousands of Frenchmen were already dead from shell fragmentation or direct hits. The rest were merely deafened and dazed. In the bottom of the trenches, the ankle-deep tide of snowmelt started to refreeze.

Then, as the sun began to fall, the first wave of German infantry advanced, debuting their newest piece of equipment: the flame thrower. Downed trees and brush exploded into fire. Smoke darkened and fouled the air. The Frenchmen who could still move crawled to the tops of their trenches and foxholes: they steadied their rifles among the clods of mud and began firing into the advancing, fire-breathing throng. Soon, they learned that if they shot the fuel tank each German flame thrower carried on his back, the tanks would explode into fire. Hundreds of Germans were immolated; the others kept coming. In another hour, the Germans were at the trenches and hand-to-hand combat became the rule. Skulls were pulped by rifle butts. Men were pinned to the cold mud with bayonets. Soldiers from both sides were shot at close range. Others were blown apart by grenades.

On that day, however, the Germans made a tactical mistake. They had bombed for too long and had not allowed enough daylight for their infantry to take the battlefield. They had also miscalculated the French Army's ability to defend itself. By about six o'clock, as midwinter night settled across these hillsides, the offensive stalled completely. There was nothing for the German infantry to do but bed down in the open fields. And in the dark, the French mounted a counteroffensive. They moved quietly along their muddy trenches, close to the Germans, then crawled over the open, blast-pocked mire on their bellies. More soldiers were bludgeoned. More men blown up. By ten o'clock that night, the battlefield was quiet. France had taken back nearly every inch of land it had lost earlier in the day.

In the hills above Verdun, that kind of fighting continued every day for ten months, then it sputtered and sparked for another two years. Before the siege was over, more than a million soldiers had been devoured by the fighting. And in what may be the most grisly statistic ever, only 290,000 bodies were ever recovered—with fewer than 160,000 of them identifiable. The remaining 130,000 dead were taken to a provisional morgue and stored, while the rest of Verdun's fallen troops—more than 710,000 men—were simply written off as lost, swallowed by explosions and mud.

The sun is coming up now, rising over the forests and long, rounded ridge lines of Verdun. The road emerges from a beech and spruce grove alongside a recently harvested potato field. Another white sign points the way. The road to Louvemont climbs a hillside at the northern edge of the field, and the furrows drop away behind. On the radio, in the growing light, a program of bagpipe music is playing. After every few songs, a Scotsman with a truly odd French accent describes what we have just heard.

The road climbs some more, turning through the shadows of daybreak. I traverse another forest, then the hill flattens. There is another sign ahead. This one is black with white lettering: "Louvemont, Village Détruit."

I stop the car and step out. There is not much around. A marble monument. A few beech trees. To this day, the earth beyond the beeches is broken up and uneven. Nowadays, the six-foot-deep explosion craters—which are everywhere—have a coating of thick grass, but they are still there, piled upon each other in a jumble. Almost eighty years after the Siege of Verdun, the battlefields here remain so unnatural-looking that astronauts can see them from hundreds of miles up. Closer to the ground, it is obvious that the shells did more than tear up the soil. They destroyed the village, too. There is nothing left of Louvemont. No little stone houses. No barns. No town square with its fountain. Nothing.

This marble monument is where Louvemont used to be, and beyond it the road droops over the hilltop. I get in the car and follow, and in a small glade a quarter-mile farther on, stands a tiny marble chapel inside a marble wall. The wall encloses a tiny graveyard with a half-dozen scattered, broken headstones inside. The marble stones are dated from the 1880s, and I figure this is where Louvemont's cemetery was once located. I walk the few steps to the front door of the chapel. The grass beneath my feet is thick with dew. The words "In Memoriam" have been carved into a slab of dark marble above the chapel door.

The church was constructed in 1931, and no door covers its threshold: a security gate keeps the curious out, but the interior is open to the elements. The chapel is small and Gothic-style, its floor plan is the shape of a cross. Its interior is big enough, maybe, to hold ten people. In its rounded apse, above the marble altar, an elaborate stained glass window lets daylight into the white-stone interior. There are statues of St. Peter and Christ set into the walls. The chapel floor is a perfectly laid mosaic of red and blue pastel rocks that, today, are scattered with the husks of fallen leaves. I stand there, staring at the beauty and craftsmanship; the memory and regret. The people of Louvemont—never able to inhabit the Zone Rouge after the Great War—built this monument to their village and its destruction. The job was small; the execution breathtaking.

THE ROAD TWISTS and turns. It passes a bombed out villa overgrown with vines, and at intervals there are little brown signs beneath the beech trees. The signs say: "Picnicking Allowed Inside This Area." Here, within the Cordon Rouge, inside perhaps the most horrible battleground of World War I, spots for al fresco Sunday afternoons have been carved between the shells.

Ahead of the car, a trio of deer is crossing the road. They disappear into the forest. It is strange here. One part of this place is mired in bloody history; another is home to deer and picnickers.

The car rounds a hairpin bend. It tilts uphill. On the left, through a large gate, is the Trench of Bayonets. This is where two entrenched battalions of the French 137th Infantry, surrounded by German forces and cut off from the rest of their army, defended this hill until—after two weeks of nonstop fighting and explosions—an artillery shell struck them directly. The day was June 23, 1916, and the blast buried the thirty or so men in their trench; their rifles—bayonets still attached—stayed leaning against the walls of what became a mass grave. After the explosion, even the Germans were impressed by the French battalion's bravery. To honor them, the Germans filled in the trench completely, leaving the Frenchmen's rifle muzzles and bayonets stabbing into the air.

Today the filled in trench is still there. A thick roof of concrete, held up by pillars at its corners, protects the trench from the elements. Beneath the roof, bayonets still spike from the dirt. Near each of them, visitors have placed small crosses, military ribbons, and the tiny, devotional paintings of saints. Ten feet above the bayonets, between the mass grave and the thick concrete roof, small and darkly beautiful birds—mostly swallows—shoot and dip through the air after the morning's insects.

The road continues to twist and run uphill, and on both sides of the pavement the ground remains broken and rumpled by shell craters. Every once in a while, a trench line twists into view beneath the beech limbs. Above the treetops on the road's right shoulder, sticking up like a fifteen-story concrete missile, is the steeple for the Ossuary of Verdun, strikingly white against the morning sun. The steeple dips behind the trees when I crest the hill, and ahead of the car is the National Cemetery, where 15,000 crosses of white marble jut from perfectly tended grass. These crosses mark the graves of some of the French soldiers who died in the Siege of Verdun. The crosses spread across the hillside for almost a mile—each of them once a life. A rose bush is planted at the base of each cross, too, and in the morning light, the roses are just beginning to open for the day. Tens of thousands of crimson buds in the dawn. Yet even the rose petals number nothing compared to what is inside the Ossuary, the long, narrow blockhouse that waits at the upper end of the cemetery. Inside that building, more than 130,000 unidentified human remains are entombed.

The Ossuary does not open until nine, so instead I follow the road to Fort Douamont, which is a mile from here, near the obliterated village of Douamont. The fort is a half-mile long and a quarter-mile wide and emplanted into the side of the longest, tallest ridge in the area. It gives a spectacular, fifty-mile vista of the surrounding hills. I leave the car in the fort's parking area, and then I am alone with the silence of a Saturday morning.

The walls of Fort Douamont are poured concrete eight feet thick, and when 420-millimeter shells (weighing more than a ton) hit the fort, their explosions cratered the walls but did not smash through. I stop to examine the concrete: it's a dark and tired-looking gray. Steel doors cover the fort's entrances, barred grates cover its windows. Everywhere—in the concrete, in the doors, in the dirt surrounding the fort—there are explosion craters and shrapnel dimples.

I follow a trail up the side of the fort to its top. The forests of the Zone Rouge stretch into the distance. Fort Douamont was built in 1885, and on February 26, 1916, just five days after the Siege of Verdun started, it was taken by the Germans without a battle. Believing the fort obsolete, the French had long abandoned it, and the Germans, having pushed the French back, took it over. During its period of German occupation, however, the fort proved nothing but bad luck. Altough its hilltop vistas helped in planning attacks, it was unfortunately situated for offensive purposes, and it had no water easily accessible. Consequently, the Germans converted it into a munitions depot and field station. Then came an accident with a large store of hand grenades. The explosion killed 679 German soldiers. Because this happened during the heat of the siege, the Germans did not have time to clean up. Instead, they mortared a wall in place, sealing off the dead. Ultimately, in late October 1916, a fire spread out of control inside the fort and the Germans abandoned it, leaving the French to retake it a few days later.

From atop Fort Douamont's concrete roof, I can see there is one area of forest where no trees are growing, where the ground is dead and gray. That is where many of the German armies were entrenched, and French shells fell there in such volume that nothing grows still. The *démineurs* from the Vaux Forest said the shells there are so concentrated you can't walk across the ground—even today. The Déminage is clearing that sector by chipping at it from the edges. It will take decades to clean up, they say. From a mile or two away, I stare at the lifelessness of the shelled out battlefield. It is French ground, pummeled to death by French weapons.

I turn and scan the horizon at 360°. Most of it is hills and trees. The only signs of man are the Ossuary's steeple and a solitary radio tower on a hilltop miles away. I begin to walk down from the fort, headed for my car. It is a few minutes before nine o'clock now; the Ossuary's doors will be open soon. Time to visit the largest tourist attraction in Verdun.

The Ossuary at Verdun is a quarter-mile long, and is made of white stone. Long, round, and low, it looks like a loaf of French bread. From its center rises the fifteen-story spire, which has been fashioned to look like an artillery shell. The resemblance is obvious: the shape of the shell's body and detonator have been etched deep into the stone.

The macadam parking area at the Ossuary is enormous, too. There is easily space for hundreds of cars—and yet, at this hour, I am alone, standing among the white lines painted to show the drivers where to park. From the Ossuary's entrance, you can see the 15,000 white crosses of the National Cemetery as they stretch toward forested hills. Near the Ossuary's massive steel doors is a bronze plaque:

NO TALKING.

NO PICTURE TAKING.

NO MUSIC.

The interior of the Ossuary is a long, narrow hallway with a rounded ceiling that runs the building's length; it feels like the inside of a gun barrel. The floor is slightly polished marble, and it catches the daylight, reflecting it in a buffed, muted way. The Ossuary's interior is lit only with sunshine, which enters through stained glass windows. Each windowpane is an orangish color, and the daylight through the glass takes on a pale, bloody crimson.

Dozens of marble coffins are arranged in alcoves that have been carved into the Ossuary walls. There are no names on the coffins, only Roman numerals to denote sectors of the Verdun battlefields. Inscribed on the interior's walls, in a stately typeface, are the names of some of the unidentified dead, soldiers who went to battle here and became forever lost, falling into eternity without a burial to mark their passage. Beneath the marble floor are the remains of some of those men. The Ossuary has been divided into sectors that correspond to the numbered coffins; all the unidentified bodies—or parts of bodies—that came from those zones are buried here, laid to rest alongside all other unidentified bodies from that sector. French. German. British. American. By the time a body reached the Ossuary, nationality had become a secondary issue. The bones of at least 130,000 men are just beneath my feet. The dead under this floor—plus the 710,000 never recovered—could have made a sizable city. Instead, they died advancing a line of battle that, through the course of the siege, wavered back and forth only a few miles. They died by explosion and gunfire, by freezing winters and the strength of each other's bare hands. Now some of them lie together under the floor, having offered up their lives for a stalemate.

How all the bodies came to be here is a gory tale. For years after the war, humanitarian organizations from the Red Cross to the Boy Scouts harvested the surrounding hills and valleys for the unidentified remains of soldiers. Originally, as is echoed in the Ossuary's interior, the dead were placed in large coffin-like boxes bearing the numbers of battlefield sectors. Together, the coffins were stacked inside an enormous provisional shed that was built in early 1919. There the bodies lay, their legacy almost forgotten, until 1927, when they were moved into the stone monument I stand inside now. Finally, in April 1932, the Ossuary was completed with international donations and opened to the public. During this time, the fields were still being cleared of corpses and skeletons. I have seen photographs of the workers in action. In some of the pictures, four or five men, dressed in heavy coats and Red Cross armbands, are carrying large, unfolded blankets by gripping them along the edges. On the workers' faces are heavy surgical masks, to help keep out stench and disease. In some of the photos, if you look closely, you can see inside the large blankets. Arms and legs are visible. In one of the photos, a muddy boot and leg hangs in the open air beyond the blanket's edge. The pants and knee joint are twisted unnaturally, in a way that makes you imagine what the dead soldier's face looks like. For the body-clearance workers, the job must have been horrible. Every day a nightmare of flies and rotting flesh. It was possibly the worst job on earth. But it had to be done—out of respect for the dead if not the war. What else were the living to do?

There is a small chapel in the Ossuary. I peek my head inside and see rows of empty wooden chairs and a marble altar. There is more stained glass above the altar. These windows do not carry tableaux from the Bible, however, as most stained glass windows do. Instead they show images of men at war. In one of them, a blue-uniformed soldier is being carried off the battlefield; explosions rumble in the background. In another, angels are transporting a horribly disfigured man to heaven.

At the center of the Ossuary's hall, near the doors to the chapel, there are two marble statues. One is called "The Private Soldier," and it is the bust of an infantryman. His uniform is purposely hard to identify—he could be German or French or British or American—but he is serious-faced and is wearing a helmet strapped tightly to his head. The other statue is a bust called "Resignation." A calm face stares from beneath the white folds of a funeral shroud, its eyes unblinking and open. From the folds of the shroud, an arm and hand extend: the index finger covers the statue's mouth. Maybe it is stifling a scream. Or quieting onlookers. I had no idea marble eyes could stare in such an alive way.

I walk outside the Ossuary, taking a deep breath of the cool, sunny morning. I start across the gravel toward my car, then see a row of windows in the white stone along the building's base. I kneel and look inside. There are bones everywhere. I can see them as far as the daylight penetrates. Vertebrae. Skulls. Tiny little bones that seem fragile and white, like lumps of talcum powder. The bony remains of thousands of torsos are piled so deep that the jumble of rib ends looks like a fish's scales. In the window's center sits a jawless skull that has been pierced behind the left ear and in the forehead. The holes are asymmetrical. No doubt they are the legacy of British officer Henry Shrapnel. Against the building support, at my window's left, thigh bones have been stacked like cordwood. I stand up, unable to look any longer. I stare down the length of the Ossuary, toward my little white car. The windows run the length of the building. It is one long, grotesque peep show.

In an area at the back of the Ossuary there is a small shop, and inside it are history books and photo slides for sale. I am drawn to the two rows of stereoscopic viewers lining one of the shop's walls. I begin flipping through the pictures, and in three-dimensional, black and white images, the Battle of Verdun comes to life: 1916 has been captured inside these solid brass boxes. The French soldiers in the pictures are slightly built and pale. They seem on the edge of moving, of shouting to me. Most of them are smiling. They have thick mustaches and shiny, dark eyes. In some of the photos, the men must be bivouacking in the remains of obliterated villages; they have set up housekeeping inside buildings with patchy roofs and broken stone walls. In others, they are digging new trenches or buttressing trenches they have already dug with log supports. In others, they are seated at makeshift tables, eating from tin plates. Their uniforms are muddy, but they look happy and cocky—even a little hopeful.

Finally, one photo makes me pull my head from the viewer with a snap. A severed forearm and hand sits on the mud. Ahead of it, there is only the bald, hilly horizon. The arm is beautifully preserved, just lying there, clean from the rain, the fingers slightly opened, the palm to the sky.

IN 1914, THE year the war started, most of Verdun's 14,000 citizens stayed with their homes in perceived safety. True, they had reason to be concerned, since hundreds of evacuated citizens from the villages above town were wandering Verdun's streets, but Verdun seemed secure against the threat of war. Then, two years into the conflict, in February 1916, as the zone of fighting slid south and east from the bogged down Somme battlefields, the Germans blasted their way onto Verdun's landscape. Within weeks, the Germans were less than ten miles from town, and Verdun's population plummeted to fewer than 3,000. Most of the people of Verdun moved all the way to Paris, 160 miles to the west. With the coming offensive and the dictum of German commander von Falkenhayn to "bleed the

French white at Verdun," all of the town—except the cathe-
dral—fell to artillery fire.

As I walk along Rue Mazzel, the town's business district
street, I pass the shrapnel-slashed stone walls of the local Jesuit
college chapel. It is difficult to believe that, after the war, people moved back into this town and began to remake their lives.
They rebuilt the handsome, half-timber houses, replastering
walls and wood-shingling roofs. They turned their city into a
candy-making center: Verdun's sugar-coated almonds are famous across France. From the street, I can see a poster inside
one of the local cafés. It is a photo of some bullets and trench
mortars that are partially covered in dirt. The poster reads:
Touche Pas. Ça Tue! (Don't Touch. These Kill!)

I LEAVE TOWN, driving north and east toward Paris. The U.S.
forces under General Pershing came through these valleys,
working toward Verdun in mid-September 1918. They had first
distinguished themselves in the battlefields along the Somme
and Marne in June of that year, when they had fought at
Château-Thierry and Belleau Wood, decisively turning back
the Germans, who had advanced along the Chemin des
Dames. Pershing's troops then turned east and battled toward
Verdun, stopping to drive the Germans from the steep,
glacially cut hills of the Argonne Forest, which lie a few miles
to the road's west. In the distance, I can see the dark trees of
the Argonne lining the steep hills, which rise sharply against
the horizon. Pershing's men did not quit there, however. After
pushing the Germans from the Argonne, they crossed the

Meuse and ripped into the hills east of Verdun, aiding the exhausted French and driving back the equally spent Germans with ferocious energy and firepower.

On September 12, with the arrival of the Americans, the momentum of the Verdun siege—and the entire war—shifted. By October 3, the Germans were on the run, and on that day Kaiser Wilhelm sent President Woodrow Wilson an entreaty for armistice, which Wilson declined even to answer. After that, every day in the hills above Verdun, Pershing's men gained back hunks of French soil. Still, as the Germans retreated, the overpowering U.S. forces were no better or braver or luckier than the other combatants, they were merely fresher. Their relative strength proved the key to driving the Germans back, but their tactical expertise made equally little sense. Before the Verdun campaign was over, more than 17,000 of Pershing's men would die as they threw themselves at the entrenched Germans in full-frontal assaults; across France, between June and November 1918, the late-arriving Americans would lose more than 126,000.

I pass through the narrow streets of another town. Red brick houses sit alongside the road. The local café, with its brown, Stella Artois beer awning shading the sidewalk, is full. At the edge of town, as in most of the villages, there is a graveyard or memorial to the French soldiers who gave their lives in the Great War. Every town, it seems, has a memorial.

The village ends, falling behind me, and I look out across the sunny fields, across the hills and valleys, toward the Argonne again. Closer to the road, black and white Holstein milk cows in pastures stare at my car as it moves by. Up ahead is an unmown grain field, barley, I think. In the center of the field, against the blue sky, a darkly dressed scarecrow towers over the crop. The scarecrow's clothes are thin and tattered; they flap and blow in the day's breeze. On the scarecrow's head is a heavy iron helmet from World War I—the German officer's type. Black. Topped with a spike.

Outside the town of Montfaucon, I come upon the American cemetery: 14,000 squared off crosses of white marble stretch away in orderly rows. No matter how I look at these rows of crosses—from the front, the side, obliquely—they are still in rows. Even in death, these soldiers are organized and work together. Each of the crosses is inscribed with a soldier's name, date of death, and a few other bits of information. Interspersed with the crosses are white marble monuments with the Star of David on them. The day is bright; the grass between these monuments is perfect and pale green. The sunlight is so clean it puts a halo around everything, as if in a dream.

I stop the car, step out, and begin reading headstones. The soldiers come mostly from the East Coast. New York. Pennsylvania. Massachusetts. It takes a while, but I finally find a marker for a soldier of the West, from Montana. In the second row is the gravestone of Frank Wellnitz, a corporal from the 353rd Infantry, Kansas. As an enlisted man, he was probably young. How young? Nineteen? Twenty? He died on November 10, 1918. A day before the war ended.

Two graves to the right of Wellnitz is a cross inscribed with the particulars of Austin F. O'Hare, a soldier with the 314th Infantry, Massachusetts. O'Hare was a private. Another enlisted man. A foot soldier. He died November 11, 1918. The day of the Armistice.

For the third time today, the weight of my surroundings compels me to leave. Around me, on this beautifully sunlit carpet of grass, I only see men dying. Arms blown off; faces blistered by chlorine and mustard gas. Eyes bleeding by phosgene, bullet holes in necks and hands and shoulders. And yet, for all of these marble markers, there is something even worse. I keep thinking of that moment in each of these soldiers' minds, that instant when death throws its private havoc over a life's loves and joys and hopes; the moment when it grows so dark it will never be bright again.

I get back in my car and drive off—quickly. I pass through more little towns, with their graveyards and war monuments bathed in autumn sunlight. I am almost to Reims, eighty miles down the road, before I feel far enough from Verdun to obey the speed limit.

ON MONDAY MORNING, a few minutes before sunrise, the *démineurs* of Le Crotoy begin the day's chores beneath an electric blue sky. By the time they are all awake and dressed, the sun is cresting the flat horizon to the east, and from the windows of the barracks, the *démineurs* can see the day's first light strike, flamelike, against the tops of the bomb yard buildings.

In the barracks kitchen, the *démineurs* sip cups of café au lait and munch brioche in the quiet. After a quarter-hour spent meditating over his coffee, one of the *démineurs*—a dark-haired, bulldog-looking man named Crisan Kowal—leaves the barracks, opens the bomb yard gate, and climbs into the cab of the new-looking orange forklift.

He fires up the machine, then drives it through the gates and toward the flat, empty, low-tide plain of the English Channel. The waters of the Channel have receded, and Kowal drives out to an agreed-upon spot a mile and a quarter from shore and begins to dig the day's six pits, where the explosive pallets will be laid. From the cab, Kowal can see the dark waters of the English Channel another half-mile out; its water churns and boils, and in the still dark morning, he can see iridescent white lines of seafoam as the waves break.

By the time Kowal is back at the bomb yard, nearly an hour has passed. In the meantime, Dominique Berlet and the other *démineurs* have been hard at work getting out the detonator cable, a large wooden spool of narrow-gauge wire, and readying its mile-and-a-half length for the day's demolitions. To do this, they test the six different contacts at the end of the cable by running an electric charge to them from the detonator plunger, a small metallic box with red and green lights. They attach an electrometer to the appropriate cable contact, then slap the plunger's lever into the box when its lights go from red to green. The depressed plunger sends a shriek of electricity along the mile and a half of cable. With each test, at each of the six contacts, an electrical charge cracks into the electrometer. The cable works. The plunger works. Everything checks out.

By nine o'clock, Kowal and the forklift have started the first of seven laps onto the tidal flat. An hour later, all the day's pallets are in their holes, their tops flush with the sea floor, and

Kowal and the *démineurs* have only to string the cable, attach the six blasting caps, and wait for the tide to return.

AFTER THAT, THERE is nothing to do but wait. Back at the barracks, there is time for an early, lengthy lunch—a rich stew and some salad. There is fresh-baked bread, too, and a healthy quantity of red wine. All the while, the sea is edging quickly up the tidal flat, climbing toward the high-tide mark. Three hours after abandoning the bomb pallets on the gray, puddled sea floor, the English Channel has once again swallowed up its low-tide zone. Four hours after burying the pallets, the Channel laps against its high-tide mark, and the bomb pallets, a mile and a quarter away, are under forty feet of dark sea water, awaiting their final charge.

At a quarter after one o'clock in the afternoon, the *démineurs* are back at the high-tide line with the cable spool. They've attached the plunger box to the spool's wire contacts, and all that remains is for the red light on the plunger box to flash green. All around the cable, the *démineurs* are in a fine mood. The day is sunny and sixty degrees, warm for the last of September in this part of France. The lunch was pleasant and tasty. For contrast to the warm day, a cooling breeze has kicked up, and a few puffy, white cirrus clouds have drifted in overhead; their shadows move slowly across the water.

Then all is ready: for the first of six times today, the red light inside the detonator box is replaced by a green glow. With a blank look on his face, Dominique Berlet presses the detonator's plunger, and for a long moment, nothing happens. Then, far at sea, a patch of the Channel's dark water gets whiter and whiter; it begins to *glow* white, and slowly, slowly, the water begins to lift in a silent bulge that seems to gather the sea water surrounding it. The bulge is rising and rising and rising—like a bulb of white moving silently into the blue sky. It is like watching a movie with the sound off. Peaks of sea water have spiked from the bulge's top, becoming spires of white against the blue sky, and the whole spiky bulge keeps going upward, continuing to climb and climb and climb in the blue sky. The explosion hurls curtains of sea water to the sides, and behind the upward path of the spires, fine white mists are now trailing toward heaven.

Finally, the noise arrives: there's a "whump-*crack*" and following that—the white peaks of sea water now a half-mile in the air—is a *boooooom* so deep and resonant that it rattles deep inside everyone's chest, rumbling against their hearts and lungs. The earth beneath the *démineurs'* feet shudders with a fast, hollow-feeling *slap*.

And that quickly, it's over. The day's quiet replaces the slowly dying rumble. Just as fast as the peaks of sea water rose, the mountainscape of white is now falling to earth with the far-off sound of rain, leaving only a misty outline of the ascent in the sky. Slowly the sea returns to itself, coming back to its dark, shining flatness; the rumbling roar of war and artillery and death has gone, replaced again by only the breeze and the cloud-drifted blue sky.

A minute passes. It is time for the second pallet to be exploded. As Berlet and the other *démineurs* attach the plunger to the next set of cable contacts, they are serious. The plunger is wired up now and its red light is on. The light remains red, red, red . . . finally, it goes green, and the cylindrical plunger is pressed down once again. As the plunger slaps into the box, the *démineurs* remain serious. Slowly, far at sea, evidence of the explosion begins again. As the water of the English Channel begins to go white, bulging above the exploding shells and bombs, the *démineurs* stare stone-faced ahead. These men in their blue coveralls know that the Déminage of France is long from over.

2

Ghosts

IN THE SPRING of 1941, whenever Adolf Hitler left home, he carried a globe in his field briefcase. Made of inlaid wood and roughly the size of a grapefruit, it was a gift from Benito Mussolini, the Italian Fascist leader and Hitler's closest ally.

Yet instead of showing an earth as God or the rhythms of the universe had created it—blue oceans, continental blotches, crenulated ice caps—Hitler's globe had only the shapes of four nations riding on its seas: Germany, Italy, Spain, and Japan. These were the countries, he had decided, whose cultures deserved to survive.

Today, the globe Hitler once possessed sits in Moscow, protected behind unbreakable glass in a rarely visited marble tomb called the Russian Museum of Military History. Under that same glass is Hitler's personal blueprint for the Nazi conquest of the Soviet Union, a plan he called Barbarossa, after the red-bearded Frederick the Great of Germany, who in the twelfth century was the last German to invade Russia. A few typewritten pages long, the Barbarossa Plan is accompanied by faded maps and, in the typewriter margins, notes in the looping, brown ink scrawl of Hitler's own hand.

His plan accounted for the disposition of troops. It made no considerations, however, for the disposition of their bones.

AS TWILIGHT FALLS on a Russian winter night, winds like freight trains sweep and howl across the flatness of the steppe. In the farm village of Peschanka, a dozen miles outside the high-rise metropolis of Volgograd (formerly Stalingrad), the season's first snow has started to fall, and its tiny, sharp flakes sift to the ground silently, then skip, wind-driven, across the furrowed croplands like a veil.

Khodykin Alexandrovitch was here in 1942, the year the German Sixth Army destroyed this place. He was fourteen years old. Standing on the frozen mud of Peschanka's main street, he is recounting the story of the German advance to me and Vasili Stepanov.

"That was August. We knew they were coming—we had known of the German advance for a month." The summer of 1942 had been exceptionally dry, even by the arid standards of the steppe, where only ten inches of rain may fall in a year. For three or four days before the Germans arrived, the people of Peschanka had monitored the approaching cloud of dust that the Nazi's tank divisions had thrown into the sky. "I remember the sky very well. Perfectly," Alexandrovitch says. "It was a hot summer sky. A flat blue sky, with the brown dust rising above the horizon. The dust was a curtain coming closer every day." Finally, as the curtain grew dangerously near — when the people of Peschanka could hear the tank division's motorized clatter as well as see its gritty plume — it was time to leave. "Our entire village evacuated in a day and a night," Alexandrovitch says. "We took ferries across the River Volga, to the eastern shore. We never knew if we would return."

In the gathering dark, Alexandrovitch removes the glove from his left hand. Sweeping his fingers and thumb inward from the corners of his eyes, he swabs places where tears have started to freeze. He pauses another moment and continues. "It was February of 1943 before we returned," he finally says. "The Battle of Stalingrad was over. The Germans were defeated — and here in Peschanka what we found was beyond belief."

Alexandrovitch raises his arm parallel to the flat ground. With a long, sweeping motion, he aims his hand across the landscape. "Our town was *gone*. Nothing left. The Germans burned our houses for firewood, pulling them down with their tanks. They probed the earth and found our family treasures, which we had buried to prevent looting. They burned our heirlooms for warmth. There was not an animal left. Not a crow or a rat. They had eaten them all."

What the Germans left behind were their dead. "Thousands of them," Alexandrovitch says. "Soldiers dead from starvation or wounds, who died after the earth froze — so they couldn't be buried. Mouths open. Heads twisted. Many of them were covered in drifted snow. Bodies were sometimes frozen together in clumps. In our streets, across fields and ditches; the dead were everywhere.

"It was so cold we soon were stripping the clothes from the dead for warmth. You cannot imagine the scene. Naked corpses on our streets, their clothes taken by people who had nothing else to keep them warm. No shelter. No fuel for fires. I remember being a boy, taking a rope and looping it around the dead in our streets. We would drag the bodies out of town, to the biggest bomb craters, then untie them and push them in. After we pushed them in, we covered them with snow to keep them cold. When the ground thawed, we covered the dead with earth. By then, the smell—" he clenches his eyes and shakes his head—"horrible."

Alexandrovitch glances up; falling snow bounces against his face. "Each spring when the snow melts, the bones of the German dead remind us what happened in the winter of 1942. They will never go away." Then he turns and walks off, shuffling up the frozen mud street in the gathering night.

My interpreter, Vasili Stepanov, shouts a thank you into the wind after Alexandrovitch. When the old man is gone, Stepanov nods and smiles. "I'll show you what he is talking about," he says. Stepanov begins leading me along the uneven street toward the edge of town, to a spot 100 yards distant where the vertical shapes of Peschanka's houses cease and the pale, endless horizon of the steppe begins.

When the last houses are behind us, we cross beneath a sagging power line that sways in the snowy wind. Stepanov slices a line in the air, his index finger pointed toward white-dusted soil. "It starts about here," he says. He reaches down, and cupping his bare hand skyward, he grabs the knobby end of a bone that is sticking six inches into the air. "*That!*" he says, pointing.

He takes a few steps further, then lunges. "Here again!" he

says, bending to tussle with a rib cage half-buried in frozen earth. All around us, human bones poke from the ground. As Stepanov kicks a butterfly-shaped vertebrae, I turn and find an upright jaw resting on the soil. A pad of new snow has collected in the jaw's interior, where the tongue should be. Ahead is a black mass. I kick it. It's a leather jackboot. Nearby, a flung-dice collection of tiny, elongated bones, a German-made leather pouch, the white, triangular curve of a shoulder blade and a stretch of intact spine that notches together like an out-size zipper. In only a few minutes, the bones of countless, unburied dead have become commonplace as wildflowers in May.

Stepanov returns to me and raises a hand, pinching his little finger so only a fraction of his smallest fingernail is exposed. "This is all you are seeing of the German bones," he says. "Even with this field full of skeletons, it makes up a tiny, tiny, tiny amount of the whole. Nothing at all, really."

Shivering in near darkness, we turn and head for the car. As we walk, Stepanov makes an offer. "If you want to see more of these things," he says, "then we must find Shtrykov. If we find him, he will show you what still exists of the Battle of Stalingrad."

Stepanov stops walking then; he turns in a full circle, taking in the endless loop of Russian horizon. "The unburied Germans go on farther than we can see," he says, still turning. "They go farther than any of us can understand."

IN JUNE OF 1941—the month and year Adolf Hitler's army of the Third Reich invaded Russia—the world seemed Hitler's for the taking. In less than a decade, he had risen from a riot-inciting, former prison inmate to German Supreme Commander; and in the last three years of his ascent—barely a thousand days—he had revived the shattered German economy and rebuilt national pride until his nation bristled with strength and vitality. Then he loosed his creation on Europe.

Hitler accomplished much of this turnabout through his "Z Plan," a program of deficit spending that immediately put more than 3 million unemployed Germans to work. While the Z Plan leaned heavily on national improvements—such as the network of high-speed roads called *Autobahn*—it also concentrated on the mass-production of Germany's next generation of battlefield weapons. If rudimentary artillery shells by the billion were the most sophisticated products manufacturing could conjure in the days preceding World War I, by the 1930s industry was capable of cranking out far more intricate objects—such as armored tanks and attack aircraft—and Hitler set his factories to making thousands of them.

A British invention of 1915, the armored tank was originally called a "land ship." It earned its modern name because, as it was boated across the English Channel to France to shatter World War I's trench-warfare stalemate, it was packed beneath canvas sheets marked "Water Tank" to deceive spies. Once upon the French battlefields, the seemingly impervious land ship was immediately dubbed The Devil's Machine by the Kaiser's army, and its arrival at the Somme helped turn the tide against Germany. But Hitler didn't just tip his spear with these mobile and armored cannons. He'd also sniffed the potential of the sky *above* the soldiers, and he'd refined military application of aircraft far past their World War I duties of reconnaissance, strafing, and light bombing. To augment the earthbound tanks, Hitler's Z Plan put attack aircraft into the sky, with four of the primary designs being the slow-moving JU-87 Stuka dive-bomber, the sleek, maneuverable Messerschmitt fighter and bomber, and Dornier and Heinkel high-altitude bombers. Of these, the Stuka was Hitler's master-stroke. Built inexpensively of low-grade steel and aluminum, the Stuka was referred to by Hitler and his generals as "flying artillery." Coming in low, at a few thousand feet altitude, the Stukas would identify their target, then dive at a steep angle, releasing bombs to fly forward as the aircraft pulled from its descent at the last minute. Though Stukas had such drag-inducing features as exposed rivets and nonretractable landing gear—which were sheathed in leather instead of metal to further keep costs low—the aircraft retained remarkable lift and power at slow speeds, and its effect in the war's early years was overwhelming.

Germany's military strategy had evolved since World War I as well. This time around, while still following the Schlieffen Plan of European conquest, Hitler's troops would rely on machines to stagger enemies with precision blitzkriegs, or lightning wars. Using attacking Tiger and Panther tanks supported by Stuka dive-bombers from his Luftwaffe, Hitler believed his army could crash through opposing fronts to slash rearward, where enemy capitals and commanders could quickly be destroyed. Then, as if subduing a decapitated chicken, waves of slower-moving infantry could sweep behind the invasion forces, mopping up leaderless armies.

It was a plan that started flawlessly. Beginning in 1938, Nazi divisions spread over the German homeland, then stepped aggressively into Austria and Sudetenland, a German holding inside Czechoslovakia. After that, Hitler's army exploded across Europe. By the summer of 1940—just two years after the initial deployment of troops—the Germans had taken the scalps of Poland, Norway, Denmark, Holland, Luxembourg, Belgium, and France. Invariably the blitzkriegs possessed such velocity that, for example, as German armor rolled into Denmark on the morning of April 9, 1940, bicyclists heading to work there thought a movie was being filmed. The same speedy hostility sundered the Netherlands in five days, while Luxembourg fell in one-fifth that time. Belgium was contained in four days, and by probing through a break between French infantry forces and the fortified wall of the Maginot Line on April 14, 1940, German tank divisions split French and British troops on the same Marne battlefields where trench warfare had raged twenty-two years earlier. Then Germany humiliated both defenders with a swiftness that left them reeling.

For the French, Nazi Germany would officially occupy their nation exactly a month after the initial Panzers hit France's soil. Hitler was personally on hand for a victor's parade—topped by a tap-dance jig—into the Place de la Concorde in Paris. As for the British, the Army of the Third Reich literally drove them into the sea at Dunkirk, where a fleet of 655 civilian boats—from fishing dories and yachts to passenger ships—was forced to ferry 337,000 troops across the English Channel to safety.

With the European continent practically conquered—as Germany was on collegial terms with the Italians and Spanish—Hitler expanded his vision. First, he ordered his Luftwaffe and U-boat submarine packs to hammer England for control of the British sky and the North Sea, but when British resolve slowed his plan—called Operation Sealion—in September of 1940, Hitler changed his mind. By December of that year, he'd ordered maintenance offensives against England and had turned his eyes east, to Joseph Stalin and the Soviet Union. Though he and Stalin had forged a nonaggression pact in 1939, Hitler had reconsidered since then. "We have only to kick in the door," the Führer said of the Russians, "and the whole rotten structure will come crashing down."

Hitler's generals were unconvinced. Behind their Führer's back, they spoke of 1812, the last time a European army had invaded Russia from the west. Then the attacker had been Emperor Napoleon of France, who in 1812 assembled 422,000 troops for his offensive: the largest army the world had ever seen. In that war, as the Grand Army had lashed across the vast Russian countryside, Czar Alexander used Russia's endless steppe as his ally. Over the summer of 1812, no matter how fast Napoleon's troops advanced across the flatness toward Moscow, the earth around them had already been set aflame, with the fire destroying any food or physical comfort the French could use. In September, as Napoleon's forces arrived in a deserted Moscow, the city was burned to the ground by Russian Cossack troops, who preferred to see Moscow turned to cinders than occupied by Europeans.

With no resources and the ferocious Russian winter approaching, Napoleon had no choice but to retreat: a long, cold, 2,000-mile march back to Paris. Along the way, hounded by Russian partisans and the czar's troops, French soldiers died by the thousands from freezing, bleeding, and starvation. By the time Napoleon's invaders returned home, with Russian soldiers chasing close behind, his army was crushed: fewer than 10,000 of the original 422,000 troops remained. As jack-booted Russian soldiers flooded the streets of a servile Paris, the czar's army ran roughshod, carving Russian notches everywhere in the French culture. Believing the service in Parisian restaurants to be slow, for instance, the czar's soldiers were known to pound their fists on tables while shouting the Russian word for "quickly": *bystro!* The result, with its focus on simple food served promptly, is France's now-famous *bistro* style of cooking.

VALERY SHTRYKOV IS a former North Sea trawler fisherman and Siberian oil roustabout with curly chestnut hair and ruggedly carved features. In the late 1980s, he returned to his family in Volgograd when Soviet fishing and petroleum exploration collapsed. Unemployed and back home, he did not know what to do at first. "I left the north to be near my family," he says. "I had no bigger plan than that."

These days, Shtrykov makes a good living by Russian standards as a guide for Germans and Austrians on the steppes, pointing out where the armies of the former Third Reich were destroyed by an encircling Red Army seven divisions deep. After fifty years of denying Hitler's loss at Stalingrad—the worst military defeat in history—the German and Austrian governments have finally returned, hoping to bury the dead abandoned by the Third Reich as it began to collapse toward the end of World War II. Since 1992, Shtrykov has helped the German and Austrian governments identify their World War II casualties, even as they lie as unburied skeletons on Stalingrad's battlefields. He has also helped start graveyards, where the long abandoned bodies will eventually be interred. It is work that has left him with an unusual collection of memorabilia — which he cannot sell, that being an offense punishable by imprisonment.

Shtrykov's apartment consists of a sparsely furnished hallway lit by a single bulb hanging on a bare wire, a kitchen, and down the hall, his study. Choked bookshelves line two sides of the room; a small radio sits on a table beneath the room's wall of windows. On Shtrykov's desk beneath the bookshelves is an opened notebook. Shtrykov is an artist, too. On the notebook's pages are pencil sketches of Russian villages not unlike Peschanka, the town where I've just seen the German bones. The drawings are delicate and assured, gray lines on white paper: the broad horizon and vertical cottages interplay for the scene's control. It is all done with the technical skill and intimacy of an Impressionist landscape painter.

Unrolling some of his hand-drawn maps across the table, Shtrykov begins pointing out the positions of Hitler's forces during 1942 and early 1943. Yet, as he explains these locations—showing me where the sixth company of this army and the third motorized squadron of that division were encamped—I become disoriented. There is no context. There are no towns nearby. Occasionally the cross-hatched vector of a rail line angles through, but that is the only familiar feature these maps show. Finally, through Stepanov, I ask about this. Why has Shtrykov neglected to put towns on his maps?

Shtrykov looks at me, a smile in his eyes. "There is no civilization where we're going," he says. "It is only the earth and the snow. Big. Empty and very difficult in the winter. It will be just as it was in the winter of 1942."

He steps away again, bending toward a large, low cabinet next to the desk and beneath the bookshelves. He reaches inside. "Where we are going tomorrow is a place forgotten by the world," he says, turning to look at me. "Until two or three years ago, no one wanted to remember it. It is sparsely farmed, not visited by people who don't live there. It is like a ghost in some ways. It is there—yet not there at all."

With that, Shtrykov grunts and hoists a large steel box from the cabinet's shelf. He carries it to the table and sets it down, opening its latch by pressing a spring-loaded lever. "What's in here," he says, flipping the lid back, "is what no one wants to think of."

Inside the box, in layer upon layer of disorder, are Nazi insignias and war medals: Iron Crosses, Knights' Crosses, SS lapel pins, large iron swastikas; swastika pinky rings and bronzed, oval awards for the battle-wounded (Nazi helmets backed by crossed swords); steel buttons and belt buckles and the small, polished swastika pins circled in red that German officers wore on their field caps; and on top of the pile, in a black leather sheath, its stainless steel hilt looking newly minted, an enormous dagger.

"Go ahead, take it out," Shtrykov says as he sees me looking at the knife. "It is an SS officer's dagger, an SSA assault knife. I found it in a bunker near where we are going tomorrow."

I reach into Shtrykov's box and lift out the heavy dagger. The handle is made of dark, beautifully turned cherry wood; the handle's pommel is stainless steel, flattened and rounded on top, for skull-crushing in close combat. Slowly, I slip the blade's length from the sheath, and its stainless steel blade glints like polished mercury in the room's light.

"I found this exactly as you're seeing it," Shtrykov says. "I have not cleaned it at all. It is in perfect condition. Worth thousands of dollars to a collector."

As I finish pulling the knife free, its broad, eight-inch blade hangs—flashing—in the air. Etched down the blade's center, in the stylized Gothic typeface of the Third Reich, are the words *Gott Mit Uns*. Shtrykov points at the lettering. "The inscription is in German, of course," Shtrykov says. "It says 'God with Us.' "

I slide the dagger back into its sheath, then hand it to Shtrykov, who looks me in the eye as he grasps it. "Hitler believed that, I think," he says, placing the dagger back into the box and shutting the lid tight. He smiles.

WHEN IT BEGAN bounding across the western Soviet Union in the summer of 1941, Adolf Hitler's Army of the Third Reich had never lost a battle. In the early stages of its blitzkrieg against Stalin, it seemed the Soviets would fold under Hitler as easily as every European nation had in the past. In Hitler's Barbarossa plan, a trio of spearhead armies—more than 3 million soldiers—entered Russia along its western border. One army went north, toward Leningrad; the central army moved toward Moscow; and the southern one was aimed at Stalingrad. Each army was to capture sixty or more miles of Russian landscape every day. After only two days, the Luftwaffe had effectively canceled the Soviet Air Force, destroying more than 2,000 of Stalin's warplanes as they sat on the ground at airfields. Within two weeks, German gunners tallied 6,000 demolished Soviet tanks. In a month, Hitler's armies were halfway to Moscow, having taken more than 1 million prisoners on the way while also capturing a chunk of territory twice the size of their homeland. Hitler, who had initially been viewed suspiciously by the German citizenry, was now a hero. Everyone, it seems, loves a winner, and many of the nations Hitler had invaded and occupied were elated by the speed and success of his Soviet campaign, further allying with the Reich thanks to Germany's seeming invincibility.

Then, out on the steppe, the Soviet Army suddenly evaporated, and the flat Russian earth stretched on for another thousand miles. Bridgeless rivers had to be forded, then endless miles of plain had to be crossed—only to be bounded on the far side with another wild river. By September, despite the fact that 3 million Soviet casualties had been inflicted in easy fighting and the northern city of Leningrad was encircled by Wehrmacht forces, the Germans were losing their edge. Supply lines from Berlin and Poland were stretching past the point of effectiveness. With the Russian winter approaching, Stalin continued his strategy of trading space for time. Still, after hard fought German victories in Minsk, Smolensk, and Kiev, everyone from Hitler to his foot soldiers believed the conquest of the Soviet Union was as good as finished. Even the hard-eyed Nazi chief of staff, General von Halder, wrote in his diary: "It is not an exaggeration to say that the campaign against Russia had been won in fourteen days."

By early October, however, German fortunes had started to fade. Red Army forces continued to defend Leningrad's city center, and all across Russia a week of raw and drenching rains left the steppe saturated, its dirt roads impassable. Snow started to fall on October 6, catching the Wehrmacht's soldiers still outfitted in summer dress. When German supply corps tried to requisition winter clothing, their appeals were denied: it would imply that Moscow might require a long, cold fight. By mid-November—with the frozen ground again able to support tanks, trucks, and infantry divisions—the German offensive lurched forward once more, despite 100,000 frostbite casualties. Hitler talked of capturing Moscow by year's end, and the Soviets, it seemed, began to believe him, too. In late November, Moscow was evacuated; even the coffin containing Vladimir I. Lenin was removed from Red Square and transported further east to safety. By early December, Hitler's army was within twenty-five miles of Moscow.

Stalin chose to make his first stand at Moscow. Having learned that the Japanese were planning to attack America and had no troops available for a press into the Soviet Union, he had moved ten divisions of his Siberian fighters—the best-trained army he had—secretly into Moscow, along with 1,000 of their tanks and 1,000 new aircraft. White-uniformed and outfitted with warm clothes that included thick felt boot liners, the Siberian forces joined the Red Army's Moscow troops to defend the Soviet's capital. On December 6, 1941, as German soldiers stuffed newspapers beneath their coats for insulation against the –15° cold, the Soviets counterattacked, and the Germans—losing their first battle of the war—crumbled. By December 25, Soviet armies had driven the Germans' middle salient sixty miles from Moscow. Still, Hitler was buoyed by the fact that his northern army continued to batter Leningrad with artillery, while in the south his forces had captured Sebastapol and the Crimean peninsula. Come spring, he felt certain his southern army would move like a dagger thrust toward Stalingrad and the oil-rich Caucasus mountains beyond.

So in March 1942, the Nazi command began concentrating on the conquest of Stalingrad, a modern, million-person showplace that Stalin had named for himself in 1925. With its steel mill, enormous tractor factory refitted for tank production, and central supply line of the Volga River at its center, it was the perfect target for the Germans to flatten, proving their setback in Moscow had been merely a false step.

Week after week, the German Sixth Army, Hitler's largest and the one that had been victorious in France two years earlier, advanced across the steppe at breakneck speed. Stalin began massing and conscripting troops inside the city center, instructing them sternly: "Not one step back." On August 23, Hitler ordered a three-day blitz over Stalingrad, a dive-bomber mauling that used every last aircraft on the Soviet front, with Stukas coming from as far north as Leningrad, more than 800 miles away. The city was decimated, but the bombing had produced exactly the opposite result the Germans had hoped for. The blitzkrieg had turned the city into a rubble fortress where every shattered wall or exposed sewer conduit could hide soldiers and where, with nothing left to defend but the soil, the

Soviets were free to fight for only the land, not the structures. "The kilometer was reduced to the meter, the planning room chart to the city map," a German officer has said. "Battles raged for every house, every factory hall, for water towers, railroad tracks, walls, cellars, and finally for every pile of rubble." Even while Soviet losses at Stalingrad rose by the thousands a week, it was the Germans who grew demoralized as fighting wore on. September ground into October, and the Germans could make no further advance inside the city. Although the Soviets sometimes defended only 100 yards of strewn bricks between themselves and the shore of the Volga, the Germans could not drive the Red Army into the river.

To the Germans, the Soviet forces were like ghosts or devils. At a grain elevator on the edge of the city, heavy German casualties were sustained when they tried to wrest the building from Soviet control. Day after day, the Germans blasted the elevator with mortars and grenades, only to see the Soviets firing back at them through every explosion's flash. When the attackers finally got inside, they were forced to fight for every room and stair. After a six-day battle, Hitler's army finally gained control of the elevator—where they found fewer than forty Soviet dead. On Mamayev Hill, the highest ground in the city, Germans and Russians clawed at each other for 158 days seeking to control the summit: When it was over, the Soviets had retained the hill, and 148,000 Germans and 47,000 Red Army soldiers had perished.

Then the early snows began, and winter had arrived. On November 10, German general von Paulus, commander of the Sixth Army, wrote to Hitler suggesting withdrawal from Stalingrad's city center. Hitler sent back orders: Keep attacking. But as it had been in Moscow, so it would be in Stalingrad. As the winter arrived, and thanks to an infusion of U.S. and British lend-lease weapons and equipment, the Red Army was finally outfitted for battle. By coming upon the fighting from the far side of the Volga, 750,000 new Soviet forces arrived almost unobserved. On November 11, more than 2,000 new Soviet artillery pieces blew holes in the German battle lines at the city's north and south. The Soviet counterattack had begun.

As Red Army forces took back the frozen steppe, German supply lines were severed, and as pressure from the Red Army increased, Paulus requested *Handlungsfreiheit*, or "freedom of action," from Berlin, hoping to withdraw his army from the city and burst through the surrounding forces and battle back toward safety. But Hitler was being assured by Luftwaffe commander Hermann Göring that his air force would soon supply the Sixth Army adequately, so Hitler denied Paulus the retreat request.

By mid-December, the Germans had nothing left to fight with. At the city center, German troops were running out of ammunition, and—freezing and starving—they were beginning to surrender. A dozen miles outside of town, the Sixth Army was starving as well. Now completely surrounded in a pocket, or *Kessel* (German word for "cauldron"), they were forced to eat foot powder and gruel made of motor oil and sawdust to survive. Every day, they became more solidly surrounded by what ultimately would become nearly 1 million Red Army troops, all of them warmly dressed and equipped with new weapons.

As the *Kessel* became contained Soviet intelligence gained a more accurate picture of the pocket. It was thirty miles wide and twenty miles deep, and inside it were more than 250,000 soldiers of the Sixth Army and Fourth Panzer divisions, as well as troops from Austria, Romania, and Italy. Soviet commanders sent Paulus an offer to surrender on January 8, granting him a decision deadline of two days. When Paulus did not respond, on the morning of January 10, a bombardment shattered the entrapped Germans with the largest concentration of field artillery in history: more than 7,000 guns, often strung at a density of 170 pieces per kilometer.

"As a result of the catastrophic supply situation, the battle strength of the troops is falling rapidly," Paulus radioed to Hitler on January 20. "Sixteen thousand wounded without care. With the exception of the Volga front, there are no defenses, no protection, no wood. Army has begun to disintegrate. I plead once again for *Handlungsfreiheit*."

Hitler declined. Instead, the Führer promoted Paulus to the rank of field marshall. Since no field marshall of the Reich had ever surrendered, Hitler was suggesting that Paulus's only option was suicide.

Instead, on January 31, Paulus went to the Soviets and began to discuss the terms of his surrender. When the moment came, on February 2, Paulus presented himself in Chuikov's headquarters and, when given a ceremonial dram of liquor, Paulus promptly proposed a toast to the Red Army. Since early January, more than 150,000 Germans, Austrians, Italians, and Romanians inside the *Kessel* had died. Upon surrender the German commander took pains to see that the remainder of his army—fewer than 91,000 soldiers—would be taken care of.

The Soviets assured Paulus they would do what they could

for his forces, but Red Army supplies were short as well, so the Germans received little aid from their captors. Of the 91,000 troops to survive Stalingrad, more than 50,000 died of disease and exposure within a month. Only 5,800 of the 250,000 soldiers once trapped in the *Kessel* ever returned home. Added to the more than 250,000 German dead from the fighting in Stalingrad, the destruction of Hitler's Sixth Army became the worst defeat in military history.

Hitler was broken by his loss at Stalingrad. During the remaining two years of his life, the once-weekly orator gave just three major speeches in public. He became removed from his generals and spent long days walking the grounds of his headquarters accompanied only by his dog, Blondi. At dinners, rather than discussing events of the war or plans for his Thousand Year Reich, Hitler began giving long, rambling discourses on dog training. And all the while the Soviets closed in from the east. The next time the soldiers of the Red Army would fight the Germans for control of a city, they would be shooting at one another down the long, broad boulevards of Berlin.

ON THE MORNING after visiting Shtrykov's apartment, Valery Shtrykov and Vasili Stepanov are waiting in my hotel's lobby. Outside, the night's storm has given way to endless blue skies and temperatures below zero. In the icy brightness of a new day, the city gardens and domed, columned Gorky Dramatic Theater across Volgograd's central square have been blanketed in pure, glistening snow. People hustle along wide sidewalks, which have already been shoveled. In their thick coats, tall leather boots, and fur hats they look warm and purposeful. As I ready for the day—with Stepanov helping me into a thick wool coat—I cannot help staring out the lobby windows at the city's classicist architecture. Down the road is a large, three-story building topped by a spire and a red star: the rail station. Another of the structures hulking around the graceful square is the telegraph and telephone center, which boasts a real hammered-gold facade. Made of quarried and faceted stone, every building on the square evinces the enormous "Stalin Gothic" style of architecture that modern Russia is known for, beautiful and profoundly impressive in sheer scale. Looking at them through the windows, I keep reminding myself that all of them—all of this city, in fact—has been completely rebuilt since 1943. As we walk to the car, I ask Shtrykov how he came to be the region's expert.

"Except for my years in the north, my whole life has been here," he says. "Even my kindergarten school was here. That is where I first began to look at the ground. My school was where a former German depot had been, so during the day I would sift the earth for things and carry them in my pockets. As I grew up, I played on the abandoned tanks and explored the underground bunkers. By the time I was sixteen, I didn't have any money, but I knew where German goods were on the steppe, so I began selling their war equipment to collectors and museums. I sold pistols and helmets and name plates. Then a law was passed saying such sales were treason, so I stopped. During that time, I had also found many documents that helped me locate where different divisions were encamped. Though, of course, I don't sell those, either."

These days, according to Shtrykov, a new black market in

German artifacts has sprung up. Due to privation since the former Soviet Union broke up while simultaneously embracing free market economics, premiums are now placed on valuables and unique collectibles, putting the old German graves and the unburied dead under a new wave of Russian attack as teenagers scoop up any knives, guns, identification tags, buttons, or medals they can find. These days, a German helmet sells for about $25, an I.D. tag $5, and an Iron Cross more than $50. The price for a well-preserved pistol or knife begins at $200, which is more than most Russians make in two months. Hoping to gather as many dog tags as possible as the plundering continues, Shtrykov has taken to visiting the sellers of these artifacts in Volgograd and outside the Hotel Intourist in Moscow. When he finds one with an identity tag, he writes the serial number down and turns the information over to the Germans and Austrians. "At least if I can't find the body," he says, "I can tell them that another missing-in-action case can be listed as deceased."

Our car arrives at a crossroad familiar from last night. To the left, a mile or two distant, is the village of Peschanka—where I first saw the bone fields. To the right, the steppe stretches on forever, unpeopled and snagged only occasionally by a line of trees or the deeply etched ravines that Russians call *balki*. We turn right—into the emptiness—and immediately the road becomes snow-drifted, with our sedan slamming through the piles of snow and fishtailing wildly on untracked roads. In minutes, we are completely alone with the sun and snow; the flatness of the steppe has swallowed all the civilization we've left behind.

"Was this part of the *Kessel?*" I ask Shtrykov.

"Right here? Yes," he says. "We have just passed where the Twenty-ninth Motorized Division was encamped. Ahead is where the Sixth Army and Sixteenth Infantry were bunkered. That army was enormous. It stretched for miles and miles."

A half-mile in front of us, a wire fence encircles a small plot of land, and Shtrykov asks our driver to stop at the fence and wait while he shows me something. "We will begin with the fate of the Russians here on the steppe," he says through Stepanov. "We will begin with Russian prisoners of war."

After the car stops, Shtrykov, Stepanov, and I step out into the day's frigid brightness. Though I am wearing a thick sweater, knit cap, heavy coat, and gloves, the gusting wind cuts cleanly to my skin, making me shiver. "Enter this way," Shtrykov says, waving for Stepanov and me to walk inside the fence. "This is where a German concentration camp for Russian soldiers was established in late 1942. There were no buildings here, and as the winter came and the temperature dropped, the Russians began to freeze and starve and die. About 4,000 or 5,000 Russians died here. All POWs. The living ate the dead. They ate each other. Terrible."

In front of us, on a tall welded-iron stand, is the iron sculpture of a torch whose metal flames rise toward the sky. "This is for the Russians," Shtrykov says of the sculpture. "The Germans called this place Hartmann Stadt, Hartmann City in English. It was named for William Hartmann, the German general who oversaw the camp. In January of 1943, he grew so despondent for both the Russians and Germans that he walked to the edge of the camp and began firing into the Russian prisoners—only to be shot by his own sentries. It was a suicide of a kind. Hitler, when he heard of Hartmann's death, didn't view it as a loss. He said it proved that all Germans were prepared to die for the Nazi cause."

Where are the Russian dead buried? I ask.

Shtrykov points ahead, to a long slope that ends at a *balka*. "There," he says, shaking his head. "A long pit. Mass grave."

As we start toward our car, Shtrykov says, "Russia lost twenty-seven million people to the Germans in the Great Patriotic War, which is what you call World War II. That was one-fifth of our population. You must remember that as we see things today. You must remember what Russians did to Germans is comparatively little. Keep in your mind what Hitler's armies did to *us*."

We get back in the car and drive on, the quality of the road deteriorating as we plow deeper into the endlessness. "It was my collection of German identification plates—what Americans call dog tags—that got me involved with the Germans," Shtrykov says. Before German reunification in 1991, he goes on, the number of Germans looking to mourn their lost soldiers on the Stalingrad battlefields were few. Every year or so, Shtrykov would get a request from private citizens in Germany or Austria or Romania asking about the fate of someone's brother or father. As Shtrykov had spent much of his life collecting identification plates and documents on the battlefields, he slowly became known for pointing people toward areas where their relative's remains might be found, where the living could come to mourn. Then, in 1991, as the reunified Germans began to address their collective past, an Austrian television producer named Walter Seledec arrived on the steppe with a film crew. He was searching out battlefield evidence for a documentary commemorating the 50,000 Austrians lost at Stalingrad. Shortly after Shtrykov showed Seledec the bone fields for the first time, the cameras began rolling, and in August of that year, when the program was broadcast, the public's outcry was deafening. Newspapers ran headlines reading "THE DEATH FIELDS OF STALINGRAD," and "BONES WITH IDENTITY TAGS"; and the monthly magazine *Wiener* ran a full-page photograph of a fallen skeleton still laid out on the grass in its German uniform, including boots. The caption read: "No cross. No wreath. This unknown soldier never made it into a mass grave. Today, he lies in the steppes outside Volgograd exactly as he fell fifty years ago. His shirt and uniform buttons still lie between his ribs."

With the horrific publicity, Shtrykov says, he became besieged by Germans and Austrians, all of whom wanted his help in identifying the fate of the Third Reich's troops. The Austrian Black Cross contacted him. As did the German Volksbund. In the spring of 1992, Shtrykov went to work with the Germans, who asked if he could locate any German graveyards. "I told them, I can show you fifty graveyards *a day*," Shtrykov says. "They couldn't *believe* it."

At first, Shtrykov took the Germans to graveyards that had already been plundered, reinforcing the idea that any identification of their war dead should be undertaken quickly. Then he began showing where troops had gone unburied, and the bone field scenes spurred the German officials to action. Within

weeks, Shtrykov had helped establish the first of four graveyards inside the *Kessel*, places approved by the Volgograd government. The Germans and Austrians made provisions to pay
for the graveyard's material upkeep and made promises that all
labor provided would be Russian. "Four of us worked that first
summer," Shtrykov says. "Two brothers—who are friends of
mine—and me, and a driver. Each of us made about $900 a
month, and each day we would begin work about four o'clock
in the morning, since afternoons were very hot. On many days
we exhumed bodies until eight o'clock at night. We would put
the soldiers' remains in plastic garbage bags, searching care-
fully for the identity tag that went with the bones, so we knew
his name and serial number." When Shtrykov and his co-
workers would come upon a mass grave, he says, they would
simply dump all of the bones—the femurs and skulls and
ribs—into a garbage bag along with the identity tags. "It was
not precise at the mass graves," Shtrykov says, throwing up his
hands and shaking his head at the futility. "These were often
places where Russians were merely clearing their towns of the
German dead, or where the Germans had been burying their
casualties just to get them underground. These were not organized burials." When a load of bags had been collected and
itemized, it was stored in a warehouse at Rossoshka, a town
nearby; while the list of identity tags was passed to the appropriate nation. Since then, the governments have been working
to inform family members that wartime remains have been
found—then the bodies are buried once again. After a year
spent getting the German program established, Shtrykov has
worked the past three years with the Austrian Black Cross. So

far, nearly 2,000 soldiers have been identified and about 430 buried.

OUR CAR FOLLOWS snow-piled roads farther and farther into the steppe. Turning this way and that, we track along a barely visible road climbing the sides of *balki* and emerging again across the flat, snowy plains. We pass a narrow clump of trees, inside of which a German Army motorcycle and its sidecar sits, new snow dusting its age-blackened steel.

"Look there," I say to Shtrykov, pointing.

He smiles. "Once in a while," he says, "you'll find something large out here. But motorcycles are about the biggest things now. The last Panzer tanks and armored carriers have been removed, though I know of two tanks that are submerged in a lake, so the authorities don't know of their existence. I'm keeping their location to myself, until perhaps I can legally sell them to a museum."

I ask about local people being injured by unexploded ordnance, and Shtrykov frowns and shakes his head. "Each spring, as the land mines and artillery shells come to the surface again, a few children are hurt, and that is tragic," he says. "But more often, it is farm animals who die in blasts. Last year, near Rossoshka, five hogs were blown up at one time. Dozens of cattle die each year, too."

The car makes another turn, crossing onto a wide, sloping plain blanketed by snow. As our sedan rattles across the field's five- or six-mile width, Shtrykov pats the car's driver on his shoulder. "Stop here," he says.

We step from the car again, and Shtrykov thrusts out a hand, blocking my progress into the field. "Look around," he says. "Look hard, and tell me: What do you see?"

I squint into the untracked snow, and slowly—as my eyes grow accustomed to the glare—the blanket I once thought was perfectly flat assumes subtle relief. Sticking from the snow in any direction are bones. Between the furrows, femurs jut into the air, ribs and hips and ulnas and shoulder blades poke from the snow, too.

As we begin into it, crusted snow again crunching beneath our boots, thick thigh bones and narrow clavicles are everywhere, as are plates from pelvises and the knuckled sculptures of elbow joints. I stop and gawk while Shtrykov keeps pushing ahead. A few hundred yards into the field, with bones jutting up all around his feet, Shtrykov turns and looks back to Stepanov and me. "On this field last year, I found a lot of Romanian and Italian soldiers," he says. "And a lot of soldiers from the German Sixth Army, too. It was a large encampment, and I have found some wonderful knives and medals here. There were two different graveyards in this field as well as the unburied dead, which are—as you can see—very many. The graveyards are filled with soldiers who died in the center city fighting, who were buried before the ground froze." He lifts a hand and turns in a circle, taking in the vastness of the field. "How many died and were never buried here in January of 1943?" he asks. "Can anyone ever know how many were right here?

"Think about it, a landscape like this is where they lived that winter," he says. "You can imagine the problems. It is flat and open. There was no place to hide more than 250,000 men.

There was no water other than melted snow. Little food. There was no wood for heat or cooking. They must have known they were waiting to die."

I look around, and seeing the endless scattering of legs and ribs among the snow-covered furrows, I am reminded that this is now a farmer's field—though one thick with human bones. "How do they plow this?" I ask Shtrykov.

"It is not too bad plowing here," he says. "The farmer's plowshares break up the bones. Still, in this field and some of the others around here, there are times when a farmer comes to a place where the skeletons are simply too numerous." Shtrykov shrugs. "When the bodies clog his plow," he says, "the farmer will usually get down off his tractor and pile the bones at a corner of the field. I will show you such a pile."

While Shtrykov is telling me this, a truly odd notion hits: Despite the fact that we've spent fifteen minutes poring over snowy skeletons that stretch to the horizon, I haven't seen any jawbones or heads. "Where are the skulls?" I ask.

"The skulls?" Shtrykov says. He lifts his hands and shrugs again. "Over many winters, they freeze and break into smaller plates. Or, just as often, farmers' plows splinter them."

He pauses for a moment. "You would like to see skulls?" he asks.

I nod.

"Then that's next," Shtrykov says.

THE PITOMNIK AIRSTRIP was one of the three Luftwaffe bases inside the *Kessel* at Stalingrad. Overrun by Soviet tanks in January 1943, nearly every soldier stationed there died in the assault. As we drive toward it, Shtrykov points at a line of wide, deep pits dug into a *balka's* ravine at the roadside. "The Forty-fourth Austrian Division was encamped here, as were parts of the Twenty-ninth Motorized Division of the Germans," he says. "Six to ten men lived in each bunker. These pits follow this road for miles, all the way to the town of Rossoshka. The Germans spread out their army for a reason. If the Katusha began to fall around them, casualties would be more limited."

During the Soviet campaign, if the German version of terror in the sky was a dive-bombing Stuka, then for the Soviets it was the Katusha. A mobile rocket system with eight steel launcher rails and sixteen dynamite-tipped rockets—two projectiles were attached to each rail—Katusha barrages packed a horrific wallop. Invented in 1940 and called "Stalin's organ" for the way the finned missiles *whizzed* away musically while the launch tracks stood like organ pipes, Katushas could be mounted on truck beds for mobile systems, or they could be lined up by the dozen as batteries along the ground. When deployed in unison, hundreds of Katusha rockets could blast the opposition in unison, decimating both the enemy's numbers and its resolve in a single volley. When Hitler's forces first saw the Katusha used in the defense of Moscow, they were terrified by the weapon's force. Yet it was during the fighting at Stalingrad, especially on the German-controlled land beyond Mamayev Hill and inside the *Kessel*, that Hitler's forces came to characterize each Katusha attack as death itself.

As we turn off the main road and onto a still smaller trail, Shtrykov tells the driver to stop the car. We get out and

Shtrykov begins walking across a square, 600-acre field ringed on all sides by brushy trees. Ahead, almost invisible in the snow, deep rectangles seem to have been carved into the soil. As we come closer, the rectangles turn into underground bunker entrances, which drop twenty feet into the earth before flattening out and burrowing underground. These days, although you can see which direction the passages led, the tunnels have been sealed by dirt. "These were some of the Sixth Army's deepest bunkers—for officers," Shtrykov says. "Inside are square chambers with sheet-metal walls. There were once many good treasures in these, if you didn't mind the dead."

I kick at the snow: in the dirt beneath is a corroded metal oval. When I pick it up, I can see green oxidation along its bronze edges. Turning the oval in my hand, I find the worn shape of a Nazi helmet backed by two swords: it is a medal for the war wounded. Shtrykov, seeing my find, begins poking around the soil, too. He finds a piece of German field radio and the lens of a gas mask. A little more kicking unearths Shtrykov a pair of small binoculars caked in frozen mud. As he throws the detritus into the bunker's deep entrance, I put the medal in my coat pocket.

"Beneath this field was a network of tunnels," Shtrykov says. "In 1943, when the dead began to pile up and things looked lost, the Germans would fill the bunkers with fifty or sixty bodies and blast the entrances closed. Some of the bunkers had side chambers, so it is hard to estimate exactly how many dead may still be under this field." Shtrykov points around the snow, which undulates with plowed furrows. He shows me a half-dozen exposed bunker entrances, their locations almost hidden by snow and uneven earth.

In another few minutes of driving the back roads—after passing an enormous field where a German graveyard was plowed to chaos before the bodies could be identified—we arrive at a pond fed by a small, iced-over creek, the River Rossoshka. Beyond it, a long, flat farmer's field recedes into the distance. This, Shtrykov tells me, was the Pitomnik airbase. "The airstrip was there," he says, pointing to the field. "But what you want is this way."

Ahead of us, littering fields that are blown with snow, the rounded shapes of skulls and the pickets of arm and leg bones are everywhere. There are tens of thousands of bones spreading away from us in every direction. Shtrykov bends forward and lifts a pair of round, white skulls from the earth. Each of Shtrykov's hands cradles one in the air. "Because of the *balki*, there has been no plowing here," Shtrykov says. "The skulls have not been broken up." He puts the skulls back down, walks two or three steps and grabs up two more skulls, lifting them to show me. "These men all died defending Pitomnik, an airfield where supply planes had stopped landing," he says, putting the skulls back down.

I walk away, looking at the endless skulls. On some of them, I can see only the paleness of their smoothly rounded backs. On others, the ovalesque holes where the spinal columns once attached are pointed toward the sky. Some show eye sockets or the blade-shaped triangles where noses once were, or they show rows of upper teeth and the dark seams of nasal palates, or the corrugated junctions where two cranial plates have split, leaving the skull cracked wide open so snow has sifted inside. And there are not just tens of these skulls—or even hundreds. There are thousands.

Ahead of me, another frozen feeder stream runs through the bottom of a small *balka*. The dry, gold stalks of tall grasses and cattails stand above the ice, rattling in the frigid wind. Beyond them, on the *balka*'s far side, a row of five skulls stares at me. Each skull has somehow been left standing upright on the soil; positioned as if on a shelf. The dark sockets once occupied by their eyes seem somehow blacker, thanks to the whiteness of the snow around them.

I have seen enough. I turn and head for the car.

"You are ready to go?" Shtrykov shouts to me.

"Yes." I tell him. "We can go back to the hotel now."

"So now you understand that the job of identifying and burying the dead is something like impossible?" he asks as we walk toward the car.

"Yes."

"Bone fields like this are everywhere here," he says. "There are hundreds of them. We will never be done cleaning them in my lifetime; perhaps not in the lifetime of my grandchildren. It's too vast."

Back in the sedan and headed for Volgograd, Shtrykov smokes cigarettes and stares quietly through the windshield's filmy glare. He directs the driver down a road, then points out a ragged pile of bones and darkly rotted uniforms: a cairn as tall as a man and maybe ten feet across. It was made by a farmer whose plow was clogged. Later, when we pass a lonely quadrangle of iron posts in the midst of a broad field, Shtrykov points at it and turns to face me. "That was once a field hospital, and at least sixty Germans are buried there," he says. "If you would like, we can stop and kick in the snow, to see what we might uncover. We might find a few old German transfusion bottles made of glass. I have found them here before. I have even found some with the blood of Germany still in them."

ON JANUARY 13, 1943, three days after the initial Soviet assault upon the *Kessel*, a German soldier of the Sixth Army, Rudi, began a letter to his wife this way:

> My dearest Greti,
> Be kissed and kissed by me a thousand times, dear Greti, believe me, this is the most difficult letter I have ever had to write. Now, I must write you openly and honestly and admit that the situation is very, very serious. I don't want to say that this letter will be the last one I write to you. God forbid. But you must be prepared for anything. When we are forced to give up the whole thing and surrender to the Russians, which I no longer doubt, then I won't be able to write you anymore. Dear Greti, don't take it too tragically, you know that I will try everything to survive, of that you can be assured. Also, you must always keep in mind that this fate that has come upon me has also hit a quarter-million human beings. . . .

Fifty years after this letter was written and mailed in the *Kessel* field post, a copy of it finally arrived in Austria. Postmarked on January 15, 1943, it was one of more than 300 letters that were captured by the Soviets after the German surrender, letters which were immediately relegated to a dusty corner of the Soviet archives. Then, in the spring of 1992, as the Austrian television network ZDF began piecing together a five-part documentary, "Decision at Stalingrad," with the Russian TV network Ostankino, a package landed in the hands of ZDF associate producer Karin Hübner. "Inside were copies of all these letters from soldiers inside the *Kessel*," she says. "Letters that had never been delivered. Letters from sons to mothers, fiancés to fiancées, lovers to lovers; husbands to wives; fathers to children."

In October 1992, Hübner released a statement through DPA, the German wire service, stating that ZDF had come upon several hundred unmailed letters from the siege at Stalingrad and was seeking to deliver them. "It was amazing," she says. "Within a week, more than 13,000 people telephoned requesting information about the 300 letters. Nearly every family in Germany lost a father or son or uncle in that war. They had never been able to express their questions or grief for the mystery of the deaths, because of shame from the German loss and the atrocities in World War II."

Beyond the problems of people's deaths or relocations, an unusual set of practical obstacles awaited in the addresses themselves, since after the destruction of the Third Reich, even the names of streets had been changed. No longer were German thoroughfares and public squares named for Hitler's Nazi leaders; in the wake of World War II, places such as Hermann Göring Strasse or Adolf-Hitler Platz were quickly rechristened.

Consequently, Hübner was forced to concentrate almost exclusively on the addressee names and the cities the people had lived in in 1943.

Hiring ten full-time interns to help her collate and cross-reference the data, Hübner ultimately was able to deliver 61 of the 300 letters. "When the people would receive these letters," she says. "It was always very emotional. They had spent fifty years forgetting the men who had sent them the mail. The living had kept on with their lives, despite the *Vermisst*: the mystery of their loss. When these letters connected the living with the dead, you could see old loves and friends return—back from where they had been dropped and forgotten. As people read the letters, their pain was very obvious on people's faces and in their tears. It was very sad and very personal. After fifty years of forgetting, the pain of remembering was almost worse."

Today there remain 239 letters sent and never received. Letters whose tone and character vary amazingly, considering the gravity facing the Sixth Army in January 1943. One soldier, who has not eaten in days and who was driven partly mad by the relentless artillery barrages and Russian cold, free associates across a page: "Hunger, hunger, hunger, and then lice and filth." Another writes of valor, comforting his daughter and imploring his wife. "Be proud," he writes, "because we did it for you, for all of you, and for our beloved homeland." Another documents the collapse of a twenty-two-year-old bunkermate, who on Christmas Eve cries uncontrollably. Another delineates his slow starvation, then adds with brave irony that there is "too much to die from, and too little to live on." Another tells of a Luftwaffe transport plane that left the *Kessel* airstrip at

Gumrak overloaded with German wounded. As it took off, it pitched to one side, throwing its human cargo against one wall; the unbalanced plane rolled, crashed, and exploded across the steppe just beyond Gumrak's snow-blown runway.

The delivery of the sixty-one messages to their rightful possessors was the subject of a special Christmas program on ZDF. "For the people of Austria and Germany, there is obviously a huge, unspoken need to mourn the dead of Stalingrad," Hübner says. "The Germans were both aggressor and victim, and that situation remains very complicated in their minds. I cannot say how deeply the guilt and inability to mourn goes, but I know in some Germans it is there—and it is not easy to untangle."

What of Rudi and Greti? I finally ask. Rudi, whose letter runs four full pages—and tells of transport planes carrying German wounded having solders vainly clinging to their landing gear as they take off—ends this way: "Let's hope for the best, and our life will be even better, our love ever greater and deeper. Now darling Greti, trust in our Savior, for he has not and will not abandon me. Warmest greetings and a thousand kisses from your Rudi."

Hübner pauses for a moment, remembering her trials to find Greti. "I finally found Rudi's younger sister," she says, "who is now very old and quite weak." When Hübner contacted Rudi's sister, she was told that Greti had married Rudi in 1936 and that Greti had waited for him until after the war was over—even though, during the time her husband was away, Greti had taken a number of lovers. After the war, when Greti heard nothing of Rudi for a year, she took up with another man. In

1949 she had a child by him. "Greti is dead now," Hübner says. "Rudi's sister never spoke with Greti after Greti began taking lovers. She said Greti became a bad person. Rudi's sister told me: If you send me a copy of Rudi's letter, I will only tear it up and destroy it. I hate Greti, even in her death. I will never forgive."

ANOTHER DAY, AND an Intourist guide and interpreter named Margarita Efremenkova is showing me downtown Volgograd. A native of the city, the black-haired, fur-coated Efremenkova was born after the war and before the city was renamed in 1961.

She begins our tour at Tsaritsa Gully, a broad *balka* that runs through the city and into the Volga. The day is sunny — and almost unbearably cold. As we stand in a howling wind where the gully meets the river, Efremenkova turns and looks upstream at the string of apartment buildings that follows the river's western bluffs. "This is one of the places where fighting was the worst," she says. "Ferries carrying Russian soldiers from across the Volga landed just upstream of here, and the forces would fan out along this shoreline and fight the Germans for every inch. The Red Army often defended only 100 yards of land between themselves and the river. Casualties on both sides were very high."

In late 1992, shortly after the Volgograd government started granting Austria and Germany places to bury their dead, it was also suggested that a series of German-underwritten monuments be erected around the city. The monuments, the Germans insisted, would be absolutely apolitical, and it was hoped that one of the largest memorials could be built at Tsaritsa Gully. "When news came out about the proposed monuments," Efremenkova says, "our people were in an uproar—especially the veterans. It was as if the war was still on! They said, 'No. There will be no monuments paid for with German money in Stalingrad. Those nations will never be allowed here.'"

Instead, Efremenkova says, a playground is now being built on both sides of Tsaritsa Gully. "It was decided that the best monument to the Russian sacrifices at Stalingrad would be a place for children to grow strong," she says. "A place for them to enjoy their lives." Looking at the playground under construction, with its now frozen earth torn up by bulldozers to make room for basketball courts and swing sets, I think back to the 1942 photos of the shattered city along this wide ravine. In the pictures, soldiers lean against the *balka's* sloping sides, pressing themselves into the brick-strewn dirt to avoid German bullets and shrapnel. In the pictures, they carry round-magazined machine guns and Kalashnikov carbine rifles, and they look exhausted and cold and filthy. Beyond them, the buildings of the city are completely destroyed; ragged sawtooth walls jut in the distance. Now, looking along riverside of a rebuilt Volgograd, which stretches for twenty-five miles along the river's western edge, there are buildings and outdoor pavilions as far as I can see. As my gaze runs along the wide park—with its outdoor theaters and eateries—that follows the Volga's banks to the horizon, it seems impossible that in 1942 all that my eyes could take in was a shattered, smoldering ruin.

Up on this unprotected bluff, the combination of wind and

cold soon drives us to the car. Efremenkova directs the driver to Mamayev Hill, a low mound that towers 126 feet above the Volga, highest point in Volgograd. Today, on the hill's summit is the concrete and steel sculpture of Mother Russia, the largest statue on earth. Standing 275 feet tall and brandishing a steel sword that weighs 279 tons, it was completed in 1967, and since then more than 60 million Soviets and Russians have made the pilgrimage to see it. As we step from the car back into the cold, Efremenkova says that, although the statue is impressive, the story of the two armies butchering each other as they grappled on Mamayev Kurgan (as it is called in Russian) is the most dramatic of the Stalingrad battle. After the war was over, as the Soviet people began to clear the hill of casualties, equipment, and unexploded ordnance, 500–1,253 bits of shrapnel covered every square yard of the hillside. And because the destruction was so horrific, neither a tree nor blade of grass grew on the scorched hillside for three years afterward. "The killing is storied to be so heavy," Efremkova says, "that in the spring of 1943, as the snow turned to water, the runoff was pink with blood."

From the road, a long walkway leads up toward Mother Russia on its summit. At the base of the hill, tended rows of gigantic plane trees line the corridor, beyond which are smooth meadows of grass. Halfway up the hill, you climb past a series of reflecting pools and sculptures. There, centered on a flat pavilion, is the stone sculpture of a bare-chested and stern visaged soldier which, if you stand directly in front of it, has been positioned to block a view of Mother Russia beyond. Beyond the soldier, with Mother Russia again in sight, the corridor widens to about eighty yards and becomes a sweeping stairway.

Along both walls of the stairs, a massive relief sculpture tells the chronological story of the Battle of Stalingrad, with Efremenkova pausing to tell me of one legend in particular. Pointing at the carving of a Soviet soldier almost hidden at the sculpture's top, Efremenkova says that his name was Vasili Zaitsev, and that he was a Soviet sniper. "He was extremely good at his work," Efremenkova says. "And he would be called in any time the Germans made gains up the hillside. He could kill with one shot. Hitting Germans even inside the wooden doorways of their bunkers." When Zaitsev had killed more than 240 Germans, the Third Reich sent all the way to Berlin, summoning their best sniper, Heinz Thorbald. For days, the two assassins stalked one another through the ruined city. "In the end," Efremenkova says, "Zaitsev killed him."

Climbing still farther toward the Mamayev Hill summit, to the right of the walkway is a pantheon whose red mosaic interior is inscribed with 7,200 names. The names, picked at random and built with tiny slivers of tile, represent just a few of the 47,000 Soviet troops killed on Mamayev Kurgan, and they are guarded by jack-booted, goose-stepping Russian sentries even today. As I stop and look at the names, the doleful strains of Schumann's *Träumerei* drift through the icy air. "That music is played all day and night, every day of the year," Efremenkova says.

We continue climbing, until, after an hour of slow walking in bitter wind and cold, we are at the top of Mamayev Kurgan, standing near the feet of Mother Russia. From the summit, it's obvious why the hill was a strategic necessity: it's the highest ground for miles, and the whole battle zone can be seen from this one place. To the south, the city center is perfectly visible. To the north stands the Red October steel mill and the tractor factory, which in 1941 was converted to crank out hundreds of Soviet T-34 tanks a month, even as fighting raged on Mamayev Hill. To the east is the mile-wide Volga, and, to the west, beginning just beyond Volgograd's outer city high-rises, are the steppes, flat and snowy and endless as ever.

IN A CONFERENCE room at Volgograd's enormous city hall, a group of elderly, well-dressed men and one woman sit around a polished wooden table. They have convened here to speak about the Battle of Stalingrad. The only people in the room who *did not* contribute to the defense of Stalingrad are me, Margarita Efremenkova, and Stanislav Glindzhev, the Volgograd city manager. A dark-haired man in his late forties, Glindzhev wears half-moon glasses at the end of his long nose, and he takes control of the meeting immediately. He wants to tell me about Volgograd today; describing the city's fiftieth anniversary "Days of Victory" celebration of May 1995. "It cost *four billion* rubles," he says, which translates to about U.S.$4 million. "But for that, the city has something truly memorable, something that helps our children better understand events of the Great Patriotic War. To help them remember the losses of Russian troops and more than 100,000 of our city's civilians, plus the brave rebuilding of the city. We have new monuments, too. One of them, along the Volga, commemorates the BK-13 ferry boats, seventy of which were sunk by Stukas while moving soldiers and civilians across the river in 1942."

"What about the Germans?" I ask Glindzhev through Efre-menkova. "Will the Germans be able to build a monument to the fighting?"

"The agreement between Russia and Germany is about graves only! Not about feelings!" Glindzhev says, nearly shouting. "We have given the Germans places for graveyards outside of town; that is all they're allowed. It is not possible to push the wheel of history back! The past is a guest in today's reality! They can bury their dead, that is participation enough."

Was it difficult to clear the ruins and unexploded ordnance during the rebuilding? I ask.

"That was a long time ago," Glindzhev says. "We haven't found unexploded weapons in a long time — except out on the steppe, where a farmer will sometimes come upon one. When that happens, the army is dispatched to clear it away. In the city, we have only found two or three sea mines in the past few years. The Germans used to drop them into the river, where they would float and blow up the BK-13 ferry boats. They have all been duds. Waterlogged."

I ask about the blitzkrieg. The one woman in the group, Valentina Petrova, says she was a nurse during the siege. Sitting next to me in a blue dress with a sweater draped over her shoulders, Petrova speaks slowly. She remembers that the Stukas were outfitted with sirens, and as they began their bombing dives, picking up air speed, the sirens' pitch would rise to a deafening shriek. "There would be this noise, noise, noise . . . then *boom!*" As nurses, Petrova and her comrades would sing to the soldiers from their first aid stations beneath the buildings. "We would stand in basement doors and sing to keep spirits up," she says. "Amid the falling bombs and artillery shells, the music was wonderful. We would sing a song that went: I am your little toy doll. . . ."

Then, seated in the chilly, fluorescent-lit conference room, she begins to sing in a spindly voice that rises stronger and stronger with each verse. Soon, she is lost in the song and won't stop, with the Russian melody winding and looping through the air. Tears are in her blue eyes, and she is nearly out of breath with each phrase. As the song reaches a crescendo, she pauses, unable to go on; then she breaks down, weeping.

Alex Zhukov, another veteran and a bald man with thick eyeglasses, says that the fighting became so commonplace it was as if life had always been that way. "When the dive-bombers would strike," he says, "the braver soldiers would sometimes taunt the more terrified ones. We would say: You need two pairs of pants when the Stukas come. You need one pair to wear during the bombings, and a second pair to put on when the bombings are over—so you can change out of the pants you've soiled!"

The people around the table chuckle. Feodor Pekarsky, director of the Memorial Complex on Mamayev Kurgan, quiets everyone by raising a hand. "I was a foot soldier during the entire battle," he says. "I fought every day in Stalingrad, and what I remember was the endlessness of it. It was: 'Go there,' 'Defend there,' 'Shoot there.' That's all I remember. Only later, when I studied the siege as the memorial director, did I realize the seriousness and the breadth of the fighting. In 1942 the Germans were upon us so quickly it was impossible to gauge how large the fighting was."

"What about the Germans?" I ask the group. "How do you feel about the Germans today?"

Around the table heads shake, and no one says a word. I look to Margarita Efremenkova to ask what's wrong, and she asks Pekarsky. He answers at length. Then she turns back to me, and her face has grown stern. "If you would like to ask about the fighting, they will try to answer your questions. If you would like to ask about the rebuilding of Stalingrad, they will answer. But about the Germans, they are still very angry. Even after these many years, about the Germans they have nothing to say."

THAT AFTERNOON, FOLLOWING the icy wind that ripped through Volgograd all morning, low, iron gray Russian snow clouds return. In a rented car, Vasili Stepanov has joined Margarita Efremenkova and me for a ride out to the village of Rossoshka, where he will show me the first completed *Kriegsgräberfürsorge*, or German graveyard. But before we do that, Stepanov wants me to meet a friend of his.

A light snow is sifting earthward to another frozen mud street at twilight. As we walk through the shanty village—its alleyways bounded on both sides by loose board fences to keep tall mounds of hay inside—the place is deserted. Inside each yard, between the fences and the haystacks, dogs have burrowed into the straw to escape the cold. Warm inside their shelters, they stick their heads between the fenceposts, barking at Stepanov, Efremenkova, and me as we move along the uneven ice in the growing dark. The dogs' racket ricochets off the wooden shacks, then rolls onto the emptiness of the steppe beyond. The village seems deserted and clinging to the flatness of the steppe as if held tight by an enormous buckle. Gusts of wind make whirring sounds across the fields, lifting fallen snow and throwing it into whorls that spin wildly above the ground. Finally, somewhere ahead, we hear a metallic *clang*-clanging that might be human-made. As we get closer, a man is working outside in the cold. He is overhauling his tractor, and engine parts are strewn across a rough wooden table directly behind him. A kerosene lamp sits on the tabletop, and as we come near, we can see he's an old man wearing insulated overalls and a heavy sweater. His face is weathered, round, and wrinkled. He wears a billed engineer's hat topped by a knit cap. We ask if he has seen Stepanov's friend lately, if he knows where the friend might be.

"No," the farmer says, clutching a rusted pipe wrench in his left hand. "This is a small village, yes, but I don't know your acquaintance very well."

I suggest to Stepanov that we ask about the Germans. Stepanov puts my request to the farmer, and he says yes, he will hear a few questions, provided his name isn't used.

"Were you in Rossoshka during the German attack?" I ask.

"Yes," he says, pulling a rag from his back pocket to wipe his hands, which glisten with dark grease. "But Rossoshka was not here then. It was down the road, near where the German graveyard is now."

Why did the town move? I ask.

After the war, the old farmer says, the people of Rossoshka returned to find only a plain where their homes had once stood. The Germans had destroyed everything, just as they had done in Peschanka, fifteen miles away. Just as, in fact, they had done all across Russia. Rossoshka was resettled a mile or two farther north. "This is a better site for a town than the old Rossoshka was," the farmer says. "It is closer to the river. And anyway, after the Germans destroyed old Rossoshka, we could not go back there. The ground there was stained by the tragedy—and the German dead were everywhere."

The old farmer's eyes turn back south, toward the *Kriegsgräberfürsorge* and the place on the empty steppe where old Rossoshka once stood. "The Germans still occupy land where my house once was," he says, pointing. "They are dead. I am still alive. Even now I am angry."

As he stares into the distance, a look of resigned determination has hardened on his face. He slaps at the air. "I don't think the anger will ever go away in me," he says. "Not until we are all dead, not until the heart of every Russian who fought the Germans has stopped will our anger toward Germany die. It will not happen until we are all dead."

NIGHT HAS ARRIVED now. And back out on the steppe, the paved road is empty and snow-blown. As we drive deeper into the *Kessel*, Stepanov points out the village of Gumrak, where both a Luftwaffe airstrip and a field hospital were located during the war. It is also the place where Rudi—the German soldier who sent off his last letter to Greti in January 1943—disappeared into history; lost even more completely than his words of love on the page. Today, we know what happened to

Rudi's letter and to Greti, but there is still no clue as to Rudi's fate. He was never heard from again. He is one of the remaining 148,000 souls of the Third Reich whose lives were extinguished and abandoned on these steppes more than fifty years ago.

From the car's front seat, Stepanov turns to me and points beyond the windshield toward Gumrak. "Today we believe a German cemetery with 2,500 to 3,000 bodies is located over there," he says. "Unmarked graves. Germans who died in center city fighting, who were buried before the ground froze."

Stepanov turns forward again and we drive on. Suddenly, in the middle of a broad field in the winter dark, Stepanov signals for the driver to stop.

Inside a low wire fence at the roadside is the *Kriegsgräberfürsorge*: a patch of flat, snowy earth that stretches from the pavement toward the eastern horizon. In the soil, rows of low, rectangular indentations are barely visible beneath the snow. Each is a grave; the name of each grave's occupant has been marked on a small square of paper and staked to the ground like a headstone.

I stoop to read a few names, but there is nothing. The ink has bled and faded completely away. As I look up, watching the staked papers blow and flutter on the wind, Stepanov says that there's been talk of getting metal identity plates for the graves, but those will come later, after exhumations have finished.

As Stepanov and I stand among the grid of graves, the dark of night has replaced twilight completely. "There are 135 Germans here," Stepanov says, sweeping his arm in a circle through the night and the falling snow. "It doesn't look very impressive, but I think it is an important place — for both Germany and Russia. After fifty years of trying to forget, this is where we begin to remember."

Away from the road, at the far end of the graveyard's plot, two white birch logs have been notched and bolted together. They make a cross that rises fifteen feet into the air. On top of the cross rests a rusted German helmet, its scalloped edges and pitted iron surface capped by a dusting of white. We walk closer, then stare for a moment at the German helmet, in silence. White bits of snow fall from the darkness above. A dog barks in the distance. Finally, the icy wind and falling snow grow too cold for our upturned faces, and we start back for the car.

3

Playground

IT BEGAN JUST before sunrise, January 27, 1951. As the dark, sweep-wing shape of an Air Force B-50 bomber streaked above the Nevada desert sixty-five miles northwest of Las Vegas, noise from its engines filled the empty valleys, scattering antelope and coyotes toward the mountainsides. When the aircraft crossed above a Joshua tree–studded valley called Frenchman Flat, it banked left—up and away—and from beneath it dropped Able: a 1-kiloton thermonuclear bomb.

A few minutes later, at something less than 1,000 feet above the ground, Able's blast ripped open the dawn. Its heat turned Frenchman Flat's sand to pale green glass. Its flash awoke ranchers in northern Utah. Its shock wave shattered windows as far away as Arizona. As the explosion's light and sound dissipated, the radiation cloud it created rose to join upper-atmosphere winds coursing east across the bulk of the American continent. Over the days to come, the breeze-borne radiation began sifting gently upon an unsuspecting nation. Nuclear fallout contaminated wheat in South Dakota. It found milk in Massachusetts. It was breathed by crabs and oysters in Chesapeake Bay. In the eyes of the U.S. Atomic Energy Commission, which had ordered this first atomic bombing of America's own soil, the test had been a complete success. Everything had gone without a hitch.

Over the next twelve years, 126 atomic weapons would be atmospherically detonated above the Nevada Test Site, a 1,350-square-mile emptiness nestled inside the Air Force's top-secret Nellis Air Force Base. Each of these explosions would spread roughly the radiational equivalent of Ukraine's 1986 Chernobyl reactor fire across an unknowing America. At the test site, these "shots" (as they were called) became so common that downwind in Las Vegas citizens blotted their breakfast bacon near kitchen windows in hopes of spotting atomic mushroom clouds rising in the dawn. For protection, the people of Las Vegas were eventually advised to wear strips of photographic film pinned to their clothes as makeshift radiation detectors. (If the film's black color shifted to polka-dot white or pale green, they had been exposed.) Often, on mornings when shots were pre-announced, local ranchers would bundle their children up and drive them to the edge of the test site, then they would wait for the flash, which was always followed by a brilliant pink-purple column stretching toward heaven, like something from a religious painting. And all the while, the test site grew more saturated with radioactivity as the fallout continued spreading east on the wind.

According to National Academy of Sciences and United Nations cancer research, radiation-associated cancers from atmospheric nuclear testing will produce at least 400,000 deaths by the year 2000, killing twice as many people as died at Hiroshima and Nagasaki. To combat this, in 1963, the United States and the Soviet Union signed a Limited Test Ban Treaty, forbidding nuclear tests in outer space, under water, or in the earth's atmosphere. In response, the world's governments began testing atomic weapons underground. Since 1963, at least 828 underground tests have been conducted at the Nevada Test Site, dimpling the earth with exactly as many neighborhood-size craters and making 1,350 square miles of American desert uninhabitable for the next 5,000 years.

At a dozen sites around the United States where nuclear material was manufactured for use in bombs, the ground and surroundings have also been contaminated and, doubtlessly, cancers and radiation have cost American lives. Which leads to the ultimate irony of America's nuclear weapons program. Since the end of World War II, the only victims of United States' nuclear bombs have been its own citizens and landscape.

"YOU'RE GOING TO be surprised by what's out here," Jim Boyer is saying as we exit Interstate 15, passing a sentry post and heading up a two-lane inside the test site's outer ring of chain-link fence. "These days, everything looks normal."

In the world surrounding the Nevada Test Site, I am already starting to discover, the concept of *normal* is relative. As we roll through the desert toward a "badge checkpoint" at a second security gate three or four miles ahead, I can't help thinking that everything surrounding the test site so far has been downright strange. Right now, for instance, as we cruise this empty road an hour north of the fastest growing city in America, the car we're driving looks outwardly like a Buick sedan. Because of a Department of Energy experiment, however, its trunk and back seat are crowded by the black-shrouded, pressurized tanks of the natural gas it uses as fuel. The dark-haired, semi-retired Boyer himself has exhibited a few non-garden-variety behaviors, too. When we got into the car sixty minutes ago, he proceeded to wipe down its interior with alcohol-saturated cloths and dampened paper towels. Then, with the passenger area sanitized, he slipped his hands into a pair of cotton work gloves—so he wouldn't have to touch the car's steering wheel or dashboard controls. He is still wearing the gloves now (and he will wear them all day, any time we're in the Buick). By way of explanation, he has offered only, "I hate filth."

"Yeah, there are animals and vegetation on the test site these days," Boyer says. He points outside, toward the southwest Nevada landscape of spiny mountains and spiky cacti. "These days, all but the hardest-hit portions look a lot like this. It's back to being Nevada desert."

I stare at the emptiness, knowing that if parts of the test site look normal, it is not because the Department of Energy has left them alone. During the 1970s, in the wake of the Limited Test Ban Treaty and more than 100 atmospheric blasts, the DOE—which was established in 1977 so control of the U.S. atomic arsenal would not fall to the military—endeavored to repair the landscape by fixing what it could. In places like

Frenchman Flat, where nuclear blasts had melted the sand to a scabby, bubble-pocked sheet of glass that covered perhaps 30 square miles, I've been told that bulldozers scraped up the top six inches of soil and buried it in bomb craters.

When I ask Boyer about this program, he falls silent. "They didn't *bulldoze* it," he finally says, exasperation crowding his voice. "They used road resurfacing machines. They had a *slew* of those things. Scraped off the top layer of glass and scorch—six or eight inches maybe—then dumped it into a crater and buried it. All gone. Then they let the plants and animals come back."

Ahead of us, the second guardhouse looms. Beyond it waits the town of Mercury, Nevada, where 4,500 Department of Energy workers and their families once lived. Now, after all nuclear testing was halted in 1992, it stands virtually empty. Boyer stops the car in the guardpost's shade. Camouflage-dressed soldiers, behind dark sunglasses and carrying machine guns, walk from the sentry station, examine our paperwork, and wave us inside. We enter the uninhabited grid of Mercury's streets, where prefabricated housing from the 1950s now stands empty and flyblown.

"Hey, want my favorite story about America's nuclear weapons program?" Boyer asks, as we pass a gas station that dispenses propane fuel.

I nod.

"A nuclear weapon wasn't used in hostility until 1992," he says. "How can that be?"

"I don't know," I tell him.

Boyer smiles and bobs his head jauntily. "Well, that was the year these Japanese scientists came over and visited. Somebody spilled the truth: the Hiroshima and Nagasaki bombs were never classified as weapons. They were tests—since nobody knew if they'd *work*. Well, they worked, and the Japanese scientists made a stink to Washington about those bombs still being called tests, so—*very quietly*—our government changed their description."

Boyer's white cotton gloves grip the steering wheel. In the desert morning's glare, we crest a rise notching two low mountains, and ahead of us sits the wide, pale basin of Frenchman Flat. "It was named for a French mineral prospector who lived here before the federal government," Boyer says. "After that, the Atomic Energy Commission built a town out here and conducted fourteen shots in the open air, to see what things might withstand the blasts—from a civil defense perspective." To the road's right, a sun-faded wooden billboard announces:

RADIATION HAZARD

TOUCHING OR REMOVING SCRAP OBJECTS IS PROHIBITED

THIS INCLUDES BLASTED DEBRIS

FUSED SILICA, METAL FRAGMENTS, ETC.

To our left, spreading across the valley, are artifacts from the atomic past. A U.S. M-60 tank, sacrificed to learn what nukes would do to conventional weapons, stands scorched and irradiated inside a fence festooned with yellow, CAUTION CONTAMINATION AREA signs. Ahead of that, a one-story auto court motel stands in tumbledown glory, its brick and concrete-block walls shattered. Ahead of that, a rail trestle with both concrete and steel supports towers above the sagebrush, its rails melted into curly remnants, its steel rail-tie supports bowed in looping sags. Beyond that, a bank vault stands alone on the sand. "Most of this stuff was erected before Priscilla shot," Boyer says. "Priscilla was a 37-kiloton device. That means it was equivalent to 37,000 tons of high explosive. The shot went off June 24, 1957. It was the largest test conducted at Frenchman Flat. The device was attached to a balloon and detonated 700 feet in the air."

As we ride beneath the railroad trestle, Boyer eases the car to a stop. "This was called Bailey Bridge," he says. "After Priscilla, it was a mass of twisted metal. We cleaned up most of it, but this is pretty much what it looked like. It stood 1,800 feet from Priscilla Ground Zero."

Can I get out and take a picture, I ask?

Boyer shakes his head. "Best not to," he says. "If you want photos, you can get out over there." His white-gloved hands point ahead toward the collapsed, melted-steel remnants of some domed air raid shelters that stood 1,200 feet from the blast. "You know what we learned from those?" he asks, steering toward the shriveled shapes and smiling. "We learned that if you're 1,200 feet from a nuclear blast and you're shielded by six inches of aluminum or steel . . . all you've got is bad news."

Our car circles the bunkers once, and Boyer stops near a livestock fence draped with more CAUTION: RADIOACTIVE CONTAMINATION AREA signs. "If you want to click some pictures, you're free to get out and do it here," he says. "But don't be too long. Just the other side of that fence is still off limits—for its proximity to Ground Zero."

As I step outside into the desert morning's brightness, Boyer finishes his thought. "Me?" he says. "I'll just wait in the car."

More than fifty years after the experimental "Trinity" shot in New Mexico ushered atomic weapons into the world on July 16, 1945, the U.S. nuclear weapons program rumbles dangerously and expensively onward, paradoxes trailing behind. Beginning in 1994, for example, in a good-faith effort to comply with a global comprehensive ban still in draft form, the U.S. stockpile of 16,750 nuclear warheads was slated to be reduced by half. At the same time, however, on the Nevada Test Site, where a nuclear device has not been detonated since September 23, 1992, thanks to moratoriums, a new $110 million warhead assembly plant was being completed. In 1992, in an effort to be more forthright, the DOE began to roll out information about the United States' atomic program, a plan whose projects included injecting "test populations" of human guinea pigs with radiation to showing that—over the past fifty years and completely behind the scenes—the "scaled back" American nuclear weapons program continued to drive a secret $1 billion-a-year economy, a business rivaled only by the American automobile industry in breadth and cash flow.

Away from public scrutiny, the DOE created the K-25 complex in Oak Ridge, Tennessee, the second-largest building in the world after the Pentagon. It funded a program called "Orion," a top-secret sister to NASA that designed and tested nuclear blast–propelled spaceships to be used on long, interstellar journeys. It operated "Plowshare," a project that found nonmilitary applications for nuclear weapons, including the single-blast digging of harbors and canals. It created a "Weapons Miniaturization" arm, where atomic bombs were scaled small enough to fit in a woman's handbag, allowing for their placement to be more surgically precise while creating less radioactive fallout. It funded the development of a nuclear jet, which was to be sent aloft to fly nonstop, like a sentry, along the edges of enemy nations, guarding and harassing them from a safe distance. The implementation of all these projects, plus the nonstop creation of plutonium for continued testing of nuclear weapons designs, has so far cost the United States more than $4 trillion.

Simultaneously, the U.S. government has irradiated more than 2,000 square miles now proposed as American "national sacrifice zones," lands like the Nevada Test Site and the Hanford Nuclear Reservation in Washington State, which because of their high radioactivity are off limits for thousands of years. Despite its public renunciations of nuclear projects, in 1995 the U.S. government spent the first of an annual $1.5 billion on the National Ignition Facility: a project at California's Lawrence Livermore Lab where—with nuclear blasts outlawed—weapons designers can produce the effects of thermonuclear explosions using football-field-size lasers to explode tiny pellets of nuclear fuel, further honing their understanding of atomic weapons detonation.

"IT'S AS IF the government has sanctioned a *playground* for nuclear physicists and engineers," Ted Taylor tells me over the telephone. Taylor, a gray-haired, large-eyed former bomb designer for the Los Alamos National Laboratory in New Mexico, is one of the atomic weaponeers who turned renegade against his tribe. A deputy scientific director for the Pentagon's Defense Atomic Support Agency during the 1950s and 1960s, Taylor designed bombs and oversaw the Orion spacecraft and Miniaturization projects. "Back when I was designing bombs at Los Alamos, I was completely protected," he says. "I worked and lived with my family behind a wall of secrecy—and I was well provided for. I was never told to meet a budget. I never knew what my budget *was*. I never had to write a proposal for a new bomb design. I just walked down the hall, to the largest computer on earth at the time, and I told the operator, Preston Hammer, that I wanted to run some numbers on a new device, one where the plutonium was milled like so. . . . If the numbers checked out, we built and tested the weapon. That was all there was to it. I was encouraged to create and test weapons as fast as I could."

Those were the heady days of the U.S. nuclear program, when a guaranteed one shot a month would go off at the Nevada Test Site, and as many as ninety-eight weapons were tested atmospherically in 1962. "It was addictive," Taylor tells me. "I was *addicted* to the idea that I could think up new nuclear weapon designs and then, with the federal government's encouragement, build them and blow them up in total secrecy. I dreamed of nuclear explosions at night. I lived them during the day. It was abstract violence, total control of the universe coupled with infinite destruction. There's a great sense of personal power attached to that. It was easy to get hooked."

He had protested the Hiroshima and Nagasaki bombings as

a student at the University of California. The story of how Taylor came to be a creator of nuclear arms is not without a certain irony. "I'd flunked my Ph.D. prelim tests, so it was obvious I was never going to make it as an academic physicist," he says. "Instead, even with my anti-nuke history, I was rescued by someone prominent in the nuclear weapons program, a man who understood that my ability as a physicist lay not in numbers but in imagination. Next thing I knew, the U.S. government was sending me back to get my Ph.D. and I was a bomb designer. Which led to a lot of fights between my ex-wife and me: We kept trying to reconcile the idea that I was opposed to what I was doing but I was being well paid for it. We had started a family. There weren't many good jobs available for physicists. And, yes, even at the time I had to admit that designing bombs was the most interesting and challenging job going. Back then, it was on everyone's mind."

During the years Taylor worked as one of America's top bomb designers, his creativity and exploits became legendary. "I didn't get to the test site very much," he says. "But I remember that once I thought—what the hell—I'll do something fun. It was a stunt, but as we were waiting for a shot that was delayed, I saw this little parabolic reflector lying in a junk heap next to the control room. It had a tiny hole in the back, I don't know why, but I looked at it and thought: I wonder if that could collect enough energy from the blast to light a cigarette?"

Pointing the reflector toward the sun, Taylor found its focal point, then he stuck a Pall Mall into the hole and fixed it into place with some wire. "Just before the shot, I lined up the mirror with the blast zone," he says. "After the shot went off,

I came back out of the control room and looked down and saw a little burning hole had been lit by the explosion, about a quarter-inch from the cigarette's end. So I puffed it—and it lit. It was the first nuclear-ignited cigarette. In those days, even though the weapons' indescribable power is what drew you in, you didn't really think about the damage the weapons could do—you saw them as intellectual challenges. Everything was like that cigarette: a stunt waiting to be pulled off."

To combat the terrifying destructiveness of the arms they were creating, nuclear weaponeers adapted a language of euphemistic denial that is still spoken on the test site. When designers—and most DOE employees—refer to the weapons, they call them "devices," or, less usually, "gadgets." The weapons' test explosions are unfailingly called "shots," and the weapons-grade plutonium inside each implosion bomb—its radiation deadly to humans if not shielded by lead—carries the casual term "ploot." The hundred millionths of a second that "shots" take to explode is measured in an equal number of "shakes"—as in the shakes of a lamb's tail. There are "jerks," which refer to the amount of energy given off by 500 pounds of high explosive. And because, in the lexicon of nuclear weapons, a jerk remains such a low number, blasts are registered in "kilojerks" and "megajerks." (A 15-megaton shot called "Bravo," the largest the United States ever tested and equal to 1.5 million tons of high explosive—carried 60 megajerks.) Even the bedrock event itself, the splitting of an atom, has a euphemism. When the cross-section of an atom to be split is identified—an area encompassing roughly one septillionth of a square centimeter—it is known as "the barn wall."

Ted Taylor quit the nukes business, to the best of his recollection, "sometime in 1965." "I can't say there was one day, one event, that set me against the program. It was more a slow realization that I didn't need to be doing this anymore, that it was *insane*. We had enough nuclear weapons to blow up the world by hundreds of times. The designs were good ones. They worked. And I thought: what I'm doing has become immoral. So I got out."

Almost immediately he began working with other concerned physicists and scientists and in 1977 he was invited to join the exclusive anti-nuclear-weapons group called Pugwash. In December 1995, they were co-awarded the Nobel Peace Prize. "I really think that we can put the nuclear genie back in the bottle—or back in the lamp; which is how the story actually goes in *Tales of 1001 Nights*," he says. "It may not be the same bottle or lamp the genie came out of, but we can still seal it away again. The weapons are a symptom of something deeper. It's not a biological need, like for food. It's a boundless desire for power. These days, we understand the destructiveness of nuclear weapons—and we can save ourselves or destroy ourselves with that knowledge. The world, as a global population, has become Prometheus. The choice is ours."

WHERE THE Frenchman Flat Road bisects the Nevada Test Site Highway, a coyote is sleeping on the pavement. "There's one of my little buddies," Jim Boyer says, stopping the natural gas car in front of a startled yet groggy animal. "The test site is a wildlife refuge. You're not allowed to harass wildlife out here. You get fired for it."

The coyote slowly stands; it trots to the road's shoulder. Boyer rolls down the driver's side window to speak to the wild dog. "Hey, little buddy, how ya doin'?" he asks. "Hey, what's goin' on?"

The coyote walks to the car door, standing perhaps three feet from Boyer's nose. It is motionless on the pavement; it sniffs the wind, its dark eyes stare into Boyer's. "They don't know fear of man, the animals out here," he says. "They have no reason to fear us, so they're curious."

With his white-gloved hand, Boyer rolls his window back up, and we continue north along the highway. About twelve miles ahead, the road rises over another low mountain pass, where atop it sits another guardhouse. "Beyond that checkpoint is the Forward Area," Boyer says. "In 1958, protests from down-winders—the population living downwind of the test site— grew so loud that the Atomic Energy Commission, who had control of the site at the time, moved everything further north. They wanted to get the tests farther from Las Vegas and the population traveling the interstate highway."

A few miles before the guardhouse and to our left, built into a hillside, is the DOE's new Device Assembly Plant. A long wall of whitewashed, loading dock doorways, the 100,000-square-foot facility is buried beneath the foot of a mountain, only its truck-unload bays showing in the sun. "That thing cost $110 million," Boyer says, his white glove pointing. "In the future, if we ever begin nuclear testing again, we'll assemble all the devices right here, on the site, instead of over at the Pantex plant, outside Amarillo, Texas."

Because of "accident potential," Boyer says, the walls and doors inside the Assembly Facility are more than three feet thick. The underground structure is also covered with dense layers of gravel, so the building can withstand and contain a nuclear blast in the unlikely event a device accidentally detonates inside.

At the top of the pass, Boyer steers the car to the guardhouse, and another camouflage-dressed soldier steps out, point-ing a black M-16 automatic rifle at our car. He inspects our paperwork, then spots my overnight bag; it has been tossed into the car's back seat, where it rests on the tanks of natural gas.

"What's in there?" the soldier asks, gesturing at my bag with the point of his gun.

"Clothes," I answer.

"I'll need to have a look, please," the guard says. "Will you step out of the car and open it?"

I do what the sentry asks, revealing a white cotton shirt and my exercise clothes.

"Okay," the guard says, waving us ahead and returning to his hut without looking our way again, as if he's already forgotten us.

Back in the car, as I repack my clothes, Boyer apologizes. "There are sensitive areas within sensitive areas out here," he says. "And we're heading into one of the most delicate." We drive on, cresting the top of the pass. Ahead of us stretches a thirty-by-forty-mile basin called Yucca Flat, across which round "subsidence craters" dimple the desert. Each crater is an inverted cone, left behind by one of the 828 underground tests conducted there since 1963, the year the Test Ban Treaty ended the 99 atmospheric tests already detonated above the valley.

From the mountain pass altitude, the underground tests have left the flat looking like a lunar landscape.

Ahead and to the right of the road, a crane stands above the desert. Beneath it, a tall scaffolded cylinder rises from the earth. "That's the site of an underground test that was terminated just before the moratorium," Boyer says. "What happens is they dig a hole, like a deep well, then they use the crane to lower the device and some complex measuring machines and sensors into it. They fill the hole with sand and other materials that are specially designed to keep the radiation and radioactive gasses inside the earth. By then, cables have been attached to the sensors to send back information about the shot; that is, until the shot's heat melts everything within a few milliseconds of detonation. Still, as the blast's heat grows and expands, the information is already on its way up the cables, so we learn a few things about each shot before everything melts."

We pass the crane and cylinder. A white trailer home is parked nearby. "That's where the above-ground instrumentation is housed," Boyer says, pointing. "When the shot's over, its fireball has carved out an underground cavern. If you were to dig down there, you'd find fused silica. Like melted Coke bottles. Eventually, the cavern collapses, leaving the subsidence craters on the ground's surface, which is what you saw from the top of Yucca Pass. You can't walk over one of those subsidences, though. They're off limits. Radioactive. They're *hot*."

Depending on the size of the device and the instrumentation committed, Boyer tells me, each shot "costs somewhere between a few million dollars and ten million dolllars." He also says that while the subsidences are off limits, other craters aren't. "Ahead of us there," he says, his white glove gesturing, "is Sedan Crater. It was part of the Plowshare program."

In the Plowshare project, which ran until July 1962, nuclear weapons were tested for nonmilitary applications, such as moving mountains, building canals, and diverting rivers. Its total budget remains classified, but there were thirty-four known Plowshare shots before "Shot Sedan" on July 6, 1962. What Sedan proved, like no shot before, was that a high-yield nuclear bomb buried a few hundred feet beneath the soil could make a big hole in the ground. As Boyer talks about the program, he steers the car off the main road and onto a gravel side-spur, parking near a sandy berm. He suggests we get out of the car to have a look at the crater. It's the only time — other than stops in paved towns for coffee and lunch — that Boyer sets foot out of the car all day. (Only later do I learn that he does so at Sedan Crater because, as a scheduled stop on most test site tours, the radioactive sand of its walkway has been scraped up and replaced by nonradioactive gravel, making it safer for visitors.)

Boyer strolls to a break in the earthwork berm. As we walk through, the landscape in front of us yawns open into a deep, conical pit. "There it is," Boyer says, smiling. "The Sedan Crater. Proof a nuclear device could build a harbor."

Ahead of us, a wooden walkway ends at a railed fence along the crater's edge. Attached to the fence, a sign announces Sedan Crater's statistics. Dug by a 104-kiloton device buried 695 feet underground, the Sedan Shot left a hole 320 feet deep and a quarter-mile across, displacing more than 12 million tons of sand and rock. What's not announced on the sign, according to scientists at the University of Utah, is that the downwind hazard from this one shot released such massive radiation doses into the air that children's thyroid glands in Utah received far more than the permissible dose of the radio-isotope iodine 131, plus as much as 700 rads of radiation, when whole-body doses of 600 rads can be lethal. What is also not said, but I was told by Dick Nutley, a systems analyst at DOE, is that during the shot—which Nutley witnessed—the soil displaced was flying so quickly away from the explosion that, due to the blast heat and mere friction with the air, flying sand and rock burst into flame; igniting as it sailed through the sky for miles, becoming fiery, melting blobs.

"That's one hell of a hole," Boyer says, smiling, as he uses my camera to snap a picture of me at the crater's edge.

AROUND THE U.S. Department of Energy, they call it the "Physics Problem." These days, if one subject has the DOE's concentrations focused, it is this: In places where plutonium and some forms of radioactive waste have been used or are being stored, it will take 12,000 years before the stuff is no longer dangerous. "There's no way to speed up the decay," says James D. Werner, director of the DOE's Environmental Manager's Office of Strategic Planning and Analysis. "That's an immutable law; it comes down to time and physics. The only way to make it safer is to isolate it. In some cases, we'll need to be *very* patient—for thousands of years."

Until 1989, when the Department of Energy established an Office of Environmental Management, few inside the agency had given long-term thought to the compounds, fuel rods, and wastes their programs were creating. "Instead, everyone thought: we'll come up with a fix in the future," the dark-haired, mustached Werner says. "Well, the future is here, and the system will now break down if we can't bury stuff at the Nevada Test Site. It's all unregulated by design, so they've been burying stuff in unlined trenches all around the country for fifty years. No one is allowed to control it; the government wanted it that way. Because of that, we don't even know how much radioactive material and waste is currently out there. It's only been in the past two or three years that we've started inventorying it, trying to gauge the storage costs for the future."

In 1995, Werner published the first ever baseline environmental report for the Department of Energy, "Estimating the Cold War Mortgage." His report pointed out, among other things:

- In the United States alone, there are at least 10,500 radioactive sites that need to be stabilized and secured for the indeterminate future;
- There are no viable, long-term storage areas or plans;
- At current levels, if the DOE authorizes no more nuclear materials creation, the maintenance of existing wastes until the year 2070 will cost more than $230 billion.

"It's a quarter-trillion dollars," Werner says, with a hangdog grin. "When I told the President's Office of Management and Budget the figure, they looked at me like I had two heads. They said, 'On our books, only the national deficit is going to cost more.' And I said: 'Hey, don't shoot the messenger, the Cold War created the problem.'"

In Werner's unprepossessing DOE headquarters office, five floors above Washington, D.C.'s Independence Avenue, near the Mall, graphs and charts crowd the walls. Thus far, they add up to very little. "We're just beginning to understand the vastness of the program over the last fifty years," he says. "It's taken us two years to start getting a handle on what's buried where. Most of what's been done so far was undertaken in complete secrecy."

At the Idaho National Engineering Laboratory, for instance, where nuclear energy testing has gone on since the 1950s—and where the nuclear airplane was developed in the early 1960s—a long, sloppy history made it common practice to dig long trenches and toss in barrels of nuclear waste. When flooding occurred, as it did during spring snow melts, the barrels often floated to the surface and security officers were dispatched to shoot holes in them to make them sink. In another INEL trench, near which the DOE recently built one of the largest robotic cranes on earth (capable of digging and lifting ten-ton objects from the ground, while also grasping a glass bottle without breaking it), X-ray-style gadgetry has scoured the subsurface landscape and spotted scattered fifty-five-gallon drums of waste, wooden boxes, and a radioactivity-imbued ambulance beneath the soil.

"The engineers and scientists who were doing this, they knew what was happening," Werner says. "But they were protected by national security, they didn't have to care. They knew there was nowhere safe to store this waste. So, for instance, they kept it liquified in big tanks at Hanford, with motorized stirrers to keep the liquid moving; that way, maybe it wouldn't get hot and explode. At the test site, they buried it in open, un-lined pits. That kind of behavior went on everywhere: at Savan-nah River in South Carolina. At Rocky Flats, Colorado; at Oak Ridge, Tennessee . . . tell me when to stop, or I can go on al-most forever."

Werner is the first DOE officer charged with making right a half-century of atomic environmental damage. "You have to understand, with this stuff, there's no such thing as cleaning up," he says. "Radioactivity is an *unfixable* problem. You can't do it. This stuff exists, and the physics problem makes some portions of it a reality for thousands of years; even the fastest-degrading and lowest-level waste remains problematic for decades. So the way I see it, my job has three stages: identify where the problems are; isolate and stabilize those problems; and figure out a way to keep people out, so nobody gets sick or dies."

Werner has few answers. "We don't even know if our culture will be *around* then," he says. "We don't know if our language will be the same; even our iconography. So while we should definitely establish some sort of nuclear priesthood, which passes information down across generations in certain areas, we also need to find an unmistakable symbol. How do you tell people in the future: Don't dig here."

Since 1979, two major studies have been done to generate such a symbol. "Both said that physical symbology or language can't work," Werner says. "But both advised comparisons with natives who controlled ancient lands in different parts of the world. In the American Southwest, the Anasazi inhabited areas with cyanide- or arsenic-contaminated springs. In Australia, natives lived near exposed uranium ores. Both groups used the same symbol to warn others, to say: Don't go here, because people get sick. They drew snakes on rocks. It's a simple symbol, one analogous to something else you should watch for. When it comes to a symbol that tells people in the future that we've screwed up the landscape and they shouldn't use it, I favor the snake."

"THE ATMOSPHERIC TEST Ban is what killed the nuclear-powered rocket," Boyer is telling me. "In 1963, as I understand it, the project was all up and running, then the treaty papers were signed and no nuclear blasts could be detonated in open air—so the program was scrapped. Just abandoned."

It's late in the afternoon now, as we drive into another broad valley west of Yucca and Frenchman Flats. I'm inadvertently discovering just how large the infrastructure of the test site is. In the desert's harsh daylight, the taupe-painted laboratories and buildings across the test site's breadth are virtually invisible against the sage, stone, and distance. But suddenly, as the sun begins to duck behind mountains, immersing the valleys in shadow, light-sensing exterior floodlamps at many test site buildings have started flicking on—and everywhere, dotting the basins, small, yellow-lit cities have started popping out.

Right now, we are driving out of a pass crossing tall mountains to the west of Yucca Flat, and as we round the brow of a hill, a large, three-story building stands suddenly visible up a spur road and away from the pavement. Two miles farther west, there is another group of buildings. They were all erected to house laboratories, probably for the rocket project, known as "Orion," Boyer is telling me. They were abandoned in the mid-1960s. "Nobody's working up there anymore, I don't think," he says. "Though I don't know that for a fact."

If the devastation in the previous valleys is what's impressive about them, here in Area 5, a mountain range away, what's truly mind-bending stands five or six miles ahead, where the 1,500-foot needle of BREN tower rises into the sky, its pointy end taller than any building on earth. "It's an acronym," Boyer says. "For Bare Reactor Experiment Nevada. They would raise and lower unshielded nuclear reactors up and down that tower, leaving them at different altitudes, to see effects of radiation on things."

Boyer loops his white-gloved hand in an arcing motion, pointing over a low rise in the valley floor. "Back over there," he says, "they built a whole Japanese town, to see how radiation affected building materials and Japanese houses. Little paper houses. It's all falling down now. Old age."

The BREN tower may also have had something to do with the Orion project, Boyer says, though he isn't sure. Other "shot towers" had certainly figured in Orion's past. As did Ted Taylor. In the years before 1951, the year all nuclear testing was transferred to the test site, America did many of its atomic shots on island atolls in the South Pacific. During that era, someone whose name is lost to history noticed that when the legs of shot towers had layers of "scorch carbon" coating them, they weren't destroyed in a detonating weapon's heat. So one time on an atoll called Eniwetok, during a shot of Ted Taylor's called "Viper," physicist Lew Allen suspended some basketball-sized steel spheres coated with graphite from cables on the shot tower. After the shot, although the blast's shock wave had flung the spheres away from ground zero, they were virtually unharmed, prompting Taylor to begin pondering Orion. If graphite-coated spheres came through OK, Taylor reasoned, what if an enormous rocket shielded on the bottom by a graphite-coated steel could direct blasts downward and away? What if subsequent detonations, one every few seconds, just kept coming? Couldn't the rocket fly a straight course for Mars or beyond? Couldn't it break all gravitational pulls? At planetary opposition (when Earth and, say, Mars are only 35 million miles apart), the trip would last—what?—perhaps three or four months, given the speed that blast waves propel objects?

We drive closer to BREN, circling it on paved roads. "I don't know much about the rocket program," Boyer says. "There were a lot of projects out here that didn't go anywhere. And I only arrived as DOE news media contact in 1981. So many of the old, abandoned programs, well, I just never had much familiarity with them."

Ahead of us, however, stands a project Boyer *is* familiar with: a long, low ridge of dense, volcanic stone called Yucca Mountain. In the late 1980s, the U.S. Congress chose Yucca Mountain's impervious stone over two other sites—the basaltic earth of Hanford, Washington, and the salt beds of Deaf Smith County, Texas—for the first, regulated atomic waste dump in the United States. "They've been doing feasibility testing over there for a few years now," Boyer says. "It's where, someday, they plan to bury nuclear wastes and the spent fuel rods from nuclear reactors."

During our tour, Boyer has shown me two other places where nuclear waste or spent cooling rods have been stored. Both have been in deep, mining prospector's shafts, tunnels dug into mountainsides. After eleven spent fuel rods from the DOE's Turkey Point Generating Plant were placed inside a shaft at the Climax Mine, near Sedan Crater, for instance, explosives were detonated inside the shaft to collapse it. "From tests at Climax, and from other tests at Yucca Mountain," Boyer says, "we're getting an idea of how durable these places are for long periods of time. To the DOE, it makes sense to bury the waste out here, since this place will remain off limits for a long time anyway."

Not everyone agrees, however. And in 1994, after nearby earthquakes shuddered Yucca Mountain and environmentalists made civilian concerns about groundwater contamination more visible to American citizens and their congressmen, the Yucca Mountain Storage Facility was plunged into a cycle of rethinking; a period where America's nuclear waste remained suspended in limbo across the nation. "I'd take you out to Yucca Mountain now," Boyer says, "but there's not really much to see. Looks kind of like a construction site. There are a few long trenches, but that's about it."

Instead, in the coming night, we follow another highway southeast, back toward the town of Mercury, Interstate 15, and Las Vegas. As we drive, Boyer tells me his history. A New Mexico newspaper man, he joined the DOE in 1981 as media-relations point man in Las Vegas. During the 1980s, he attended many of the underground shots himself, broadcasting them live on radio. "My first year, I was the 'shot caller' on fifteen of the nineteen tests," he says. "I counted them down live on the radio, had TV and newspaper reporters out, too. It was fun. I became semi-retired in 1995. Now I'm a subcontractor, though I still give tours to media people."

"Why did you retire?" I ask.

Boyer pauses for a long minute. "Last year," he says. "I got hit with a buckshot load of cancer. All through my stomach and pelvic area." The propane car rolls up the empty highway for another minute. Boyer's white gloves grip the steering wheel. Outside, sunset's light covers the desert with a warm gold. Finally, Boyer speaks again. "I want to make sure you understand," he says "My cancer had nothing to do with my work at the test site."

How do you know that? I ask.

"I know it didn't," he says. "I just know."

IN THE EYES of the U.S. government, there are seventy-two ways its citizens can die. According to the U.S. Department of Vital Statistics, citizens can perish from cancers, viruses, wars, disease, old age, and automobile accidents. There is no category, however, for death due to nuclear radiation. The government computers, much like Jim Boyer, will not accept it.

Over the dozen years that open-air nuclear tests were conducted on the test site, a grayish-white ash of fallout would sift almost daily into the lives of local citizens. Termed "a low-use segment of the population" in some of the Atomic Energy Commission's documents, the ranchers and rural people of Utah and Nevada began, after a while, to find the "nuclear snow" unnerving. Their children would play in it, often until it burned their skins. As testing continued and their livestock—especially sheep—began to die or present birth-defect babies in growing numbers, area adults started to yowl. In the downwind town of Annabela, Utah (population 187), when three cases of leukemia came to one street in a year—the usual statistic is three cases per 10,000 people—and cases of bone cancer and thyroid cancer sprouted elsewhere across town, civic fathers grew voluble and furious. To combat growing outrage, the Atomic Energy Commission sent operatives to live in dozens of downwind communities, where they made themselves helpful by fixing bicycles, assisting the elderly by carrying packages, and showing AEC-made movies in high school gyms. In larger towns where the protests were especially loud, such as St. George, Utah, the AEC eventually showed people that all was well by making movies of *them*, using local people as their stars.

"Have you ever seen that PR movie, *Nuclear Tests in Nevada*?" Jay Truman is asking. "Hell, that whole movie was made with people from St. George."

Truman, the bearded and rough-hewn founder-director of Downwinders, a powerful, anti-nuclear advocacy organization, grew up in the southwestern Utah town of Enterprise. "I was born in December 1951," he says. "Eleven months after atmospheric testing started. I was conceived at its beginning. So it's always been there for me. One of my first memories in life, in fact, is going out to where we had cattle on the farm and sitting on my father's knee, and we watched the sky light up with an A-bomb. It was extremely frightening. It still scares me. I've never been comfortable with it."

By the time he was "ten or twelve years old," Truman says he'd seen neighborhood friends become ill and die of leukemia, even as new children were born with birth defects. "I used to go with my father when he'd haul potatoes and hay to the town of Mesquite, Nevada," Truman says, "and on some days there'd be roadblocks, and they'd say: 'Go home and wash your car. Stay inside.' Well, it doesn't take much of that before you're skeptical. I'd always had the problem of being inquisitive, so as I began to look more closely at what the government brochures said, and as I compared it to what I saw around me—livestock damage, birth defects, dead sheep, roadblocks—well . . . I could see the government was feeding us absolute lies."

One day, Truman remembers, a prospector who lived near his parents' ranch came over with his Geiger counter. "He'd been nagging my father to get rid of our milk cow," Truman says, "and he put a Geiger counter on the back of the cow, and it registered radioactive. Then he put it on its mouth, and it registered. And then he put it on its udder—and the udder was the hottest, by far. I didn't drink any raw milk after that. There was also mother's uncle, who was a store owner downtown. He wore a film badge to detect radiation. He also ran the town air-monitoring station. I used to watch him change the tapes and recalibrate the monitors, and I used to hear his conversations with AEC guys who'd come to pick up his findings. They'd say things to him they wouldn't say to anybody else, like, 'You folks really had a hot time up there the other day.' Things like that. They knew we were getting dusted with radiation constantly, but they didn't care."

At age fifteen, Truman himself became ill with cancer, a lymphoma called Waldenström's disease. Ultimately, he survived, but since then he's had, as he puts it, "all the usual problems, thyroid trouble, arthritis, gout. I've run the same course as everyone else who was born and grew up out there." On this January evening, as a new, twenty-inch layer of non-nuclear snow sifts onto the roof of his home in Lava Hot Springs, Idaho, Truman's furor remains vital. "Nobody who loves their country wants to think the rising leukemia and birth defect rates in town are caused by our government's own hand," he says. "Back then, we believed the weapons we were testing were important for national security. So they couldn't be bad, right? Instead, the most important thing we've learned is that nuclear development can't exist without the government having to lie. Whether it's Russia or France or America; the government has to deny the truth or citizens won't allow it. You have to kill your own to play with the nuclear toys. And we're not talking about an accident. We're also not talking soldiers going off and knowing they may die. We're talking genocide."

"What's so amazing," Truman says, suddenly almost whispering. "Now, at the end of this century, we've all become Downwinders. We all have nuclear fission products in our system. We all have little, atomic bits of Nevada Test Sites and Russian nuclear tests and Nagasaki bombs in our bodies. The battlefront collisions of soldiers and armies, they don't have to happen anymore. Now, nuclear waste from before we were born can damage generations after our grandchildren. How reckless have we become? I only hope to be around when cancer rates finally start to drop. So when doctors say, We've finally cured cancer, I can say back: No way, what's happened is the latency period from the nuclear elements in our cells is finally ending, because atomic testing was outlawed."

BACK IN Las Vegas, Jim Boyer drops me at a casino; the one place he knows I'll be able to find a taxi to the airport. As we've driven back into the city, past suburbs that seem to stretch forever, we've been discussing the growth of Las Vegas, whose 800,000 population has more than doubled in the past decade.

"I sometimes wonder if the test site would have been placed where it is had Las Vegas been growing so fast back then," Boyer says. "But at the time, we had to move testing out of the South Pacific, and we had to keep testing. Those were the realities of the age. The situation was difficult, which people today seem to forget. It's easy to be a Monday morning quarterback forty years after hard decisions had to be made. But still, it makes you wonder."

As I open the door of the natural gas–powered Buick to step out, Boyer says, "I don't think the people who set up the test site were evil. I think they were just like us." He nods. "Hell, they *were* us," he says.

4

Torn Leaf

VIETNAM, 1965–1975

BOMB CRATERS. As my Cathay Pacific flight banks above the runway at Hanoi's Noi Bai Airport, through the aircraft window, ragged pocks dug by long-cold explosions become visible at the runway ends and spread across Vietnam's green, rice-paddy patchwork to every horizon.

The holes were left by U.S. B-52 airstrikes. More than twenty-five years later, they remain tattered pits, big as houses. In the flare of a summer twilight, the craters—now filled with water—scatter far beyond where my eyes can find them individually. The most distant ones give away their locations only when sunlight bounces from their surfaces to my eye, glittering and flashing from their hidden positions in fiery, blinding blips.

Thirty years ago, during Vietnam's war with the United

States, Noi Bai was called Di Phuc, and it was among the largest airbases in North Vietnam. For three years beginning in March 1965, U.S. explosives rained upon it, pummeling the ground in a "sustained pressure" bombing that began as Operation Rolling Thunder, then became an everyday affair. Now, in a nation where protein has always been scarce, the Vietnamese have pivoted American force to their advantage. They have knit the craters together with a system of dikes and levees and filled them with water and fish. In an act of almost magical transmutation, Vietnam has turned destruction into life. But then, for nearly 2,000 years, necessity and history have taught the Vietnamese to pull war inside out at every opportunity, their efforts a continual struggle to make sense of war's legacies.

BEFORE I WENT to Vietnam, a friend who'd traveled there suggested I not bring short pants with me. He wasn't thinking about Vietnam's ravenous tropical insects, or the infections that might attach themselves to my exposed legs. He was thinking about history. "If you wear shorts, you'll remind the Vietnamese of the French, who wore shorts when they occupied Vietnam," he said. "The association makes the Vietnamese angry. Believe me—they live with their past every day. So wear long pants, even if you have to sweat."

On the ground at Noi Bai and wearing a pair of khaki trousers, I step from the jet and onto the glare of the airstrip, where soldiers in olive-colored uniforms direct me toward the terminal: a flat, low, water-stained blockhouse a hundred yards away, a building whose glass doors are opened wide in the summer heat. As I walk across the pavement, late-day sunlight blasts down through a pale and cloudless sky. Up close, the Noi Bai terminal is even more crumbling than at a distance. Constructed of cinderblocks smeared with plaster, it still shows the hard edges of a former military post, a place now softened by humidity, rain, and time.

Just beyond the customs desks, a medium-sized Vietnamese man with plastic-rimmed eyeglasses and a thick mustache is waiting impatiently. He's alone, and above his head he holds a sign with my name penned on it. Vu Binh is with the Foreign Press Office at Vietnam's Ministry of Foreign Affairs, and I have spoken with him a few times on the telephone. For the next ten days, he will be my guide.

Binh (pronounced "Bing") is not the Vietnamese I would have expected. At thirty-four, he's a year younger than me, making both of us too young to have fought in his nation's conflict with the Americans. He is the son of a Vietnamese provincial governor and educator, and Binh turned down a Harvard Business School education to work in Vietnam's embassy in Bombay, from which he returned last year. I nod to him, raising a hand. He smiles, then gestures to a soldier-crowded anteroom at the right of the customs desks, telling me to go there.

In minutes, soldiers are counting the U.S. dollars I carry. They shout questions in Vietnamese about the ways I have completed their immigration forms. Binh interprets. "Why do you leave this space blank?" they want to know. "Why do you want to see an old war?" On other, shouted questions, Binh answers without keying me to the subject of the exchange.

"I keep telling them you are a guest of our government," he finally says to me. "That's all they need to know."

Still, the standoff continues; the customs officers detain me. They stare and smoke cigarettes. They sip green tea in their little, airless room. Vu Binh is calmly leafing through a month-old copy of *U.S. News and World Report.* I understand the suspicion. Ever since 207 B.C., when a general named Chao T'o annexed Vietnam for China, one global power or another has been trying to slip Vietnam's foot into a colonial shoe. And the Vietnamese—in their own docile style—have never gone quietly. Vietnam's past is crammed with stories of hopeful imperialists destroyed in violent insurrections. Whether the account is driven by the scholar Ly Bon, who overthrew the Chinese in 543, or by Ho Chi Minh, who defeated the French Army at Dien Bien Phu in 1954 and left Vietnam divided into North and South along a Demilitarized Zone, or DMZ, the strategy for staving off enemies has always been the same: Allow the more powerful aggressor inside, then confuse and patiently destroy him with your home-side advantage. During these regular struggles to freedom, the Vietnamese have sacrificed life and land when necessary. Later, after the aggressor has gone, the Vietnamese have always reasoned there will be time to absorb and make right their private losses. In 2,000 years, it's a plan that's never failed.

THE LOWER LIP of the chief customs officer extends beyond his upper one, and in the airport terminal's heat, it works gently up and down. Above the wide set of his Asian eyes, his balding head sweats beads thick as sorghum. A dark line of perspiration tops the tight collar of his uniform. Finally, for no discernible reason, the head official stamps my passport with a big, red star, then he collects my entrance tax—and I'm inside.

On the twenty-mile ride into downtown Hanoi, I look out at rice paddies filled with peasants knee deep in the shimmer of watery fields. Farmers wearing rags and conical hats of woven reed are busy planting germinated rice. They bend and pull the young stalks from swampy paddies, then transport them across dikes and into elevated fields nearby, where they'll bloom to maturity. Water buffalo are everywhere, too, their sweep-back horns and muscled brown bodies like something bolted together in Detroit. Nearer the roadside, a few workers are making their way from the fields toward home, and as they step from the water of the paddies, I see they're wearing shorts.

Though I've only known Binh for an hour, I test our relationship. "I've heard the Vietnamese don't like Westerners wearing short pants," I say. "It's supposed to remind you of the French. Is it true?"

"*Hoh!*" Binh snorts. "*Hoh!*" The noise comes so quickly it sounds as if I've punched him. Inside it, a whole spectrum of emotions has spilled across the car: surprise and irony, a little bit of shock. It takes him a moment, but as the car passes a small, bombed out pond where fishermen with dip-nets swish the brown water, Binh finally answers. "In the Vietnamese language," he says, "our word 'the American' is the same as the word 'the Beautiful.' We are a practical people, and we remember only what we can use of the past. Now we think the Americans can help us. So—" he opens his hands in the air, rolling them at the wrists with a magician's *presto* motion—"we love the Americans."

Binh pronounces the dual word for beautiful and American: *my*. He says it again slowly: *mee-Hee*. As an afterthought, he adds: "The Vietnamese see similarities between themselves and the Americans. Both are a mix of cultures. Both won independence with their own blood. Neither of us is like the French—not imperialists. It is a tragedy about the war, since today the Vietnamese see Americans as their brothers."

I go back to looking out the window, only to realize over the next mile or two that Binh has evaded my question, so I turn and ask again. "If I wear shorts among the Vietnamese," I say, "will it make them angry?"

We continue along the road in silence. "Yeh, yeh . . . yes," Binh finally says, blinking behind his eyeglasses. "It is better, I think, if you don't wear short pants in Vietnam, especially in the North, where Ho Chi Minh beat the French. Yes. It is better not to do that."

I settle back in my seat, watching the peasants and rolling bicycles, pondering sprouting rice, converted bomb craters, and the increasing density of huts as we approach Hanoi. If I'm to understand how modern war has affected Vietnam, I will have to get inside the minds of the Vietnamese people. If wearing short pants carries complicated levels of historic meaning, what of more important things?

IN 1965, U.S. forces sent to fight in Vietnam were confident their resources and weapons could stop communism cold. During the next eight years, as 2 million American troops passed through Vietnam, they would be forced to use every piece of military equipment in the U.S. arsenal—with the exception of nuclear warheads—in an attempt to stop the North Vietnamese and their Viet Cong counterparts in the South from uniting under socialism. The Americans would detonate the equivalent of 250 pounds of dynamite for every person living on the Southeast Asian subcontinent, dropping more bombs than were used by all sides in World War II. U.S. soldiers would fly fixed-wing aircraft of every imaginable size and speed, from propeller-driven Cessna spotter planes to supersonic F-4 Phantoms to the Boeing B-52 Stratofortress, an eight-engine tactical warplane capable of carrying twenty-two tons of bombs and dropping them with precision from nine miles above the earth. A fleet of more than 1,000 offshore vessels, including patrol runabouts, inflatables, destroyers, cruisers, battleships, tankers, and aircraft carriers, would amass off-shore. Soldiers would use gadgets that found the enemy through his heat, light, sound, seismic movement—and even smell. They would crater the earth with millions of artillery shells and mortars, and drop more than 3 million tons of conventional bombs from aircraft. They would use jets to spread napalm, an explosive gelatin of gasoline that roasted villages and victims alive. They would spray the landscape with more than 11 million gallons of chemical defoliants that melted away nearly a million acres of obscuring jungle. They would drop "pineapple" cluster bombs by the hundred thousand, bombs which, at explosion, rammed thousands of steel fragments into any flesh available. They would implant hundreds of thousands of land mines, throw thousands of hand grenades, and fire endless numbers of bullets, of which, according to their government's own figures, 100,000 were expended for every North Vietnamese soldier killed. Tallied up, U.S. forces inflicted more than $300 million in damage on Vietnam each year—at an annual cost to the U.S. government of at least $900 million. And it was all spent in a war the Americans never meant to win, only to tie.

In Vietnam, American soldiers were deployed to stop the spread of communism. In the years since World War II, communism's shadow was drifting across a world "safe for democracy" like that of a hungry eagle over a rabbit. No one had to remind any American of the age that Soviet space capsules had beaten American ones into orbit, or that Red Army tanks had recently rolled into Poland, the Baltic states, or Hungary.

The U.S. intervention failed for one reason. The North Vietnamese and their socialist-leaning comrades in the South would endure anything—even starvation and death—to achieve the goal of a united country once again. Unbeknownst to most Americans as they entered the war, it was already too late. In fact, it had been too late since the French abandoned the North in 1954—after losing at Dien Bien Phu. At that time, U.S. president Dwight Eisenhower had heeded his advisors, who had told him sentiment for a united Vietnam under Ho Chi Minh already had solid support in the South. By 1961, when President John F. Kennedy decided to send his 12,000 U.S. "advisors" into South Vietnam to prop up its democratic government, the insurgent National Liberation Front, or Viet Cong, had already organized and spread across the nation. By 1963, Americans in Vietnam required 50,000 U.S. special forces to ensure their safety. On August 4, 1964, when North Vietnamese gunboats were said to have attacked the U.S. destroyer *Maddox* in the Gulf of Tonkin, President Johnson authorized "all necessary steps, including the use of armed force" to defend democracy in South Vietnam.

By the end of 1965, 185,000 U.S. troops were stationed across

South Vietnam, and they faced the impossible task of distinguishing democratic friends from Viet Cong enemies. As U.S. ground troops wandered through the swamps and dripping jungles of South Vietnam and the DMZ, tigers, elephants, shrieking birds, and five-man Viet Cong "fighting cells" could be encountered at any moment. The bulky Americans with their heavy equipment were as visible as flies on a windowpane, and they soon learned that friendly human contact could be as unpredictable as the overgrown landscape itself. On one day, finding a jungle village behind its encircling bamboo hedge, Marine or Army infantry grunts might meet friendly natives who offered food and water. The next day, having been infiltrated by Viet Cong soldiers or North Vietnamese regulars, the same village would erupt in sniper fire and grenades.

Helicopters—developed in the years after World War II and refined in America's Korean War—could move in minutes from high mountains to swampy lowlands, velocitizing the fighting by quickly traversing landscapes it would have taken foot soldiers days to cross. In Vietnam, anywhere U.S. helicopters landed, the soldiers disgorged might encounter a hidden wedge of the population secretly against them. Across the war's eight years, 12,000 of these green steel pterodactyls would swarm Vietnam's lush back country like wasps on an orchard of windfallen apples. Before the war was over, more than 8,000 would be shot out of the sky. Compounding the velocity, helicopters effectively lifted forces from one battle situation only to drop them into another, exhausting soldiers through mobility. In World War II, a typical American infantryman served four years and saw 290 days in the active battlefield. In Vietnam—

thanks to the efficiency of the helicopter—the same number of battle days was experienced by U.S. troops in less than thirteen months.

A further complication was a shift in the character of U.S. military force during the war, a reality that ultimately affected its public support. In 1965, the Americans coming ashore in Vietnam were steeped in the ways and attitudes of professional soldiery, and they wielded the latest war-making technology with seasoned understanding. Within a few years, however, these career soldiers had cycled through their time in Vietnam, and they were replaced by conscripts fresh from high school hallways and college campuses. These younger, less experienced fighters were less convinced that democracy in Southeast Asia needed to be defended. As the war crushed on, increasingly fought by young, duty-minded men locked in a ground soldier's bloody reality—Kill him or he kills me—the deep bruise that is America's experience in Vietnam began to form. By the late 1960s, state-side support for the war had shriveled, and U.S. soldiers in Vietnam were questioning their role. Even twenty-five years after the war's end, the wisest path in Vietnam remains a mystery. No matter which side of the issue an American at the time came down on—defend democracy or let another nation fall to communism?—recollections of the age are guaranteed to leave everyone wincing.

IN HANOI, on the morning after my arrival, there's little evidence war ever visited Vietnam at all, much less dropped 100 tons of bombs on it each day for three years. Hanoi is a city of boulevards choked by endless hoards of bicyclists where ancient trees arch above the roadsides. In the city's oldest neighborhoods, 600-year-old huts of tile and mud line streets and alleyways, while in newer sections (which are still 200 years old), French-inflected architecture—with its plaster exterior walls, elegantly carved doors, and slate roofs—lends the place a distinctly European air. In the marketplaces, the rhythms of Hanoi seem not to have shifted for centuries; shoppers haggle over pigs in tight wicker baskets and vegetables piled on ancient wooden tables.

Our first stop is the Army Museum. At the entrance, a Soviet MiG 21 fighter on a pedestal seems to fly above the shredded, tin-can wreckage of a U.S. B-52. Inside the museum, which with smooth-tiled floors, custard-yellow walls of plaster, and a red-tiled roof looks as Vietnamese as any building in Hanoi, the politicized knick-knacks of a war won by the People sit inside glassed cases. The bloodied shreds of a twelve-year-old boy's anti-aircraft gunnery bandana is on iconlike display. As is Ho Chi Minh's bulbous Bakelite telephone. As is a letter written to a father, which recounts his only son's death under fire—then requests that the father step into his son's place on the battle line.

In the next hall, a map of the Ho Chi Minh Trail is bolted along one wall. Nine thousand miles in total branching length, the trail's network of jungle paths and mud roads looks like an electrician's wiring diagram. Apocryphal as the stories may be, tales of Vietnamese peasants and the Ho Chi Minh Trail make for powerful legend in today's Vietnam. In truth, in the rainy, muddy landscape of narrow Vietnamese mountain valleys, the one thing American technology was incapable of overcoming was the insectlike volume and tenacity of the people moving along the Ho Chi Minh Trail. With a seemingly endless supply of muscle power, the North Vietnamese silently transported supplies for an army hundreds of thousands strong 500 miles south, then turned around and conveyed casualties north. One story is recounted over and over to me during my visit: A Hanoi peasant was recruited to carry two artillery shells along the trail's 500-mile length. As he walked south with his cargo, he slept with the shells next to his head every night, dreaming that his two shells would be the things that broke the Americans' back. Finally, after a month of walking—slogging across rice paddies and mountains, through mud and heat and rain—the peasant arrived at the DMZ, where he watched his shells fired off in a matter of seconds. Then, as a subsequent peasant's cargo was slid into the breech, the peasant began to sob, seeing his month-long effort already forgotten. "Go back to Hanoi and get more shells," a commander barked at the peasant, leveling a pistol toward the peasant's head for inspiration. The peasant walked back to Hanoi in tears, then gathered up another pair of shells and started south again.

Ahead of us now, arranged along a gallery's back wall, the museum has a display of U.S. listening devices. Steel-tipped and battery-powered—with rubberized sound-, light-, or heat-sensor antennae that resemble spindly, four-foot trees—U.S. aircraft dropped tens of thousands of these "ears" along the Ho Chi Minh Trail, only to have them destroyed every time the North Vietnamese encountered one. Behind the sensors is a "typical" bicycle the Vietnamese used to transport goods south during the war. Boards have been lashed onto the bicycle's handlebars and frame, allowing it to be loaded with nearly a thousand pounds of supplies while the driver, walking alongside, steered the rolling warehouse south like a pregnant cow.

"Fifty-six thousand American bombs exploded on the trail," Binh says, reading from a Vietnamese-language plaque hanging on the wall. "There were 111,135 battles with the U.S. Air Force there. Twenty-four hundred American aircraft shot down. Two thousand, five hundred major combats left a combined 10,300 G.I. soldiers and Vietnamese dead."

Binh points to his arm, where goose bumps have risen. "Sometimes, when B-52s would carpet-bomb the North's troops, whole battalions would disappear under the bombs," he says, slapping his hands lightly together for emphasis. "Thousands of men, gone at once. It is amazing."

Ahead, a whitish stack of what looks to be skulls turn out to be American fighter-pilot helmets. Inside glass cases are vials for malaria pills, boots, spoons, and handmade fishing lures the Americans crafted for recreation. On one wall is a photo of Kham Thien Street. The most populated thoroughfare in Hanoi, it had been shattered during the most aggressive B-52 air strike against civilians of the whole war. The bombing, which lasted for eleven days in December 1972, was ordered by President Richard Nixon, whose emissaries had been in peace talks with the Vietnamese for months, only to see them mysteriously depart the peace table in Paris and return to Hanoi. To drive North Vietnam back into bargaining, Nixon initiated the Christmas Bombings, and here in the museum, the result of the pounding is shown in grainy, black and white photos that hang on the walls. The pictures have few humans standing in them. Instead, they show only chipped and broken rocks, like a moonscape. There are no cars. No omnipresent Vietnamese bicycles. Somewhere in each of these photos, the houses and pavement of Kham Thien Street must have existed, but it's not evident where. Instead, there is only rubble and sky.

Can you take me to this place? I ask Binh.

"Yes, yes. Of course," he says. "But you will see nothing unusual. Now, it looks just like any of Hanoi's other streets."

Binh shrugs. He looks across the warehouselike floor of the museum's Great Hall. At the room's center, the M-79 Soviet tank that crashed the gates of the Presidential Palace in Saigon—to "liberate" South Vietnam from democracy in 1975—stands guard. "Here in Hanoi," Binh says, "land is too expensive to leave it destroyed after the war. Out in the countryside, we can turn the bomb craters into ponds to grow fish. But in the city, land sells for as much as $10,000 a square meter. We can't afford to leave it unused."

OLD HANOI IS arranged in a grid of thirty-six streets, and each bears the name of what can be bought there, or what trades are plied along its sidewalks. There's Fish Street and Silver Street and Paper Street. There's Silk Street and Herb Street and even Tin Street (where I saw sheets of galvanized tin being hammered into perfectly square air-conditioning ducts by artisans, a nod to modern commerce). And a half-mile southwest of them runs Kham Thien Street, the busiest thoroughfare in Hanoi.

When the U.S. bombing of North Vietnam started in 1965,

American pilots didn't aim for Hanoi's ground structures; instead they scattered explosives across the unpeopled landscape outside town. They pelted rice paddies and jungle hammocks. They hit roads and trails but missed the enormous and vulnerable dike system along the Red River, which—if hit—would have flooded and drowned hundreds of thousands of Vietnamese civilians. Once in a while, to remind the Vietnamese they were being generous and not inept, American bombers would decimate an isolated Vietnamese army camp or ammunition depot with a sharpshooter's accuracy. Each day, the bombings proceeded with President Johnson's complete endorsement, Johnson himself often signing off on both the daily missions and their results. "They can't even bomb an outhouse without my approval," he was known to boast.

As the war ground on, the leash of American benevolence began to chafe, and benign shows of force were not appearing to work. So when Vietnamese negotiators broke off peace talks in Paris in December 1972, President Nixon decided the United States had been restrained long enough—and Kham Thien Street bore the brunt of his frustrations. It lay due south of Ho Chi Minh's lakeside home, an open, screened building the Vietnamese leader steadfastly refused to evacuate, despite the constant threat of air raids. It was also close enough to rail lines that if an errant bomb fell and disrupted train service, all the better—since Soviet arms were suspected of being funneled into Vietnam by rail.

Beginning on December 18, U.S. bombers flew nearly 3,000 sorties over a corridor between the coast city of Haiphong and inland Hanoi, each aircraft dropping as much as twenty-two tons of explosives on civilian targets. During the eleven days and nights of the Christmas Bombing (ironically, December 25 was the only day the Americans *didn't* bomb), the mile-long stretch of Kham Thien Street was pounded on five different nights, and one night, December 26, left behind a stripe of absolute destruction in the B-52s' wake. When the entire offensive was over, more than 1,300 citizens of Hanoi were dead, a deceptively small number of casualties, since the city had virtually been evacuated for almost a year. Most of the casualties were invalids too sick to be moved, or people who had been day visitors caught in Hanoi before heading back into the less densely populated Vietnamese countryside.

Near the center of Kham Thien Street's length, Vu Binh asks our driver to pull to the curb, and Binh and I step out into the throb of bicycle and foot traffic. Binh points at the roadside, then looks obliquely up the street. "Here is where the picture you saw was taken," he says, motioning at the long rows of ancient-seeming houses and shops fronting the street's sidewalks.

Bicycles and scooters move noisily along the pavement. Ahead of us, a woman pushes a cart heavied by beans and cabbage. Just behind us is a small memorial to the bombings. A bronze sculpture of a woman carrying a dead child is raised on a dais five steps high. Yet no one is stopping—or even acknowledging—the sculpture: it is as if the memorial exists in a parallel universe.

Binh grabs my arm. He turns me to face the buildings along our side of the street, where a narrow alley leads away from the sidewalk. The alleyway branches, and a half-dozen slim paths lead to the doors of dozens of narrow houses tucked side-by-side. "We are now in the tube houses," Binh says. "These are all over the old quarters of Hanoi. They are an ancient style of living, where whole neighborhoods can't be seen from the street. The houses are narrow, only a few yards wide, and they can stretch for 100 yards. Inside each of them 150 people may live, 40 or 50 families inside one house, with a central hallway connecting the few small rooms each family calls its own."

Steering me to the open doorway of one of the tube houses, Binh points inside and I peer along its central passage. In the darkness, columns of light from widely spaced windows slice across the hallway's murk. Along the hall's length, dozens of people are talking and hanging laundry and gesturing in conversations. "You can see why these houses were evacuated during the war," Binh says. "A direct hit from a bomb would kill many, many people. A 750-pound bomb off a B-52? It could wipe out five or six of these houses by itself."

A man brushes past us on the narrow path, and Binh stops him, asking questions in the clipped syllables of Vietnamese. When he is finished, Binh points down another of the forking paths. "That man said we should walk this direction," Binh says.

Ahead of us, to the left, is a small, custard yellow hut of plastered brick. Its roof is flat; its thick wooden door is open. Binh pokes his head inside and introduces himself. Then, waving me up, he introduces me, too. Inside the hut—which is furnished only with an Indian rug, a mahogany pallet bed, and a low table—a nearly naked old man is sitting on the bed, wearing only unbuttoned green trousers. Le Thanh Lang is sixty-four years old, and on December 26, 1972, he was an evacuee who had returned to Hanoi with his eldest son and daughter-in-law to collect a few things and check on their house. "We had decided to stay in the city overnight. It was eleven o'clock when we heard the sirens, so we went for the nearest bomb shelters," he says, shaking his head and looking at the floor. "We were separated on the way, and they ended up in one shelter and I in another. When the bombs began to fall a few minutes later, the first one to fall struck the shelter my son and daughter-in-law were hiding inside. Everything on the street was destroyed. Everything. The bombing that night killed all twenty-seven people inside the shelter where my son and daughter-in-law were hiding."

Mr. Lang moves slowly from the bed to the rug, where he sits with his feet folded upon his knees. He invites us inside, and, removing our shoes before sitting on the rug, we join him.

Each day after the bombings were over, Mr. Lang says, the North Vietnamese Army sent out weapons experts with metal detectors to search for unexploded bombs, although they never discovered any. Instead, on every pass, the explosives teams learned the American weaponry had worked perfectly, leaving behind only destruction and new craters after each night's onslaught. "In that night," Lang says, "they said at least twenty-nine 750-pound steel bombs fell along this block. Right here."

Did he live in this place then? I ask. On this piece of property?

"Yes," he says. "Right here. This house is all new, of course. After the bombings, there was nothing left of the old one. This new house took me twenty-four years to build. It cost $5,000."

Lang stops and smiles: behind his lips, his teeth sparkle with gold caps. "I just finished this house a month ago," he says.

So where has he lived for the past twenty-four years? I ask.

"Here, part of the time," he says. "Before that, for twelve years, I lived in a shack I built from remnants of other houses. Windows and walls I'd scavenged and pieced together. I had a roof of only waterproof paper." He smiles. His teeth flash. "After that bombing, I had a paper roof," he says.

Lang bobs his head and smiles weakly, his capped teeth glinting gold. "I was badly injured in the Christmas Bombings," he says, pointing toward his right foot. "This ankle was completely shattered. Then it was left in the same position for many hours while I lay beneath the rubble. The cuts and smashing were very deep, it could not be fixed. It had to be permanently set into one position."

Lang sees me looking, then gestures toward his foot. "Touch it," he says. "Go ahead."

I reach forward, across the expanse of rug between us, and lay my hand on his ankle. The skin is cool; almost cold. ("That's because the circulation is very poor," he tells me.) Beneath the skin, Lang's ankle is hard and fused tight, as if it were made of steel. "They destroyed my street in one night," he says. "Everything was flattened—then they kept going. They turned me into a cripple who must move slowly wherever he goes. I had to retire from my job as a road builder, now I am forced to live on my wife's salary, about $25 a month, which is not enough. I have nine children, and they help where they can. But times remain difficult."

How hard have the years been? I ask, lifting my hand from Lang's ankle. Can he give me examples?

He shakes his head, then pinches his mouth tight and stares at the carpet. "I don't think so," he finally says. "I am glad for Vietnam. But for me, now that my house and the city are complete again, I try and forget the past."

Lang's neighborhood, house, and foot are an apt reflection of Vietnam a quarter-century after the war. It may have been devastated at one time, but now it has been made to appear completely and outwardly normal–no visibly lasting scars at all. In its way, it's proof that, in the years since the war's end, another type of battle has raged in Vietnam. Individually and collectively, every day since the liberation of the South in 1975, the Vietnamese have fought a war against remembering. Their streets can be cleaned up, the bomb craters can be converted to ponds. But a war inside the hearts and minds of the Vietnemese people continues to rage on, its enduring destruction denied even as it continues.

ACROSS VIETNAM, damage so easily seen from the windows of a passenger jet grows invisible at closer range. Buried beneath the impenetrable twin shields of socialist denial and Southeast Asian face-saving, the war and its destruction have been scrubbed to an inoffensive presentableness. And although the physical damage inflicted upon Vietnam and its people can be glancingly addressed—even rolled out for sympathy if absolutely required—the war's emotional trauma remains Vietnam's dark secret, something never acknowledged or elaborated upon, especially in the presence of Americans.

Twenty years after the war's end, the Vietnamese prefer to seek the remaining 900 American soldiers missing in action than to publicly mourn 300,000 members of their own armies never accounted for. Rather than revisit personal emotional losses, they claim to follow the teachings of Ho Chi Minh by elevating the appearance of their cities and countryside. Patching over this vacuum of introspection comes only an admission that, yes, the years during and after the war were difficult, but things seem better now. Pressed for specifics, the few Vietnamese who'll verbally reminisce flesh out their experiences in only the broadest details. In every corner of Vietnam, I am constantly told that the Vietnamese are practical people, a nation that doesn't dwell on tragedy; then I've been shown new homes and emerging business ventures.

"Part of the reason for this is that, during the war, everything the North had went into their war effort," Binh tells me as we walk the steamy, thirty-six streets of old Hanoi after lunch one day. "The people were unified and had direction, but we sacrificed a lot of individual pleasures. Then, for a time after liberating the South, we lost our way."

During the war, normal life in the former North Vietnam ceased by nationalist mandate, replaced by a unified effort toward things military. In the hierarchy of need, front-line fighters stood first in line: rice and raw materials were funneled south to the hundreds of thousands of soldiers near the DMZ. For soldiers or civilians injured by fighting or bombing, medical care was limited or nonexistent. "The suffering," Binh says, "at times it was very great.

"Then, with the liberation of the South," Binh continues, "the government decided to concentrate on industrial development, not farming. We thought we could be a factory center like Singapore or Taiwan overnight. When international manufacturers didn't approach us, we had not concentrated on our farms and our economy stopped. We were exhausted, physically and in spirit. For most, the years after the war were harder than those during it."

After the war, Binh continues, another problem infected the north as well. Inside the cloister of North Vietnam, nationalist propaganda had painted the people of the South as starving under French and, later, American constraints. In the wake of the liberation in 1975, North Vietnamese citizens hurried south to rescue family members with hard-collected stockpiles of rice, secondhand clothes, and sandals made from automobile tires. When they arrived in Southern cities like Saigon, Bienhoa, and Quinhon, they discovered their long separated family members had prospered far beyond anyone's equal under Ho Chi Minh. In the South, televisions, radios, and refrigerators were in many households, and food and clothing were far more readily available than they were in the North. The Northerners, who possessed none of these unthinkable luxuries, tried to hide their small yet magnanimous gifts, claiming to have come upon the same stripe of prosperity under socialism — but the damage had been done. Word of the South's prosperity spread north quickly. "We felt we had been lied to — manipulated," Binh says. "It was hard on the nationalist feeling. Though we still loved and believed in the teachings of Ho Chi Minh, we saw that things were more complicated than we had been led to believe. It was a difficult realization for people who had given everything to win a war. It took until 1979, when the Hanoi government reorganized its business plan and admitted to the people that they had made strategic mistakes."

On Paper Street, Binh and I stop to have some business

cards printed for me. As in other parts of Southeast Asia, the cards are handed to most any new acquaintance, and I have quickly exhausted my supply. At a deep, three-foot-wide shop fronted by glass display cases, we ask Luong Van Bu, the forty-year-old proprietor, if he can print some cards up for me within a day, since we'll soon be leaving for the DMZ. He says there isn't time. I ask about his wartime experiences. "During the war I was a student in the Ha Tuyen Province north of Hanoi," he says. "I studied mining and geology. Naturally, there was hardship."

What kind of hardship? I ask.

He shakes his head. "The same as everyone: very little food; the family was separated; there was always the possibility of bombings," he says, summing up fifteen years of life in fewer than twenty words, the long-term privation leaving no hint on his facial expression. "After graduation I worked in a coal mine in the North," he continues. "In 1980, I quit to return to Hanoi and start my own business. Owning a private business is where the future is."

We continue up the street, and Binh shows me the small "paper made" imitation cars, motorcycles, and money the Vietnamese burn to honor their dead during anniversaries of their loss. "We prepare a good meal and invite the soul of the lost person to partake," he says. "We burn incense. Then, after dinner, we burn these miniatures. They go into smoke, and our belief is that the soul of your loved one in the other world can receive it as real."

The woman running the shop we've stopped in front of steps up and speaks to Binh. She's fifty-nine years old, and has long black hair that falls over her shoulders and down toward her thick stomach—something unusual in Vietnam. Binh talks to her for a moment, then turns to me. "She won't let you use her name," he says, "but she will tell you her experience, if you would like."

The woman begins quickly. "In the war's early days," she says, "I worked by the shift at a food processing factory near Hanoi's anti-aircraft gun zone. One night, on the shift after mine, the Americans dropped bombs on the factory as they carpet-bombed the anti-aircraft guns. The factory was destroyed. A few weeks later, the factory was back to work and it was bombed for a second time. I was there. Six people were killed. A friend of mine was wounded; his wife and four children were killed. Not long after that, my husband, who was a soldier, came home wounded from the fighting. There was no social services money to care for him. I took a second job. Then the district where I used to live was bombed to nothing in the Christmas Bombings. My husband was wounded again. We had nothing. I began to have problems with my head."

Can she tell me about those? I ask Binh.

After Binh asks, she lifts a hand and makes a winding motion near her ear. She shudders. "No," she says.

In Vietnam today, it is called "war syndrome," and according to Nghiem Xuan Thue, deputy director of the Vietnamese Ministry of Labor, War, Invalids, and Social Affairs, more than 1 million people have been hospitalized with varying degrees of it since the war's end. Characterized by occasional catatonia, persistent flashbacks that can flare into violent episodes, free-floating anxiety or depression, a lack of care for personal well-being, and recurrent nightmares, the syndrome is said to follow on the heels of a profoundly traumatic or life-threatening event, an affliction American soldiers have come to know as post-traumatic stress disorder. Yet, unlike the Americans, who can receive psychotherapy and clinical help, chronically affected Vietnamese are simply placed out of sight inside hospitals and infirmaries.

Across Vietnam, on the subject of war syndrome, doctors, social workers, and government officials are altogether silent. "The Vietnamese have little use for psychology or psychiatry concerns," I am told by one social worker. "Instead, we believe the intact leaf should wrap the torn one; that is our philosophy." War syndrome victims, I am told, are treated through isolation from regular society and human compassion. Inside hospitals and care centers, their needs are provided for until, hopefully, one day they return to society after symptoms have disappeared. Because the underlying disorder is left untreated, however, symptoms may return at any time, making chronic hospitalization an enduring probability for an entire generation of war syndrome sufferers.

Later that day, in fact, Binh and I will visit Bach Mai Hospital, a 1,000-bed facility and a location smashed on three different nights during the Christmas Bombings. While there, I spot a ward of psychiatric and war syndrome cases; a quadrant where the hospital's tall, glassed casement windows are shut tight—even in the day's sticky heat. When I ask about war syndrome victims, my guide, Dr. Tran Quong Do, the hospital's deputy director, acknowledges that some sufferers are seen by the hospital, but that's all he'll say. While we walk many of the hospital's corridors, which have been completely rebuilt since the war's end, I'm never allowed near the ward with the closed windows. Finally, toward the end of my visit, Dr. Do and Binh disappear for a few minutes into a surgical ward, leaving me alone in the hospital's interior courtyard. Across the yard is the building with the closed windows; behind its glass, patients dressed in pale, threadbare gowns pass by and occasionally stare outside. I walk closer and stand beneath a spreading willow, where a few of them look down upon me impassively. They have joined the nation's 300,000 missing-in-action soldiers as the war's abandoned souls, their existence far too sensitive an issue to be publicly confronted. Cared for with government money and given all the solace available, they are human wreckage, torn leaves to be kept secret, wrapped into obscurity by intact ones. They are the price of national unity.

HIGHWAY 1 RUNS the length of Vietnam along the South China Sea. Often as rough as a South Dakota back road, it stretches more than 1,000 miles, the only thoroughfare in Vietnam to be honored by the appellation "highway."

Near Highway 1's midpoint, 300 miles south of Hanoi and just north of the imperial city of Hue, the cartographer's 17th parallel cuts across Vietnam's waist. Here, the two-and-a-half-mile-wide stripe known as the DMZ once followed the parallel, and it starkly divided North Vietnam's socialist regime and South Vietnam's democratic one.

Along Highway 1 heading north out of Hue, the U.S. presence in Vietnam is remembered in hunks of oxidized metal—

in a thousand Picasso shapes. Rounded sea mines the size of Tilt-a-Whirl cars are lined up near a small bellows furnace. Junked jeep frames and the stubby, rusty spires of unexploded artillery shells stand upright at every fifth or sixth hut. The green steel body of an armored personnel carrier, its chassis stripped away and discarded, is now a chicken coop. Like a sewer line never buried, thousands of elongated, cigar-shaped napalm pods and wing-tip fuel tanks—once dropped by American warplanes—line the roadside end-to-end, their lengths delineating Highway 1's shoulders in the growing light. More than twenty years after the Americans left this part of Vietnam, their junked past still lies everywhere.

My driver, forty-two-year-old Cao Xuan Vien, was once a member of North Vietnam's 320th Division, its elite force; and he spent six years of his life in the DMZ, fighting for his life against the Americans and their South Vietnamese Militia counterparts. Today he makes his living, roughly $4 a day, guiding newly readmitted Americans through a place where he once fought them to the death. Now he loves Americans, he says.

He turns to me, lifting a hand from the steering wheel and making a fist. "Touch this," he says through Binh. "Touch where the first knuckle meets my hand."

I reach up and gently touch his hand. As I do, he flexes it, and from beneath the flesh an unearthly-looking bulge thrusts through, purple or black, pushing against the skin, the size of a large marble. Cao laughs as my hand recoils. "Shrapnel from an American pineapple bomb," he says.

Vien tells Binh that in six years of fighting he was wounded dozens of times. He shows off the long, asymmetrical scars on his forearms, then lifts his hair to expose a streaking break in his scalp. Between exhibits, when Vien returns his concentration to the road, I try to look out the window, too. In front of the huts, bamboo food carts are being set up for the day, and their glass-fronted shelves hold tea kettles and baguettes, steaming bowls of the Vietnamese noodle soup called *pho*, and bottles of water and beer. Ahead of us, in land that rises toward hills in the west, are miles of rice paddies, all stitched together by canals and dikes and dotted by the dark shapes of water buffalo.

It's a big landscape—far more sunny and open than the claustrophobic war footage Americans were shown on TV. From my seat in this car, I can see jungles, hills, mountains, dikes, fields, beaches, and swamps. To my right, the earth gently rolls, spreading toward a line of sand dunes and the South China Sea, which lies four miles off. To my left, past the endless rice paddies, the Flintstone-like landscape of the Rockpile juts up: ancient, now-jungled volcanic spires where American jungle forces once re-grouped and strategized. And there, beyond the Rockpile, are the rain-forested DMZ highlands themselves, home to that unsnuffable lifeline of roads and paths called the Ho Chi Minh Trail.

As we roll into the rice fields, Vien is talking in bursts that won't stop until the end of the day. After his wounding, he says, he was sent to recuperate at a hospital near the South China Sea. Then, when healthy, he joined the Viet Cong, the South Vietnamese troops sympathetic with Ho Chi Minh's army. "We nicknamed ourselves the Black Tiger Regiment," he says. "We wore armbands with black tigers stenciled on them." As bandits inside pro-American South Vietnam, the Black Tiger's job was to harass the Marines and Army air cavalry at every opportunity, a difficult task, since the Viet Cong were terribly undersupplied. Vien says, "We got meals only by ambushing convoys or shooting down helicopters. If we succeeded, we ate the Marines' supplies. Otherwise, we had no food. No rice at all. Hunger made our aim very good."

Vien talks of his fervor for a unified Vietnam during those days, noting that, although the DMZ had been evacuated for years, its houses and shops were left unlocked. "We were hungry and the shops had food," he says, "but we were disciplined. We were the People's Army, so we ate none of their rice, drank none of their tea. Ho Chi Minh told us the truth. If we stole from the people, we would be stealing from ourselves."

Vien smiles. "I sort of regret that now."

Just before we turn onto Route 9, the road that will take us west, away from the seashore and into the mountains, the landscape to the road's left grows more hilly and jungled. To the right, alkaline flats and sand dunes nearly touch the pavement, their surface bone white and unvegetated. "The Marines used to call this part of the road Horror Avenue," Vien says. "Both sides shelled it and hardly anyone could pass through without meeting an ambush."

For a long moment then, Vien is quiet. When I notice the silence and look at him, his eyes are full of tears. It was 1972, New Year's Eve, he says. He and three other soldiers had only one cigarette and two pieces of candy to split for celebration.

Still, he goes on, he was happy. One of the soldiers in this group was an old friend—from Vien's hometown up north—and they had been reunited while massing for a planned 2:15 A.M. convoy ambush. "But there had been a spy," Vien says. "And at 2:11 came a B-52 strike that was like fire falling from the sky, falling all around. My friend, one of my oldest friends, he had half of his body blown away." Vien rips his right hand across himself; a tearing motion from left breast to waist. "His last words were, please visit my people. Please tell my lover that I will wait for her."

After this story, Vien says nothing for a long time. Then, finally, he adds: "I have never gone to his family. Never contacted his lover." His voice is wavering. "I have never returned home," he continues. "And because of that, at night, the ghost of my friend has returned in recent years. He speaks to me. 'Please go and tell them,' he says. And still I have not."

We turn west off Highway 1 and onto Route 9. It's rougher—by far—than the highway, and as we drive along it, I watch Vien's face. Tears regularly rise from his eyes and hang, glistening, on his lower eyelids until he wipes them away.

BEGINNING IN 1985, through a series of economic reforms called the Doi Moi, Vietnam pushed its socialist tendencies slightly aside in favor of a more market-oriented economy. Enlightened self-interest replaced collectivist farming and the foundering national manufacturing plan. Drawing attention to the iron and steel left behind by Americans (plus the rich, wet soil of the highland valleys), in 1990 the government declared the mountains of the DMZ to be a "New Economic Zone," and Hanoi staked anyone willing to move there to a fresh start.

Today, prosperity, especially with an American accent, seems to have arrived. Coca-Cola, Apple computers, and Garth Brooks cassettes are to be seen everywhere, and they exist like new friends among the rusting detritus of an American army that pulled up stakes almost twenty years earlier. Ahead of us along a roadside, two massive M-48 tanks with U.S. Army insignia are waiting to be loaded onto trucks. The flatbeds will carry them to the Vicasa—a steel mill—near Hue. Once there, they will be smelted and turned into wiring conduit and construction I-beams for the new high-rises of Hanoi or Ho Chi Minh City, or maybe they'll be poured into ingots that will be sold to the Japanese. "In Vietnam we laugh at the steel exports," Vien says, his smile resurfacing. "We joke that American war vehicles may be sold back to Americans as Toyotas and Nissans."

The higher we climb into the DMZ highlands, the less the valleys are farmed; though terraced fields still surprise us at odd turns in the road. Beyond the Rockpile, at a certain elevation, thick cotton-gray clouds form and begin to drizzle. We have now entered the upland rainforest, where indigenous Bru tribeswomen, their sarongs printed in lively geometric patterns and red bands ringing their arms and waists, are drying slices of pineapple-like carrava on the pavement.

There are no towns. Except for an occasional hut set far off the road, no one seems to live in these mountains. If this is the booming New Economic Zone, I ask, where are the people?

Binh and Vien smile. "Soon, soon," they say.

Route 9 keeps winding upward, and Vien points out valleys

where fighting occurred. He motions at knolls and river cross-ings where he once warred: "Big fighting there," he says of one spot. "The Americans had Claymore anti-personnel mines lined up across there," he says of a bridge crossing. Then, from out of nowhere, he begins speaking of the helicopter, the dom-inant motif in the entire war. During the war, Vien says, the DMZ reverberated constantly with the whomp-whomping thud of Huey and Chinook rotors. During times of heavy fight-ing, as many as forty American choppers went down in Viet-nam in a day, and until about six months ago, when the last known one was removed from a valley just over there—he points ahead—their carcasses could still be found hanging apocalyptically in the trees.

As he says this, we begin to round a turn in the road. Ahead, just as it was near Hue, the long shapes of napalm pods and wing-tip fuel tanks come into view, lining the road in profu-sion. We are entering Khe Sanh.

A MOUNTAINSIDE BRU village tucked where the DMZ con-nects with Vietnam's border at Laos, Khe Sanh has always been a native outpost, its huts scattered along Route 9 and spilling back into the jungle. In the years following World War I, it became the home of a sprawling coffee plantation owned by a Frenchman named Polaine . . . and that's all the objective facts there are. After that, depending on your source, the story's particulars shift remarkably.

Khe Sanh was a U.S. Special Forces outpost in the mid-1960s, a place where American soldiers recruited and trained

Bru tribesmen while monitoring North Vietnamese activity a few miles to the north. In 1967—the American version goes—the Marines established an airfield there, hoping for a foothold from which to stomp out the Ho Chi Minh Trail. Then, late in 1967, four North Vietnamese divisions, more than 40,000 men, massed in the mountains above Khe Sanh in preparation for an attack. Thanks to 6,000 Marine reinforcements, a half-million artillery shells, and more than 100,000 tons of B-52 bombs, the battle proved one-sided. According to the American version, the defense of Khe Sanh was successful and quick. The Marines counted North Vietnamese dead at 13,000 while listing only 205 of their own killed and 852 wounded. Ultimately—and despite the fact that Americans had held Khe Sanh since the mid-1960s—two months after the battle of Khe Sanh ended the base was deemed unnecessary and the Marines razed it, destroying everything that had stood there.

In the Vietnamese version of Khe Sanh's siege, North Vietnamese forces are said to have driven the Marines from the valley after an exhausting, 170-day drubbing. The Marines struggled into the DMZ, then slapped down an airstrip and garrison, all the while swatting at a tireless enemy they never saw. From the hillsides above Khe Sanh, the Vietnamese story goes, artillery and mortar shells rained upon the airbase, while snipers played patient hide-and-seek with the Marines. Each time a new runway was completed, rocket fire destroyed it overnight. Finally—according to the Vietnamese—in June 1968, the Marines scrapped their operation and the base was evacuated. Before leaving (and with hopes of cacheing materiel for a return), the Marines bulldozed everything, burying it in deep pits. Even the base's complement of M-48 tanks, which had been airlifted into Khe Sanh and weighed 96,000 pounds apiece, went into the red clay earth. On June 7, 1968, with casualties estimated at 5,000 Marines (plus 197 U.S. aircraft shot down), Khe Sanh was "liberated" by North Vietnam.

There is a third version of the siege at Khe Sanh: the one told by men who fought there. Far more fragmented than official recitations, it's a cordite-scented tapestry composed with scraps of terror and dark humor, like Hieronymous Bosch paintings dressed in Marine camo. There's the story of the Marine grunt who, caught up in bloodletting, cut the ear from a dead Viet Cong soldier and sent it to his hometown girl as a souvenir; then he wondered why she quit writing him letters. And the tales of hundreds of cold and starving North Vietnamese soldiers who approached the Americans wanting to surrender, only to be machine-gunned at base perimeter and left to hang—bloated and rotting—in the concertina wires like insects on an automobile grill. There were also the reports from U.S. Mission Headquarters claiming the Marines were happy, well fed, and showered every day, despite the fact that the officers' club, barracks, showers, mess tents, and beer halls had been flattened and the Marines were bunking and eating in World War I–style trenches. There were the Ranch Hands, Air Force units that spent days spraying Agent Orange defoliant above the groundfire of 40,000 enemy troops, and whose aircraft carried the cavalier motto: "Only We Can Prevent Forests." Finally, there was Luke the Gook. Equal parts NVA sniper and Marine housepet, he inhabited a tiny-mouthed underground nest on a hill outside base perimeter. By day, he shot at any Marine he could see; by night, he plinked at light-bulbs and lanterns on the base. Finally, after weeks of annoy-ance, the Marines brought their weight upon Luke the Gook, shooting back with snipers' rifles, M-79 grenades, shoulder-launch rockets, and mortars—but he just popped back up and kept shooting. Frustrated, the Marines called in helicopter gunships, which poured hoagie-sized rockets and .50-caliber bullets atop Luke the Gook's hideout—only to see him remate-rialize at the chopper squadron's departure. To end Luke the Gook for good, napalm was delivered, searing the soil to life-lessness in a fiery, orange-blue explosion. This time, when Luke the Gook announced his survival with a random potshot, the Marines cheered.

The car slows as we near a clearing on the mountainside, a place barnacled with hundreds of huts made from woven palm fronds. Along both roadsides, in house-sized piles, are mounds and mounds of scrap iron: automobile transmission cases and empty aircraft fuel tanks; helicopter blades and the planks of perforated steel that once made the airstrip's foundation; unidentifiable iron shards and shiny steel cam shafts; alu-minum fuze casings and loops of rusted tank tracks. In the cen-ter of town, we stop the car and step out. Chickens peck in the mud street. Around a pile of scrap, children are running, play-ing in the rain. As we slam the car doors, they come over, in-trigued.

"They haven't seen many white people," says Binh. "They will be curious." The children come up and reach out quickly. With pinching fingers, they touch my skin. They grab my khaki trousers. Through the rain, we walk around one of the scrap piles and toward the huts beyond. A wire-thin man steps from one hut and waves. In the cool rain, he's barefoot, wearing shorts and no shirt. "Hello, American!" he shouts in wobbly English. *"Hello!"*

We walk toward him. His name, he tells Binh, is Le Quang Dan; he's thirty-seven years old, father to two of these children. Three years ago, he came to the New Economic Zone as a "digger," but he's now resumed the career he had before. Now that Khe Sanh has a school, he is once again a teacher.

I ask Vu Binh what a "digger" does, and Binh explains they use metal detectors, shovels, and trowels to unearth iron and steel left after the fighting. "It is good money, but dangerous," Binh says. "Sometimes one digger is blown up every day by unexploded weapons. It is often very bloody, and the hospital is fifty miles away, so many victims never survive the trip. Arms and legs blown off. Eyes lost." This is not something the Vietnamese government tells its people when assessments of the New Economic Zones are invoked. Still, at $2 a day, Binh adds, digging provides some of the best money to be made by peasants in this part of the country, so a ready supply of new workers is always available.

Le Quang Dan beckons me toward his dirt-floored house. As we step near the front door, I notice a water bucket next to his well. The bucket is made of aluminum: it's an old fuze casing. In fact, the fuze activation instructions—in English—are still painted on its aluminum exterior. Then I look at the well itself. Sitting atop the well's mouth, a 150-millimeter artillery shell— longer than a child's arm—spans the opening. At the foot of the shell, Le Quang Dan has fashioned a handle; at the

rounded projectile end is a fitting to keep the shell from shifting. In between, like a common spindle, the shell's body is
wrapped with rope.

Le Quang Dan sees my surprise, then says, "We use lots of
shells. Bombs for living." With that, an unrehearsed show begins. Dan leads me inside the hut, where 105-millimeter shells
have been emptied and sawed in half—now used as flower
pots. For a moment he disappears behind a doorway; then he
returns carrying a pair of long, cast iron skillets. They used to
be napalm bombs. He's halved them and fitted them with handles, Dan says, so his wife can cook with them on the hut's
wood stove. He sets the pots down and lifts others. These, he
says, were made by pounding mortar casings flat. "We cook our
rice in them," Dan says. He laughs. He lifts a low, wide kettle
made from the skin of a pineapple fragmentation bomb. Inside
the receptacle, a thick yellow liquid sloshes. "I cook my rice
wine in this," he says. Then he steps from the kitchen into the
living room, saying he used to have many more implements
made from weaponry, but as metal has grown valuable, he's recently been selling off bits when he needs money. At one time,
he tells me, he had a large-bore artillery shell halved length-
wise that he used as a rocking cradle for his baby. "Ah," he says.
He lifts an aluminum wash basin: a former rocket tube, off an
American aircraft. Using only a hammer, he's flattened the bottom, finally attaching riveted handles to the basin's sides.

"A wash basin from a factory couldn't compare with this,"
Dan says through Binh, knocking the basin's outside with his
knuckle. "This is sturdier and lighter than anything I could buy
in Vietnam."

On a long, flat drying table in a corner of Le Quang Dan's

dirt-floored living room, he has spread an even layer of black peppercorns. "I pick these and sell them for extra money," he says. "And on weekends I still work as a digger sometimes, for extra money. There is so much money to be made now, as long as you are careful." Beyond the drying table, a blackboard leans against the far wall, written on it in jagged letters are words:

neighboring
maternity ward
respiration
artificial

"These are the words I learn today," Dan says, smiling. "Every day, my future grows."

OUTSIDE LE QUANG Dan's house, an elderly man stands atop a heap of scrap iron, tossing bits into separate piles. His name is Nguyen Gian, and he's responsible for sorting the metal that diggers bring in from the field. Gruff and wearing an insulated jacket against the cool rain, Mr. Gian says he's too busy to speak with an American. Finally, and with prodigious cajoling, Binh gets him talking, anger still tingeing his voice. "The price for different grades of metal is different," Gian says. "Rusted iron materiel pays seven cents a kilo. Shell casings, fifteen cents a kilo. Aerial bombs and aluminum, twenty cents a kilo."

Gian looks at me and shakes his head. Across his thin, weathered face, a wave of disgust grows, throwing accordions of wrinkles into his cheeks and closing the fleshy flaps over his eyes. Then he bends and lifts another piece of metal, tossing it onto a pile. "It tells me much about Americans," he says, "that you would use the highest grades of alloy—metal Vietnamese have never seen before—to make bombs against us. While we, the Vietnamese, drove you away with guns and sticks."

Then he goes back to sorting scrap.

WE CROSS THE road and return to the car. It's time to visit the Khe Sanh airbase, so Vien fires up the ignition and we drive off, slipping and sliding on the dirt road now saturated with the day's light rain. A little over two miles out, Vien stops at a side road and steps into the drizzle. "We'll never make it up the road in this rain," he says, peering inside the passenger area. "We must walk from here. It is not far."

As we begin, the rain falls harder, coming suddenly in sheets, and fifty yards ahead a skinny man steps from a hut of woven palm fronds. He waves for us to join him, which we do. Once inside the shelter, the man, dressed in Russian blue jeans and a dirty rayon shirt, tells Binh his name is Ly Cong Thang, and he's a thirty-three-year-old digger at the Khe Sanh airbase. "I dig every day," he says. "It's dangerous, but I have to do it. I want the money. Only on days like this, when the mud gets thick and is heavy to lift or use a metal-detector through, do we not work."

Inside his mud-floored hut, whose interior roof has been blackened by an open cooking fire, Ly Cong Thang holds court. His wife stays hidden in their tiny bedroom addition: an appliance-box-sized room walled by woven palm fronds. Pullet chickens skitter constantly. I'm wearing a pair of Nike hiking shoes, and one of the chicks keeps pecking at the yellow embroidered "swoosh" logos on them, thinking they're inch-long worms.

Suddenly, from outside, three ten-year-old boys come bursting through Thang's open doorway. They're carrying G.I. dog tags. Some of the tags look real, some are obviously fakes; the imposters have been pressed from soda cans recently. The real ones are thick metal and read like this:

Martinez
E
2277017   O
USMC   M
Catholic

Each of these kids tries to sell me a dog tag or two, which inspires Thang's children to begin hawking rusted shell casings from M-16 rifles. I decline all, saying that I'm only here to see the airbase.

Thang brightens, then gathers up a pair of sweat-crusted conical hats. The hats are filthy; their reed wrappings are rotted and sprung, and their chin straps are veil-sheer fabric that's been stained by mud and sweat. "Put this on," he says. "To keep the rain off your head. I show you my world."

We step outside, with hatless Vien and Binh following me into the rain. Away from us, the mountains encircling this valley are sheathed in mists that lift and drop, tearing away in spots to reveal the dense jungle beneath. We keep walking, our steps taking us over the brow of a hill, where a landscape like a post-surgery corpse awaits. There, in ripped red earth and stringy vegetation, sits the Khe Sanh airbase.

"Come on, come on," Thang is yelling. "But remember—

step in my footsteps. Live ammunition and land mines can still be anywhere." On the rain-soaked soil, it's easy to see Thang's footprints, and three minutes later, we're standing at the center of the long, bowed, red earth valley the U.S. Marines once called Khe Sanh.

There's not much here. In random patterns around us, circular, two-foot-deep holes have been cut in the soil, places where live shells have been discovered and dug from the ground. To the right of where we walk, an unexploded mortar—rusty and carrying the bulk of a sledgehammer head—lies on the red mud. Nearby is a single, waterlogged American combat boot, the red dust that coated its black leather now a paste from the rain. We keep walking, finally stopping at a monument: a stone pillar standing on the barren mud of Khe Sanh's former airstrip. On the stone memorial, in the politicized language of a nation that's bested another, a bronze plaque honors the valor of the Vietnamese people. The plaque is printed in English, not Vietnamese.

"Come over here," Thang shouts from somewhere beyond the monument. "This is where the buildings used to be."

More of the same. It's all excavations, ragged indentations in red mud. Rain pointillizes the ground, and Thang shows me a large hole where a building foundation could easily sit. He and his co-workers found an M-48 tank there, he says. The tank has been excavated. It was trucked down to Hue, to the Vicasa. Beyond the tank's hole are a few scrubby bushes. Just to the right of my footfall, the bulbous shape of an American M-79 grenade—a bubble-gum wad of metallic yellow—lies on the mud. "Watch out for *that*," Thang says, pointing.

Ahead, in a more vegetated area, are oval groupings of stones: burial mounds for Buddhists who have died clearing this ground. These are the graves of local citizens, New Economic Zone leaders. I become interested in a wet cobblestone gravesite: a mushroom-colored area rug of perfectly laid rock and pebble on the red soil. As I begin to examine it, from over a nearby hill the local children have found me again. This time, there are many more than before; maybe twenty of them. They're running toward me in the rain, carrying dirt-caked G.I. gun belts and combat boots; Zippos and grenades, cartridge belts and fake dog tags.

"Do they know where they're *stepping?*" I yell to Thang, the rain dripping off my conical hat.

"Oh, yes, *yes*," he says. Still, on Thang's face, I can see the nervousness, the anxiety that one of them may be blown up as they run, their hopes of winning a U.S. dollar destroyed in a flash of shrapnel.

Then they are all safely around me, trying to sell me war surplus. Their little faces are all pointed up at me in the rain: big smiles topped by bright, beautiful eyes and mops of jet black hair. They're little baby Vietnamese, barely as high as my belt, and they're learning their nation's new lessons well. They are risking their lives to sell what mud-caked history they've got.

I THANK Mr. Thang for his hospitality, and after returning his hat it's time to start downhill again. It's afternoon, and we have one more scheduled stop: a three o'clock visit to the provincial hospital in Dong Ha, all the way back down in the lowlands.

We've got fifty miles of rough, Route 9 driving ahead, Binh reminds, trying to hustle me to the car. Before leaving, however, I break down and buy three rifle cartridges from Thang's children.

As soon as we pass through the village of Khe Sanh, the rain lets up. Another five miles along, the sun begins peeking out again. Through the intermittent drizzle and sunlit mists, the jungle glistens. In the years since the Doi Moi, visiting scientists have discovered three new mammals in this jungle: two species of goat and one of oxen. They're the only new mammal species found in Asia since 1949, a fact made more astonishing by the idea that war has raged here almost continuously since that time. But then, that's how thick these jungles are. Their trees have leaves larger than most men; their near-vertical mountains are scattered with tiny, vest-pocket valleys. Seemingly, this place could keep anything hidden.

THE PROVINCIAL HOSPITAL is relatively modern—and in terrible disrepair. Arranged as a set of quadrants, its boxy, single-story wards open onto vegetated courtyards sutured together by covered walkways. The wards all have picture windows facing the courtyards, but much of the glass in the windows is cracked or shattered. Now, strolling beneath a walkway's roof, I can tell we're back in the lowlands: the afternoon is steamy, and the sky is a dusty, pale blue scoured colorless by the sun. Along the hospital's entrance walkway, Binh hurries ahead of me. He introduces himself to a small, stout Vietnamese man wearing a baggy white jacket, white trousers, and bright white shoes; on the man's head is a white cotton skullcap. "This is Dr. Phan Huu Tai," Binh says as I approach. We shake hands. "He's director of this hospital.

Dr. Tai begins to give a speech he seems familiar with. When doctors and nurses approach and interrupt his discourse, Dr. Tai snaps from his script, solves the problem at hand, then continues the tour, never skipping a beat. "The hospital was built in 1972, shortly after the Paris Accord was signed," he says, walking past wards filled with thin children and rickety adults. "Funds to run it were provided by the Dutch, who estimated this facility would need to be open for five years. Now it is more than twenty years later, and we are still at full capacity. No one expected our problems to be so deep, so long-lasting."

The Dutch ultimately abandoned the hospital in 1990. "They left us without any money at all. For four years, we have run a 300-bed hospital on international good will and donations from nongovernmental organizations." Dr. Tai speaks approvingly of humanitarian groups like Handicapped International of Germany, the Vietnam Veterans of America Foundation, and the British organizations Mines Advisory Group and Halo Trust. "This province, Quang Tri, is one of the poorest places in Vietnam," he says, "and we have the nation's highest casualty rates." Almost six people a day are injured by mines or unexploded bombs. Not all of them are wounded badly or seriously, but they need medical attention. And we are not simply a trauma center. There are also illness and disease to treat."

Dr. Tai ducks inside a doorway. Snaking through rows of beds, he works toward a far exit overlooking another courtyard.

Near a cracked picture window, a human form lies on its right side in a bed. The body's left arm is gone; its flipperlike shoulder is swaddled by pussed gauze. Across the torso, hundreds of open scabs spatter the waist and chest. Parts of the patient's left thigh are missing, the holes plugged and wrapped by sodden cotton. Hearing Dr. Tai coming, the patient turns our way. Its face is scabbed shut—almost unidentifiable as human. One eye is completely closed by swelling; it oozes a clear liquid. The nose has been abraded off, leaving only two holes where the nostrils once were. "This is Tien Dang Quang," Dr. Tai says. "He is seventeen years old and worked in a stone quarry near here. Four days ago, he tried to pry an artillery shell free from the pile of rubble it was trapped in. This is what happened."

For a few minutes, Dr. Tai talks with Quang, speaking in Vietnamese that Binh doesn't translate. I look around the ward, and there are dozens of similarly disfigured people. House flies—thousands of flies—thicken the shadowed air, which hangs humid and breezeless above the beds. The patients stare back at me, constellations of scabs and open sores fronted by flat, unfocused gazes.

Finally, after a three-minute eternity of buzzing flies and dead-eyed stares from the most recently torn leaves of Quang Tri Province, we move on. Dr. Tai goes outside, and after a short walk beneath the covered sidewalk, he enters another ward. There, just inside the doorway, a scabbed, limbless human is draped across a mattress. "This is Hao Luu," Dr. Tai says as we approach. "He was a graveyard worker. He was caught yesterday by an exploding pineapple bomb. A family was clearing a spot for a sister's grave—they were all killed. Only Hao remains. He already is having problems with infection and extensive tissue damage—beyond the loss of limbs. He is blind in both eyes. Totally blind."

Nurses have just finished bathing and toweling Hao Luu. They're starting to re-wrap him in fresh gauze. He lies on his back; his head tilted on the sheets, his chin thrust in the air. His body is pocked by hundreds of liquid scabs. The nurses lift his head from the mattress and rotate it slightly to begin its gauze wrap. He groans. For a moment I can see Hao Luu's full face; skin has been pulled off, exposing rhomboids of raw, pale bone and bloody tissue. There are empty sockets where his eyes once were. Dr. Tai asks the nurses how he is doing. The nurses shake their heads and glance down. Flies whir everywhere; touching down on Luu's skin wherever they can. Strangely, a feeling of relief takes me all at once: I am glad Luu doesn't know I'm in the room.

From outside the ward, another nurse comes for Dr. Tai. They exchange words, and Dr. Tai tells Binh that shortly he will have to go. They have a new explosion victim coming in a few minutes. Still, Dr. Tai says, there is something he wants to show me. We step outside, crossing one of the hospital courtyards at a diagonal. As we walk, Dr. Tai says: "We hope that, as the years go on, the ordnance will eventually be cleared completely away, resulting in fewer injuries and casualties. But right now, that is only our hope. This year, there are roughly as many casualties as last year—and the year before. So far, we have seen little decline."

At the far side of the quadrant, in the corner ward, the exterior wall's old picture window has been removed, and in its place a pair of swing-out shutters has been installed. "This is one of the good things," Dr. Tai says as we step close. "A piece of good that comes because of the bad."

A young, European-looking man steps from inside the room. He is wearing shorts and a printed T-shirt. Wire-rimmed eyeglasses rest on his nose. His name is Thierry Mulpas, Dr. Tai says, and he's come to establish a prosthetics lab. "He works for the organization Handicapped International," Dr. Tai says. "They have donated this $5,000 workshop and the instruction of Mr. Mulpas. When he leaves after five months, we will take over the lab for ourselves."

Mulpas, a thirty-four-year-old Belgian, leads us toward a large stainless steel machine that looks something like a medical autoclave.

The machine, he tells us, is a curing oven for hardening the polypropylene for prosthetic arms and legs. At a long table near the machine, plaster molds sit, awaiting their time inside the oven. This is how the prosthetics program works, Mulpas explains: "A mold is made of a leg or arm stump. Then a reverse of that mold is created by the local artisans. Once the reverse mold is created, it is cooked in the curing oven, out of which comes a hard polypropylene socket, custom fitted for the amputee's stump." When the socket is completed, Mulpas goes on, an adjustable shaft of stainless steel is attached to its base, and onto the shaft's bottom goes a vulcanized rubber foot. "It's a very good foot," he says, "impervious to water and rot. Fine for going barefoot in the rice paddies and walking home at night."

Each leg, Mulpas says, costs about $38, and while abandoned ordnance and modern land mines have inspired the invention of many low-cost prosthetic devices, none are better than this polypropylene-socketed one for the damp economics of Vietnamese life. "There is the Jaipur foot of India, for instance," Mulpas says, "but that has a leather socket. For this climate and agricultural economy, where days are often spent in water, the leather of the Jaipur limb would rot and chafe the skin of a wearer's stump. In these tropics, infection is something we worry about." Mulpas lifts a gray, foot-long length of polypropylene socket from the table. "This fits tight and never rots," he says. "And it can be filed down as the wearer's stump regains muscle that's atrophied after amputation."

Around the workshop, dozens of sockets lie scattered on the tables; others hang from the ceiling joists. Each is waiting to be filed and fitted to its wearer, while dozens more plaster casts await their reverse molds and the heat of the curing oven. At the fitting table, four Vietnamese men use motorized files and shaping tools to finish still more sockets. Their handiwork has put a cloud of fine gray dust into the air.

"How many legs will be made this year?" I ask Mulpas.

"That's hard to know," he says, shrugging. "The world has forgotten this place for twenty years. These days, we are making prosthetics not only for the recently maimed, but for those injured in the past two decades. We have much catching up to do."

Mulpas pauses then and scans the prosthetic limbs scattered across the workshop, his eyes finally coming to rest on the chaos of artificial legs hanging from the ceiling. "Probably, I would guess, we will make thousands of legs this year," he says. "Yes, this year easily thousands."

HO CHI MINH City—still called Saigon by most everyone in Vietnam—is where the Americans set up their base of operations, and where, on April 30, 1975, the armies of North Vietnam swept in and declared the South free to follow socialism, even as the last American diplomats were being helicoptered off the U.S. embassy's roof. As the end of the Vietnam War arrived, it was Saigon, center of the South's government, that surrendered; its name instantly changed to honor the North's guiding leader. More than in Hanoi or the DMZ, history should have changed this city like nowhere else in Vietnam.

But on the sidewalks of Ho Chi Minh City, I immediately see that's not the case. If Hanoi's government was victorious in the war, the commerce of old Saigon has won the peace. If Hanoi is the national capital, Saigon is the financial one. For instance, Petro (the Vietnamese national oil company) could have established its headquarters anywhere it wanted in Hanoi, but instead they took over the crumbling U.S. embassy in Ho Chi Minh City. The same goes for the world's private chemical companies, banks, and modern businesses, all of which fill skyscrapers that have started to crowd Saigon's boulevards the way they do not anywhere else in Vietnam. Along every street, the locals wear pricey sunglasses and ride expensive motor scooters instead of pedaling austere bicycles. Everyone dresses more expensively. At night, on the building walls and roofs above Saigon's wide avenues, the flashing rectangles of countless advertising signs pulse with their own rhythms, illuminating the night sky in a low-lumen dome seen nowhere else in this country. On some walls, there are three and four signs—each containing thousands of colored light bulbs—and they click on and off, on and off; selling Konica or Goldstar or Cathay Pacific or Coke.

In the heat of this afternoon, outside the Majestic Hotel—a wonderful, Art Deco high-rise where we're staying—I look across Dong Khoi Street and toward the Saigon River, watching the $200-a-night Saigon Floating Hotel and the motorcycle traffic while marveling aloud to Binh about the city's sophistication. Binh smiles. "Yes," he says. "Saigon had the money before and during the war—and they still have it now. The average worker here makes $850 a year, twice what his counterpart makes in Hanoi. Only slowly is wealth moving to Hanoi."

The afternoon air is thick as mayonnaise; the sun bright. As we get in our air-conditioned car (the first "air con" I've had since arriving in Vietnam) for a ride to Tu Du Maternity Hospital, Binh, too, is transfixed by the crowded streets. He lifts a hand, pointing at the scene beyond our car's windows. "You know," he says, "not everything wars leave behind is destruction. Look at this city. The money that's here, it is the result of occupation by the French and Americans before liberation. The money those countries brought created an economy that lasted even after they left."

Still, life in the South after liberation was not easy, Binh is forced to admit as we begin for the hospital. In 1975, the Southerners lost their identity when the North's forces finally arrived, and more than 300,000 of the South's military and civic leaders were immediately sent to barb wire–enclosed camps for "re-education." Inside these prisons, the South's former ruling class was isolated from family for periods between two and five years, forced into menial farm labor by daylight and the study of Ho Chi Minh and his teachings by night. No time limits were placed on their sentences, so the inmates' only hope for release lay with the favor of their North Vietnamese Army jailors, who would free individuals only when it was deemed their rehabilitation was complete.

For those Southerners not sent to re-education camps, life in the new, reunited Vietnam proved difficult as well. For the more than 1 million who could afford the smuggling fees — often four or five times what they could earn in a year — the only solution was to escape Vietnam and become a refugee in hopes of landing in France or the United States. Even for those Viet Cong militiamen and socialist sympathizers who stayed to rejoice in the South's liberation, fortunes slumped as they took their place in a reunited Vietnam whose manufacturing and farming plans collapsed in the years preceding the Doi Moi. "For ten years, the people were hungry and depressed," Binh says. "The war was over, and still the people barely survived. They began to wonder if they were being punished by God. Truly, there were a lot of people who thought God and the souls of eternity had turned against them."

WE TWIST THROUGH Saigon's streets, our route sling-shotting us around traffic circles and along wide eight-lane boulevards where scooters move past and around us with Brownian frenzy.

Finally, at a gated opening in a long, white wall, we turn into a large courtyard building and the car stops. The courtyard is the size of a city block. It's sunny and dotted with a quadrant of gardens where women in pajamas and hospital gowns sit in the late afternoon sun. Except for the patients' clothes—and the white-suited doctors and nurses hurrying across the courtyard's gravel—it could be a village square in southern France.

I turn and look at the scene, wondering why Binh has brought me here. He hasn't let on why we've come to this maternity hospital. He's only said, two or three times, that it's something I need to see. We ascend stairs to the second floor, and a nurse comes forward, talking to Binh. After a moment of discussion, she leads us along the balcony for a distance, then tells us to wait in a narrow meeting room. A pot of green tea and four cups are centered on a rectangular wood table that runs almost the room's length. A few seconds later, two doctors enter, Dr. Song Nguyen, an obstetrician-gynecologist at the hospital, and an obstetrical intern introduced only as Dr. Tuong. The older man, Dr. Nguyen, is thickset and balding and has a belt of hair that covers his ears yet leaves the top of his head shiny. With a manner both welcoming and comfortable, he asks us to sit at the table. A pair of bifocals swing on a black lanyard around his neck.

Dr. Nguyen pours us each a cup of hot green tea. For a long moment, we all sip quietly. Then, setting his cup down, he begins. "Thirty years since broadcast defoliation using 2,3,7,8, TCDD—also called Agent Orange—began on Vietnam's forests," he says, "we believe we are finally seeing the effects of dioxin dosing washing through our population." Reaching for a blue folder on the table, Dr. Nguyen tosses it my way, spinning it across the table's wooden top. "If you'll look at the graphs contained here," he says, "you can see clear evidences of illness and disease related to chemical agents are visible in Vietnam—especially in the realm of fetal death in utero and in a type of cancer called hydatidiform mole carcinoma. The graphs mark studies done in four districts of Vietnam. As a control, one of those districts was Saigon, where Agent Orange was never sprayed directly, but where food and water subjected to Agent Orange spraying may have been ingested."

Dr. Nguyen opens the folder for me, pointing to a graph. In 1952, the graph shows, the incidence of in utero fetal death was 0.12 percent of all pregnancies in the four districts. By 1967, when Agent Orange spraying was at its peak, the rate had climbed more than tenfold, to 1.56 percent. In the graph marking the rise of hydatidiform mole carcinoma, the 1952 rate of 0.78 had nearly doubled by 1967 (to 1.43 percent), and by 1975, as the collective chemicals continued to build in tissues, the incidence had risen more than four times, to 4.54 percent of the sample population. As Dr. Nguyen begins speaking again, he flips the page. "Of course, neither of these studies is as striking as are the congenital malformations in live-birthed babies," he says. "Look at the graph."

On the table in front of me, the graph shows an almost steadily rising curve. In 1966, the number of congenital birth defects stood at 0.52 percent for the four sample areas, a number that stayed relatively consistent until 1980, when the youngest of the children born to parents subjected to Agent Orange spraying (which started in 1965) began to reach child-bearing age. That year, the number of malformations leapt to 1.26 percent. It is a percentage that, with a few statistical drops, continues upward to this day, where 1.86 percent of Vietnam's children born in the four districts each year now have congenital birth defects.

Dr. Nguyen shakes his head. "Sadly," he says, "we cannot predict how long the trend will rise. Just as we cannot know for sure that the cause is dioxin or Agent Orange buildup inside tissues, since testing is difficult and expensive, about $2,000 for every sample, and Vietnam is a very poor nation. Still, for me, the numbers and anecdotal human evidence give strong indication of Agent Orange poisoning in the Vietnamese people, if not proof."

With that, Dr. Nguyen knocks back the last of his tea, then he introduces Dr. Tuong. "He is a good doctor," Dr. Nguyen says. "He is my resident, and he will show you what I'm talking about in flesh and blood terms." Before Dr. Nguyen leaves, he hands me the blue folder, saying "This is for you. Remember it as you write." Then he is gone.

Dr. Tuong is young—in his early thirties—and speaks a little English. In his white lab coat, with his cropped thatch of black hair, his movement is smooth and economical as he walks along the hospital's halls, past wards and laboratories. "Most of the women who've had problems are between twenty and thirty years old," he says. "They were born during the times of heaviest Agent Orange spraying."

We turn a corner, and Dr. Tuong stops on a landing where a staircase runs into a pair of locked double doors painted white. A sign above the door says: GESTATIONAL TROPOPLASTIC WARD in blocked black letters. As he searches his pocket for the key to this door, he says: "You must remember that some of the numbers on the graphs you've been shown were for parts of Vietnam where Agent Orange spraying was never done. They are not simply for the provinces around the DMZ, where the spraying of 2,3,7,8, TCDD was excessive. In those places, the incidences of what we are about to see are absurdly high. If you were to single out those provinces alone, taking their infant mortality and congenital birth defect percentages, it would tell a real story."

Dr. Tuong opens the door and steps into the large storage room. We follow—and I can't believe my eyes. From floor to ceiling, on all four walls, are shelves holding glassed tanks of malformed fetuses. One large tank, backlit by a window has what's literally a pile of babies floating in its formaldehyde; their bodies are absolutely melted together. In the faintly amber-tinged liquid, I count four heads. There are four sets of ears and hands. Between these four lives, there was only one torso. I look at the babies for a minute, pointing at them. "What happened to the mother?" I ask Dr. Tuong.

He looks at the floating mound of flesh in the tank and shakes his head. Dr. Tuong tells me that the shelves are arranged by types of birth defects, and as I circle the room, it's not hard to distinguish where one form of defect ends and another begins. Along one entire shelf, an endless row of babies have similar facial features—all of them have eyes and mouths pulled far too tight, making their dead, pale little faces appear masklike. Another shelf has babies with six toes. Another shelf, which follows a long wall and goes two tanks deep, is filled with Siamese twins. Some of these babies are attached at their heads. Others at their chests. Others at their pelvises or legs or shoulders. The room is warm and smells sharply of formaldehyde. Its windows are frosted, and the light that washes through the glass gives everything a muted, milky, surreal quality. After another minute of walking the large tiled room, taking in the horror of what's preserved here, Dr. Tuong steps to the middle of the floor. He lifts his open hands toward the tanks along the walls, then twists at the waist as he looks at more shelves. "Most hospitals in the world," he says, "they have 1 percent of these births in a month."

He pauses for a moment, still looking at the shelves crowded with floating flesh inside large glass tanks. "In Vietnam," he adds, "we see a hundred cases like this a day. At this hospital, we only keep the ones we someday might have the money to study. These? They are only a sample of what is actually encountered in a given week or month—or year."

In the United States, I tell Dr. Tuong, American soldiers returning from the war have sustained their share of birth-defect babies, miscarriages, and physical problems, too, all of which they've associated with the spraying of Agent Orange. The U.S. govenment has flip-flopped on the subject of how to compensate affected soldiers at least three times, shifting its official position on Agent Orange and dioxin across a broad spectrum, calling it, at different times, the most dangerous chemical compound on earth and of negligible concern.

Dr. Tuong smiles. "Of course they are having problems," he says. "American soldiers were present when the defoliant was being sprayed, just as the Vietnamese people were. As in Viet-

nam, U.S. tissue sampling has proved expensive and inconclusive. Which is why I believe this anectodal evidence is enough.
The existence of dioxins in tissue can be difficult to show, but
the related rise in this reality"—he gestures across the room's
glass containers—"it is not inconclusive at all."

DOWN THE HALL from the storage room, a ward of floor-to-
ceiling windows and friendly staff members awaits. This is the
nursery, Dr. Tuong says. This is where abandoned congenital
cases are cared for; where the babies even Vietnam's mothers
did not want are looked after. As we walk closer, I can see inside the ward's windows, where more than fifty children—all
under three years old and with severe birth defects—are playing with wooden blocks and brightly colored plastic toys.
They're shrieking and laughing, just like kids in nursery
schools the world over. As I stand closer to the windows, they
grow curious about me: a non-Vietnamese stranger. I walk to
the door, and they come for me as well. Dozens of them. Leg-
less ones, swinging on their three-fingered hands. Bald ones,
no arms or legs at all, writhing their limbless torsos in my direction. An armless child, who Dr. Tuong calls Duy, shuffles over
on his behind. ("He can draw wonderful pictures holding
crayons or pencils in his feet," Dr. Tuong says.) There are re-
tarded ones and ones with malformed arms or legs, too—all
coming for me.

I step through the door and put one knee to the floor, so
they can get close. Their hands and feet and mouths and bodies reach out and touch me. They grasp at my clothes, arms,

and face, obviously thrilled to have another adult on the hospital floor who cares about them. As we walked down the hallway toward this room, Dr. Tuong told me the Vietnamese government will always care financially for these orphans. He said he hoped this would be the last generation where dioxin moved from parent to child; that this would be the last generation affected by the war. "After all," he said, "the war was a finite event. Only so many bombs could be dropped. Only so much Agent Orange could be sprayed. Eventually, the bombs will all be discovered or, tragically, they will be accidentally detonated. Eventually, the dioxin buildup in human tissues will begin to dissipate. No one can be certain when the war's remnants will disappear, but eventually they must."

5

Eating the Elephant

KUWAIT, 1991

IT'S 5:35 ON a late summer morning, and in the desert surrounding Kuwait City, the temperature has already climbed to 118°—and it's rising fast as the sun clears the horizon. The Saudi Arabian border is fifteen miles to the west; forty miles to the east is the Persian Gulf. In between, in every direction, dead Iraqi soldiers lie scattered across the sand, leathery markers still uncollected three years after the end of the Gulf War.

Floyd D. "Rocky" Rockwell, mine field supervisor for Conventional Munitions Systems—the Tampa, Florida–based company also called CMS—takes a measured step across the sand, swinging the head of an olive-drab metal detector ahead of him. Behind him, twenty-two men dressed in tan fatigues and working in paired teams are doing the same thing with equal care. They are slowly crossing this desert together.

Just as they have done six days a week for the past eighteen months, Rockwell's squadron has awakened in darkness and driven fifty miles over roadless sand to this place: a strip eighty miles long and a hundred yards wide, where deadly clusters of land mines lie hidden every six feet. Each morning, they have slipped into Kevlar knickers and "last chance" vests, strapped on protective helmets, and stepped inside the looping, barbed-wire cordon that defines this mine field's outer edges.

A tiny speaker on Rockwell's mine detector screeches. He stops, then eases the detector's oval-shaped head back and forth above the earth he's just covered. When the detector emits a sustained, steady yowl, indicating the exact location of his quarry, Rockwell twists and places the detector on the sand behind him. From a pocket on his safety vest he removes a large trowel and, crouching down, etches a line in the desert—a visual reminder of where not to step. Then, with long, gentle sweeps of the trowel, he begins lifting away the gritty earth that covers the day's first find. "Because I'm working the outer ribbon of this mine field, I know I've got a Valmara 69 here," he says, taking a momentary break from his scraping. "It's a bounding mine that, if I handle it wrong, it'll leave me blown up and bleeding out here. Lying on my back and doing the funky chicken."

Slowly, with a half-dozen more scrapes of the trowel, Rockwell exposes the mine: a dark metal cylinder the size of a Thermos bottle. On its top is a spiky cone; each prong is a detonator. If touched off, the Valmara 69—known to the U.S. military as a "Bouncing Betty"—will jump four feet into the air and explode, sending thousands of hot and jagged pieces of

shrapnel across a sixty-foot circle referred to in mine-sales literature as a "guaranteed kill zone."

Rockwell rolls forward on his haunches. He pulls a carpen-
ter's nail from his vest and inserts its sharp end into the mine's
firing mechanism. He jiggles the nail—as if picking a lock—
and it slides home, disarming the mine. With the nail in place,
Rockwell unscrews the V-69's spiked top and gently extracts the
explosive charge of the mine's detonator. Placing the charge
near his knee, Rockwell pulls the rest of the Valmara 69 from
the ground, turning it on its side in the sand. "There," he says
without a hint of relief. "That one's safe."

ACROSS THE SANDS of Kuwait, an estimated 7 million land
mines were sown—and subsequently abandoned—by both
Iraqi and coalition forces during the five months leading up to
the Gulf War conflict. Since then, 4,000 munition experts
from six nations, supported by nearly $1 billion in cleanup con-
tracts offered by Kuwait, have been moving slowly across the
sand, an inch at a time, unearthing and disarming everything
they encounter.

Most of the mines, bombs, and shells have been rendered
even more volatile by a thousand days of blistering temperatures and sun. Often, in between the mines, Rockwell's men
come upon unexploded submunitions: lawn dart–sized
"bomblets" slung 247 to a brood from coalition cluster bombs.
When this happens, they have to decide if the weapon can be
cleared and disarmed by hand or whether a small piece of plastic explosive will be detonated next to the bomb, destroying it
in place. "In a mine field, you hate to blow 'em in place,"

Rockwell says. "The explosion can disrupt the mine field's pattern—which is a bigger problem, because then you don't know where the other mines have been rescattered. We try to clear by hand whenever possible. Every day or two, though, we have to blast one."

Rockwell scans the landscape ahead of us, his eyes easily finding the few bombs, submunitions, and artillery shells that stand isolated above the sand like ship's masts. These are just a few of the buried dangers this mine field contains. Although many of the mines rest in predictable ribbons, millions more have been sown indiscriminately across the desert, scattered from aircraft or by artillery shells that open in midair like clams. Now they doze everywhere in the sand, awaiting any footfall that might strike them.

The cleanup has been exacting work: hot, dangerous, and grindingly monotonous. "The boredom, nobody believes it," Rockwell says, stopping his work to turn and look at me. "You do the same thing, over and over. What keeps you honest is there's no second chance. You can't say, 'Hey, let's try that last one again.'"

Rockwell is a man awash in nervous tics. Beneath his bulletproof suit and Kevlar face mask, his neck twitches every few seconds. As does his right eyelid. As does the skin on his belly. His nervous spasms are left behind when he's working with mines, however. Then his hands and body assume a Gibraltar-like steadiness. "That's the way it happens," he says, lifting his metal detector from the sand. "You save your nerves for free time. In a mine field, you've got to be steady—or you're gone."

Staring ahead, through the shatter-proof face shield of his helmet, Rockwell slides the metal detector over the hole where he just extracted the V-69, checking it for other mines. At random intervals, the Iraqis have buried antipersonnel mines two and three deep in hopes that whoever clears this field will, during a moment of slack concentration, step forward without rechecking where the last mine came from. "It's strictly mental warfare," Rockwell says. "They do it to maim or kill a few of us when we got sloppy. To keep us thinking."

In Kuwait alone, the mines have killed more than 1,700 civilians—and thousands of sheep, goats, and camels—since the end of the Gulf War. Nearly as many coalition-nation citizens have perished clearing Kuwait's desert of mines and bombs (83) than Americans died during the fighting itself (104). In the first week of cleanup alone, all five Kuwaiti mine-clearance specialists were blown up and killed, as were specialists from Pakistan and Afghanistan. In eighteen months, only two CMS workers have been killed while detecting, disarming, and destroying the current tally of 332,193 mines. That's 769 mines a day, six days a week.

"For guys in this business," Rockwell says, smiling behind his face shield, "we all tell the same joke. It goes: How do you eat an elephant?"

He stands and waits, letting the question dangle for a moment as he focuses back toward his work. "One bite at a time," he finally says, chuckling. "The only way to eat an elephant is one bite at a time."

AT 2:37 A.M., on January 16, 1991, when the armies of nineteen coalition nations roared into the desert of Iraq and

Kuwait, they unsheathed a quarter-century's stockpile of high-tech weaponry across the sand. It was equipment Saddam Hussein and his army had never seen before. During a war with Iran in 1986, the United States had given arms assistance to Hussein, but the guns and missiles funneled to his armies had been from an outmoded stockpile. Now it was five years later, and the United States was using cutting-edge technology and playing for keeps. Since the end of the Vietnam War, computer microprocessors and satellite navigation had changed the way modern conventional war was to be conducted. Instead of sending troops into battle zones as first lines of attack, U.S. military strategists and weapons designers had found ways to send only a few highly trained soldiers into battle alongside wave upon wave of unmanned—and explosive—scouts. Missiles fired at specific targets had television cameras emplanted in their noses, giving technicians and generals thousands of miles away perfect views of the targets without endangering their forces. Computer miniaturization had also birthed the cruise missile—essentially a jet bomber without an aircraft or a pilot. Above all this flew reconnaissance jets snapping digital photos of the landscape that, thanks to their computerized format, could read the headlines on newspapers tens of thousands of feet below. Beginning on that early January morning, across the sands of Kuwait and Iraq, the United States led liberation forces of eighteen nations into battle. As the Americans unsheathed the new weapons, the fearsome precision stunned not only the Iraqis; it transfixed the world.

First across the emptiness, flying from airfields in Saudi Arabia, had come U.S. Apache attack helicopters. Painted matte black and scooting in low under cover of night, the Apaches were built narrow and faceted like diamonds to deflect radar. Piloted by two-man crews wearing flip-down night-vision goggles that also functioned like binoculars, their orders were to knock out a pair of radar sites barely inside Iraq's boundaries. At roughly four miles from their targets, the pilots fixed laser beams on the radar base's buildings and satellite dishes. Then they fired volleys of laser-guided Hellfire rockets into them, each supersonic missile using a light-seeking sensor in its nose to follow the laser's narrow track—ultimately delivering seventeen pounds of explosive and instantly reducing the Iraqi transponders to flame. When the Apaches were a little over two miles from the now-flaming radar sites, a hail of sleek Hydra 70 rockets was sent after the Hellfires. Each Hydra carried hundreds of finned darts, called "flechettes," and upon explosion at the target the flechettes spattered and ricocheted across the radar site, killing soldiers and demolishing structures with the terrifying randomness of sharpened grapeshot. When the helicopters were slightly under a mile out, the pilots opened up with 30-millimeter cannons, shooting bullets as large as railroad spikes across the now decimated landscape, each impact clawing at the remaining buildings and etching lines in the desert with puffs of sand. With the night-vision goggles, the Apache pilots could see and shoot at everything, and they pocked the duo of bases to bits, shattering vehicles and bunkers, killing any soldiers who hadn't been dropped in the earlier waves of attack. After only four minutes, the Iraqi radar was completely destroyed and the Apache mission was complete.

Thirteen minutes later, the first F-117 Stealth fighter jets—
also matte black and low-profile as stingrays—streaked in over
Baghdad. Faceted for radar deflection and swallow-tailed, the
F-117s were coated with a Styrofoam-like skin that absorbed
radar waves; they were also outfitted with a radar-sensitive
weapons system that homed in on anything targeting them—
and returned rocket fire at it. As the packs of Stealth fighters
began dropping one-ton, laser-guided GBU-27 bombs on Baghdad's communications and government centers, their forward
rockets returned fire at any anti-aircraft guns sighting them
electronically. After a few passes over Baghdad, Iraqi gunners
discovered that if they switched off their radar gear, the aircraft
wouldn't shoot at them. Word of this find spread quickly across
Iraq's anti-aircraft troops, and soon the Iraqi gunners had shut
down their targeting assistance. They were now shooting
far behind each jet's contrail; firing blindly into the night as
the F-117s began making unopposed bombing passes above a
city in flames.

Then, at 3:06 A.M., the first wave of Tomahawk cruise missiles slammed into government and military targets all over
Baghdad. Carrying orders spanning twenty-four pages of tightly
coded computer programming, each Tomahawk had been
fired from ships in the Persian Gulf. Each used its satellite-
based targeting system to follow the ocean and undulating
Iraqi landscape for nearly eighty miles before striking its target
coordinates precisely. As the first Tomahawks entered Baghdad,
eight destroyed the Presidential Palace. Another six pounded
Saddam Hussein's Ba'ath Party headquarters. Thirty of them
hit Iraq's Taji missile complex.

At 3:11, as a second barrage of Tomahawks began to fall across the city, the first wave of top-secret Kit 2 missiles knit the skies over Iraqi electrical plants. Loaded onto U.S. ships five months earlier—back at Norfolk, Virginia—Navy crewmen had at first thought them a new type of Tomahawk. Now, deployed over Baghdad's twenty power plants, the Kit 2s dropped unspooling spindles carrying long, carbon-fiber threads that draped across the power lines, shorting out the city's electrical circuits and making much of central Iraq "go midnight." There would be 38 days of this strategic "softening" before the first ground troops would invade.

The new technology became the real story. Closed-circuit pictures were televised back from guided missiles, showing their paths and trajectories—with the picture going a fuzzy gray as the missile smashed into a building or dove down a chimney and exploded. Adams land mines flung out trip wires before exploding. Laser-guided SG 357 "buster" bombs held two charges, one that exploded on impact, allowing the bomb to burrow into the airstrip or building of choice, and the second (and larger) charge then blasting the structure to bits. U.S. and British anti-helicopter mines drifted to earth on parachutes; once on the ground they were activated by air pressure changes or acoustic tremors. Once "active," they chased down helicopters on mechanical feet, exploding only when the choppers landed inside their blast zone. Cluster bombs were exploded just above a landscape, spitting hundred-loads of submunition "bomblets" across an area the size of twelve football fields before the smaller bombs exploded in unison. The fire from these submunition explosions, it was said, was like that of a nuclear blast: burning all the area's available air, the explosions created a vacuum so ferocious that lung tissue was storied to be pulled from soldiers' chests and out through their mouths. And, of course, there were still the garden variety low-tech bombs and artillery shells, the "steel" as they were now known, which—just as in Vietnam—were dropped by the ton from the bellies of B-52s and fired from American M-1 tanks, Bradley Fighting Vehicles, and gunboats in the Persian Gulf.

Three years after the war, though, it's not the five weeks of high-tech pounding—which ultimately spread fifteen times more explosives than were used by all sides in World War II— that's proved the long-term problem in Kuwait. Instead, it's a far older technology: land mines.

AT THE Al Habdan Towers, twin skyscrapers south of Kuwait City that CMS uses as barracks and offices, Walt McCauley and two other CMS executives have convened to walk me through the cleanup of Kuwait. One of the men is contracting officer Earl Hine, a recently retired army supply sergeant under General Norman Schwarzkopf, director of the battle against Iraq. The other is CMS project boss Bruce Halstead, a West Point graduate, retired Army colonel, Vietnam veteran, and munitions corporation executive. We have gathered in Halstead's large office, where the glittering Persian Gulf sits just beyond the picture windows.

A large map sitting on a nearby easel shows the 150-square-kilometer sector that Kuwait has granted to CMS for clearance. The sector has been divided into thirty-six smaller, gridded subsectors. On the map, in each of these smaller, five-kilometer areas, different cross-hatch patterns cover the squares. Dollar symbols on some of them indicate the areas CMS has cleared to the satisfaction of the Kuwait Ministry of Defense. Others have cross-hatches on them that show the landscape has been swept, but KMOD has yet to approve the job; other cross-hatchings show sections now being reclaimed by CMS workers. One sector, in a dotted pattern, has not been okayed by the KMOD, meaning CMS has to return and resweep for a few uncollected mines, bombs, or bits of weapon that KMOD inspectors might have discovered. Slashing across this grid, spanning the map like a pair of craggy facial lines, are the eighty miles of mine field that Rockwell and his men are mopping up, one inch at a time.

"We're already gearing back in manpower numbers," Halstead is saying. "We used to have 1,400 men here. Now we have maybe 200. By our assessment, 92 percent of our work is done. The rest is verification and small improvements—and, of course, getting those mines up."

McCauley, a retired Navy bomb expert, slides a packet of information across the table to me. "We've said we'll clear our sector of all weapons—and we'll do it to someone else's satisfaction," he tells me. "The sand out there blows this way and that on different days, covering and uncovering things by as much as six inches a day. The idea that we come in and say, 'Yeah, we'll clear it until we *know* it's cleared,' well, it's a bigger job than it seems at first."

I look at the packet's charts. In a prominent section on one map is a box titled "Total counts," and inside are CMS's to-date cleanup totals. In the past eighteen months, CMS workers have found, collected and destroyed 13,992 tons of artillery shells and bombs. They have collected 9.06 tons of rifles; 220 tons of grenades; 1,606 tons of mortars; and 14 tons of loose explosives—just to name a few of the ordnance categories. They have also found 3,068 Iraqi vehicles, which they have towed away to an impoundment. They have collected 265 Russian T-72 tanks and 341 artillery guns. They have destroyed 112,959 bunkers and filled in 213 miles of trenches, while also leveling 243 miles of earthwork berms. All of this is in addition, of course, to the 332,000 land mines Rockwell's crew has unearthed and destroyed. All of it is just one-seventh of what has been found and cleared across Kuwait, a landscape the size of northern New Jersey.

"You know the joke about eating the elephant?" he asks.

I nod.

"Well, do you know what those bites are made of? You know how we've had to clear non-mine-field sectors?"

No, I say.

"With men, walking shoulder to shoulder." Halstead smiles. "In 120-degree heat, walking slowly and shoulder to shoulder all day long until 150 square kilometers has been cleaned up."

AS HALSTEAD AND I ride out of town, he points out a few buildings: white-tile apartment houses, eight to twenty stories tall. Weapons from either the invading Iraqis or the liberating coalition forces have left gaping, thirty-foot explosion craters in their sides. Their balconies and windows are shattered and tilt earthward like broken bones. "Here we are, three years later," Halstead says, "and the workforce here has been banging away the whole time, but the place still isn't repaired. The Kuwaitis have the money to fix it up, but it takes time. The destruction of this country—it was amazing." Even the Al Habdan Towers was destroyed by the Iraqis, who used it as a stronghold, knocking out its sliding glass terrace doors encircling each floor and replacing them with mortared cinderblocks, turning every floor of the skyscraper into a barracks fortress.

"About here's where our sector starts," Halstead says after we've driven ten or twelve miles along the highway. Ahead of our jeep, on both sides of the road, there is only hot sand. Far in the distance, a broken oil well head spews black smoke, a remnant from the retreating Iraqis, who blew off its valve and set it aflame, just as they did 700 other wells around Kuwait, almost all of which have now been capped and contained.

"You want to see how big one of our thirty-six subsectors is?" Halstead asks.

"Sure," I say.

"Okay," Halstead says, "start looking at the landscape now." He glances at the dashboard odometer, and I stare outside the speeding jeep's window at the desert. Three minutes later, Halstead says: "Okay, we've just gone the length of one side of one quadrant. That's five kilometers—about three miles. Now square it and multiply it by thirty-six quadrants. Imagine 1,400 men clearing all of it in eighteen months."

Ahead of us, on the right, the Al Jabar Air Base sits on the side of the road. A Kuwaiti Air Force base before the war, it was captured by the Iraqis and used after the invasion. Now, all of its poured concrete hangars have been perforated by U.S. TV-guided penetration missiles, weapons whose needle noses carry TV cameras inside of them, allowing technicians removed at a safe distance to "fly" them into their targets. Looking at the shattered hangars, with huge holes cut through their concrete roofs, their reinforcing steel bars twisted like cooling spaghetti, it's obvious that each roof has been struck at exactly the same spot: in the center and at its peak.

Halstead drives toward one of the Al Jabar hangars. On the way, we pass a few of the airbase's other buildings: a field hospital, a barracks, and a low office building. None of them has any glass remaining in its windows. Their walls of tan brick are peppered with blast holes the size of basketballs. "What did this?" I ask.

"Cluster bombs and Hydra rockets," Halstead says. "These scars? They're the beauty of high-tech weapons. They say to the enemy: We know where you are, and we can reach out and get you any time we want."

Halstead pulls his jeep up to the doorway of one hangar. The penetration bomb has left its mark everywhere. Fifty yards inside the building, the roof has been driven in, leaving a twenty-five-foot mound of rubble on the floor like a stalagmite. Steel tendrils of concrete rebar drop from the roof: bent and twisted, they braid across the pile of broken concrete like lengths of nylon rope. Shattered fiberglass and alloy pieces from a jet are scattered across the large hangar's floor, too, and their trail extends out the hangar's doorway.

Since World War II, a tactical bomb's accuracy has been measured inside a rectangle sixty feet wide by one hundred feet long. Dropped from a bomber flying at 10,000 feet and aiming for that target, the number of bombs necessary before one falls inside the rectangle is the weapons technicians' test of a system's accuracy. During World War II, even using the then sophisticated Norden bombsight (a visual speed and distance calculator whose development was guarded as a secret weapon), a B-17 bomber needed 9,000 bombs to ensure a target was hit. By the Vietnam era, that number had dropped to 300, the increased accuracy having mostly to do with the advent of computers and "smart" bomb guidance systems in the war's last two years. In the Gulf War, thanks to microprocessors, laser sighting, and TV cameras inside the bombs themselves, one-bomb-to-one-target surgical precision had been achieved—and its evidence is spread all across the hangars at Al Jabar.

Halstead stands in the hangar's sunny doorway and looks into its darkness. "These weapons fly right up and knock on the door."

"What's it like cleaning this up?" I ask Halstead.

"High-tech and smart bomb arrangements aren't too bad," he says. "There's one explosion, some extensive damage, but it's limited. It's economical." Halstead turns and points toward an already cleared section of Rocky Rockwell's eighty-mile mine field. Far in the distance, we can see looping barbed wire that crosses a mile south of Al Jabar. "I'll tell you the tough thing to clear," he says. "It's those mines. They don't cost much to lay down, but they're expensive as hell to take up. And they just go on forever."

AT THE END of the century, the age of land-mine warfare has arrived. And it stretches far beyond Kuwait's borders. Around the globe, land mines crowd the soil in more than sixty countries. In Angola alone, where two decades of no-holds-barred civil war has left 20 million land mines in the earth, 120 people are killed by them each month. In Cambodia, 18 million antipersonnel mines have been implanted, and health workers there calculate that, thanks to Khmer Rouge mine-laying teams, 4,000 people are killed or maimed each year, and 1 of every 236 Cambodians has lost a limb or eye to land mine explosions. In Afghanistan, 12 million mines were laid during the 1980s war with the former Soviet Union. Today, with fighting ended and the Afghan nation exhausted, the cleanup is slow and mines remain strewn across mountains and lowland pastures, on footpaths and roads, in irrigation canals and urban alleyways. In the former Yugoslavia, an estimated 6 million mines have gone into the soil. In northern Somalia and the Mozambique highlands, millions of mines ring villages and water holes like silent sentries. Never hungry or in need of sleep, the mines have replaced fallible human soldiers; they not only stop humanitarian aid from flowing in but keep refugees from flowing out as well.

"Land mines are so plentiful and cheap, as little as $3 a throw, that their numbers have become staggering overnight," says Patrick Blagden, demining expert for the United Nations. "They're now so pervasive that—and this is terrible to admit— we can't even calculate how large the problem is."

Worldwide estimates on the number of uncleared land mines vary, but the figures tossed around are relentlessly impressive. In 1994, the U.S. State Department said upward of 85 million mines were spread across fifty-six nations. Other computations, though, run far higher. The United Nations, for example, claims that somewhere between 105 million and 200 million mines may be emplaced in sixty-two nations worldwide. The International Committee for the Red Cross says as many as 300 million mines may now be indiscriminately scattered across sixty-six countries. That figure works out to one mine in the ground for every sixteen people on earth. No matter how many mines are implanted worldwide, it's a problem that the United Nation's Blagden estimates will cost $200 billion to $300 billion to clean up. "The mine clearance costs are yet another dumbfounding aspect to this," Blagden says. "Over the next twenty-five years, we'll have to commit between $300 and $1,000 to clear every $3 mine currently in the ground. Obviously, the economics of this kind of warfare are devastating. Figuring out how we'll pay for the mine clearance is as difficult as the mine clearance itself."

Blagden, a retired brigadier with the British Army, works at the UN building in New York, some 5,000 miles from the sands of Kuwait. The walls of his office are festooned with UN-printed banners from mine-field zones worldwide; each uses international symbols and a host of languages to warn of mine-related dangers. One of the larger banners, handed out in northern Somalia, has a dead camel printed on it; above the camel is a message in Arabic and the silhouette of an exploding mine. Another, for Afghani refugees, has vertical columns. In each column is a different type of mine: a trip-wired hand grenade on a stick; a large, steely cylinder; a green disk.

"We have no idea how long mines in the ground will stay operative," Blagden says. "But we know they're waterproof and stable, so other than something coming along and setting them off, what's to stop them from lasting fifty years? A hundred years? Or longer still?"

Blagden places a puck on his desktop. "There you are," he says, gesturing. "That's one of the most plentiful buggers out there. A Chinese-made Type 72 antipersonnel mine. It's all plastic, except for the slightest bit of metal in its firing mechanism. Virtually undetectable once in the ground."

Blagden unscrews the mine's top. He pulls the disc into two parts—like halves of a yo-yo—then points out the black, tarlike explosive inside. "There are millions of these, tens of millions, in the ground worldwide. And when as little as six pounds of pressure is placed on one, it's capable of blowing a foot and lower leg clean off, amputating right up to the knee. Nasty. Very nasty."

In the world today, some 340 types of mines are manufactured in forty-eight nations. Some of the makers, like those in China and Romania, are state-owned. Others like the Italian maker Valsella or Thiokol in the United States are private manufacturers trafficking specifically in government contracts; agreements that, among other things, prohibit them from disclosing the numbers or varieties of mines they produce. All told—and not counting knockoffs fabricated in basements from El Salvador to Southeast Asia—Blagden says 10 million to 30 million mines are produced each year.

Blagden turns back to a gray cabinet behind his desk which contains several other mines, and extracts a Valsella 2.2, a larger mine made of molded plastic and tan in color, roughly the size and shape of a Frisbee. "If I were to go to Valsella, the maker of this mine, for example, and ask how many of these they made last year and whom they sold them to, they'd respond by sticking two fingers up my left nostril and escorting me to the door.

"Valsella won't even admit it makes mines," Blagden continues, "although we have ample evidence that they do." After his retirement from the British Army, Blagden spent five years working for a private London-based company called Royal Ordnance, which was awarded the mine-clearance contract for the British-assigned sector of Kuwait. During his year in Kuwait's oil fields—before the United Nations enlisted him ("Under slight duress, I might add," he says)—Royal Ordnance workers pulled 524,000 mines from their sector of Kuwait, including numerous specimens of the Valsella 2.2, like the one in front of me. "That Valsella," Blagden says, jostling the tan mine on his desktop, "they can *say* they don't make these things, but I know differently. I've viewed their handiwork in the field."

BACK IN KUWAIT, Rocky Rockwell is starting to step slowly forward again. Ahead of him, he eases the head of his mine detector slowly above the desert floor. The battery-powered detector, made by a Viennese company called Schiebel, is a green painted, amped-up version of the metal detectors used by beach-going treasure hunters on weekends. Its batteries and sensors are checked twice daily, and CMS minesmen have proven the Schiebel detector to function well in temperatures to 55° Celsius (about 131° Fahrenheit). On most days, the temperature reaches 55° Celsius by 10:30 A.M., at which time mine sweepers mark the day's progress with staked flags and retreat to safety. "The temperature restriction is why we start working before sunrise," Rockwell says. "Otherwise we'd never get any work done."

One last time, for confirmation, he swings the detector over the hole left by the V-69; the speaker on the detector remains silent. "That hole's clean," he says, moving slowly to his right, easing the detector's head a half-inch above the ground. "There should be an 'A' pattern arrangement of mines just over here," he goes on. "It'll be the first of six 'A' configured ribbons across this field." This configuration, he explains, is an anti-tank mine ringed at twelve, nine, and three o'clock by smaller (and nearly undetectable) antipersonnel mines. A moment later, Rockwell adds that NATO has another approved configuration, a "B" pattern, which is the circle of antipersonnel mines without a hefty, anti-tank mine at its center. What concerns him most though, he says, are those zones around the world where antipersonnel mines have been sown randomly, without consideration for who'll follow. This happens mostly in Third World nations, where insurgencies, civil wars, or genocide leave NATO and UN protocols ignored. Still, land mines aren't scattered indiscriminately only by renegades, terrorists, or small-potatoes despots. During the Gulf War, coalition forces used rocket-launched, scatterable-mine systems to lay more than 1 million mines along the Kuwait border and around the Iraqi city of Basra. Still, the problem remains most grave in the Third World, where poverty and long-running civil wars haven't allowed convalescence. "You go to a place like

Cambodia or Angola," Rockwell says, "and your odds of finding mines are astronomically high. Like Mardi Gras beads on Fat Tuesday in New Orleans."

After another half-minute of slow searching, Rockwell's mine detector begins to growl; just beneath the detector's flat, rounded head, a circle of greenish plastic is barely visible. "There we are," he says, his voice muffled slightly by his helmet's face shield. "A Chinese-made Type 72, an antipersonnel mine with real teeth."

Rockwell sets the mine detector down. He kneels, then trowels another line into the sand. He lifts the mine gently from its sleep, then turns it over in the air. It's the same mine as in Blagden's office, except three years of harsh sun has pitted and faded this specimen's plastic top. "See what the elements do to these things?" Rockwell says. "In some cases, sun and blowing sand will wear the plastic clean away, which can make a mine *really* squirrelly to work with." Rockwell places the mine between his hands, then unscrews the disc. He separates its top and bottom, and points out the tarry explosive inside. According to Rockwell, the Type 72 is highly unpredictable: its detonator being a sheer plastic diaphragm that's sensitive to downward pressure. Once the diaphragm is depressed, the explosion cannot be stopped.

Rockwell removes the tiny metal "booster cup" from the mine, the primary charge that sets off the larger explosive. He screws the mine's halves together again and leaves it standing—sideways on edge—in the sand, the signal to cleanup crews that this mine has been disarmed. "All done," he says.

He stands and lifts the mine detector, swinging it over the

newly made hole. "Nothing here," he says. A foot to the right of the hole, the tan, rounded top of a Valsella anti-tank mine—the same, Frisbee-sized one Blagden has in his office—is flush with the surface of the desert. "That's the anti-tank mine, it's the centerpiece of this A-pattern group," Rockwell says above the prodigious squawk of his mine detector. "There should be two more Type 72s here, too," he adds. "We've already pulled the mine in the nine o'clock position, but there should be one at twelve o'clock and one at three o'clock. Sand has covered them over. Anyway, I'll bet they're here."

Rockwell eases the mine detector's head a foot further into the mine field, to where he believes the twelve o'clock–positioned mine should be. The detector begins to growl. "There's the one," he says. He swings the detector's olive green head a foot to the right of the anti-tank mine's large, tan disc: to the three o'clock position. The detector makes a scratchy groan. "There's the other one," Rockwell says. He sets the detector down and removes his trowel. He etches his lines; then pulls the anti-tank unit first, flipping it over and deactivating it by tightening a single screw with the tip of his trowel.

After turning the anti-tank mine on its side—and double-checking the hole it's left—Rockwell kneels forward. With easy, gentle scrapes of the trowel, he begins to peel away sand in a slow search for the next small green disc.

AS EXTREME AS the working conditions for CMS minesmen are, the advantages afforded CMS technicians in Kuwait pale beside the existences confronting mine-field workers worldwide. In Kuwait, CMS employees live in hotel-like suites, with air conditioning, three catered meals a day, in-room kitchens, and cable TV. In Fahaheel, a mile down the road, are a half-dozen good restaurants: Chinese, Middle Eastern, even pizza joints. Kuwait is a Moslem nation, which makes possession of alcohol illegal, but a few CMS employees home-brew gin and often throw Thursday night parties. And if parties aren't a minesman's idea of fun, the Al Habdan Towers have a sparkling and complete health club. Or, there is the opportunity of late afternoon snorkeling and scuba diving in the surprisingly lucid waters of the Persian Gulf, which lap just across the Coast Highway from the barracks towers. The beach, of course, is still mined.

Mine workers elsewhere in the world are less fortunate. In Nicaragua, mines are cleared by hired soldiers in heavy, lead-filled chest and leg shields, often without the benefit of metal detectors. They move forward an inch at a time, pressing steel rods into the ground ahead of them at a practiced, thirty-degree angle, hoping their probes will hit the inert sides of mines rather than their explosive tops. When the day is over, they return home by whatever transportation is available. All for $6.60 in wages. Until 1992, conditions in Iraqi Kurdistan were tougher still. From May until September of 1991, unpaid volunteers were forced to crawl the edges of suspected mine fields, prodding the earth ahead of them with sticks or steel rods until safe perimeters had been established and roped off. In the months between May and September of 1991, more than 2,000 land-mine victims were treated at two field hospitals in Iraqi Kurdistan. Since that time, humanitarian explosives experts from Middle East Watch and the crack Mines Advisory Group of Great Britain have arrived and sped mine clearance in Kurdistan along, also establishing high-quality field hospitals to treat the finally lowering tide of victims.

Although the sophistication of mine-clearance techniques varies around the world, everyone involved acknowledges that mistakes carry the same, universally unhappy end. So, for each CMS mine sweeper, workdays are chiseled into clear, half-hour eternities. During the first thirty minutes a minesman works, he is either feeling his way across the ground with the Schiebel detector or acting as spotter for his partner (who's using the detector) by following roughly ten feet behind and double-checking his movements. "We switch positions every thirty minutes," says Bill Smith, a CMS mine specialist, "so our concentration doesn't burn out. Then, after your time with the Schiebel, you follow behind your partner. That way, if the sweeper gets a growl on his detector that he doesn't acknowledge—or if his mind wanders or he does something unusual—the spotter is there."

At thirty-eight, Smith has already had a full career as an explosive ordnance technician with the U.S. Army; he's been married twice and already has four grandchildren. "I don't know," he says, grinning. "Maybe my life's just got a fast metabolism."

After two and a half years in this desert, working for United Nations forces before signing on with CMS, Smith has come to take long days and unexpected events in stride. Often, while clearing this mine field, he'll be on his knees, reaching for a mine, and a kangaroo rat or dhubb (a grayish, eight-inch lizard) will zip beneath his hand, exploding from the shady burrow it's carved below the mine. Other times, as CMS deminers are working near the Iraqi border, Saddam Hussein's sentries will fire volleys above their heads.

Smith's most unsettling experience as a minesman took place in March 1993, when an anti-tank mine exploded in his partner's hands. "I'd just switched jobs with my partner, to be spotter for him," Smith says. "We were walking back to work and we saw two anti-tank mines. My partner just reached down and pulled one up. It was a bad habit he had: pulling mines when I was too close. And I thought, 'Son of a gun, he's doing it again.' So I said: 'Hey, man, wait 'til I get into position before you start pulling mines.' "

His partner had happened upon a mine with an anomaly called a floating pin, which renders it explosive to any kind of jostling or movement. "Well," Smith goes on, "he had a second bad habit, which was to knock his trowel against a mine to get caked sand off of it." According to Smith, whose back was turned at the time, he heard a tap, then a second tap. "On the third tap," he says, "the mine detonated. And our mine detector—which is nineteen pounds and five feet long—it shot past me at ballistic speed. This was a big mine, an anti-tank mine, not a little antipersonnel pop. And the blast wave hit me, and something big caught my shoulder, which spun me around, and I felt something hit me, *real hard*, in the belt buckle."

The explosion pushed Smith from the cleared section of mine field into the dirty, uncleared part. As he struggled to recover his balance and keep himself from tumbling onto mine-strewn sand, Smith says, "I looked back at my partner, and there wasn't much left of him. His arms and legs were gone.

Blown away to nothing. I looked down, and I was bleeding pretty well from my left thigh. And the rescue team came out, working their way across the clean part of the mine field toward my buddy and me, and my buddy was still talking out loud; even with his limbs gone, he was coherent. The downed-man team had to hold my buddy's head down, so he couldn't look up and see what happened. They got us into a med evac chopper, *fast*, and he stayed alive for three more hours."

The next day, three employees quit the CMS force, with the company buying their airline tickets home. "Nobody gave them a hard time about it," Smith says. "That's the thing. Everybody knows that you can't be worried or nervous in a mine field. If you are, you're no good to yourself—or to the guys you're working with."

For Smith, however, the way back led across the barbed wire. "I knew I had to go back out there," he says. Three weeks later, after the artery in his thigh closed, he returned to work. He is still picking shrapnel out of his skin. "It works its way to the surface over time," he says. "I've had to pick some of my buddy's bones out of me, too. I had a big piece of him lodged in my lip. It just came out recently. A long sliver of bone."

Smith lifts a hand, and spreads his thumb and index about two inches apart, regarding the distance between his fingers closely.

Although he still has a constant ringing in his ears, which he characterizes as "a thousand crickets in my head," and regular nightmares—where the blast jolts him awake—Smith continues to clear mines. "It's what I do," he says. "And when we get done here, I'll go and do this same thing somewhere else."

To maintain their confidence, most mine clearance specialists incorporate various lucky touchstones and rituals into their workday. One CMS employee has been eating the same food every day for months; another follows a strict dressing regimen each morning; another describes his meticulous shaving routine and the mantras he recites while traveling to and from the mine fields. ("Some of them see themselves as artists with supernatural powers of survival," says Rockwell of the technicians.) For Smith, as he goes to work each morning, he says a prayer and wears a hunk of luck around his waist. "I don't kid myself," he says, looking at his belt. "A higher power has something to do with why I'm alive. You can be the most experienced guy in the field, and if you get the wrong mine, your number is up. Like that blast? I should have died, but I was wearing my lucky belt buckle. A big rectangular brass thing from my Army days with Explosive Ordnance Disposal. That shrapnel hit the buckle just high of center—or I'd be dead. That buckle has a dent a half-inch deep in it, and I'm alive because I wore that belt on that day. How's that for lucky?"

DESPITE THEIR HUNDREDS of variations and dozens of manufacturers, land mines are easily divisible into two distinct groups. The larger ones, anti-tank mines, have their genesis during the end of World War I, when German trench soldiers in France, trying vainly to beat the newfangled armored tank, buried large artillery shells and left their fuzes exposed in hopes a "land ship" would rumble across. By World War II, sturdy and devastating anti-tank mines had been developed; and in a testament to the longevity of these units, each year anti-tank mines laid by Erwin Rommel's Afrika Korps of the Third Reich are still unearthed and disarmed along the Libyan seacoast. But by and large, anti-tank mines are a small problem these days. Essentially a defensive weapon that slows the approach of armored tanks and vehicles by disabling them with massive explosions, these mines generally weigh thirty pounds or more and won't detonate unless hundreds of pounds are pressed directly upon them. Also, thanks to their high metal content and overall heft, anti-tank mines are easily detected in the ground, allowing whole fields of them to be safely swept— over time—by small groups of men.

At the other end of the spectrum are the antipersonnel mines. Inexpensive, readily available, and nearly undetectable once in place, they have quickly replaced mortars and bullets as the favored weapon in small-scale conflicts, disagreements where troop size or financial limitations force military leaders to maximize assets. Antipersonnel mines were developed as a way to protect anti-tank mines toward the end of World War II. Nowadays they come in at least three different styles: from the basic, foot-triggered models, also called "blast" mines, which shred lower limbs; to trip-wired hand grenades on stakes; to shrapnel-throwing beasts called "directional" mines that look like modernist sculptures (and can be implanted by low-flying aircraft, helicopters, or field artillery shells). With all antipersonnel mines, the principal purpose is to maim rather than kill, since an injured infantryman is more burdensome to military support staffs than a dead one. Antipersonnel mines are widely considered the cruelest and least discriminating weapon of war. During the past decade, they have become the largest source of war-related injury in the world, maiming and killing at least 26,000 people each year, an estimated 80 percent of whom are civilian women and children.

"Who makes 'em? I'll give you an international list as long as you want to hear," says Gregory Fetter, an analyst with Forecast International, a company based in Newtown, Connecticut, that follows the defense industry. "But no one will talk about it. You may get position papers out of some of the makers, but that's as far as it'll go. These makers want to protect themselves and their industry. Which is larger than you can imagine. Why should they disclose how many mines they make—or who they sell to? Especially since, after they sell their mines, they're not even certain where the mines will end up. These things have an *incredibly* long shelf life. They can be stockpiled and re-sold, then restockpiled and resold again. They're literally impossible to track."

Fetter has followed the sales from one Italian company to sources in Spain, Norway, and Holland. "But when those shipments get to their destinations, the paper trail ends," he says. "It all turns into a shadow. Those mines I tracked, they could be anywhere in the world now. The arms traders run the show. It's all done under the table. But every nation is making them, and everybody is making a lot of them."

The United States alone, says Fetter, has made somewhere upward of 5 million conventional land mines since 1970, not to mention more than 75 million mines for scatter deployment by artillery shells (known as a "multiple-launch system submunitions"). "It's gotten to where the only way to estimate the number of mines out there," he says, "is to monitor the profits of the mine manufacturers—and to follow the rising number of casualties. It's a grim way to gauge business, yeah, but that's the only halfway reliable information we've got."

ONE EVENING I accompany Earl Hine of CMS to the KMOD Central Collection point: the vehicle dump where tanks, weapons, and vehicles from all seven subsectors have been dropped. Hine calls it "The Boneyard."

Off and on, as we've driven the twenty miles up the Coast Highway, Hine talks about CMS's contract with the KMOD. Initially, it was an agreement for eighteen months of ordnance clearance, and CMS has lived up to its end of the bargain. But now, with only about two weeks left, the KMOD has changed the rules. Now, it appears, CMS is responsible for clearing debris from every inch of the sand. In the past few days, in fact, the KMOD has visited two of the CMS subsectors for final inspections, and both subsectors have failed. "They find a little scrap of metal out there," Hine says, "and they give us the thumbs down. So we've got to go out and clean it up again with a comb. There's no ordnance left, only metal—but the rules have changed. To an Arab, a signed contract isn't what it is in America. In the Mideast, if you have a signed contract, it means you officially can renegotiate its terms."

Still, Hine also knows that CMS is lucky to have gotten into Kuwait at all. In response to the growing land-mine hazards worldwide, there are more than twenty different private mine-clearance companies all keenly competing for the same lucrative clearance contracts. Some of the organizations, like

Britain's Mines Advisory Group, are humanitarian agencies, nongovernmental and nonprofit groups that provide medical treatment along with the demining. They stay afloat with money made from demining agreements and contributions. Others, like $130 million-a-year CMS, are commercial enterprises that pay entry-level workers as much as $90,000 a year and are often owned by multinational corporations. CMS is American-located, but it happens to be a division of Deutsche Aerospace, which in turn is owned by the German giant Daimler-Benz. The arrangement left four other American demining companies screaming foul when CMS was awarded the American-based clearance contract in Kuwait. There are other arrangements as well: the French Sofremi, for example, is a partnership agreement between the French government and private defense contractors.

The Boneyard is south of Kuwait City. Hine steers our jeep through an open gate, then brakes it to a stop. To the right, extending for a half-mile or more, the brown barrels of thousands of field artillery pieces poke skyward. There are 105s, 175s, 205s—and a dozen other calibers and variations. They're still mounted on their wheeled carriages. Hine and I get out of the jeep and walk to the cannons. I lay my hand on one. Even at sunset, its solar-heated iron is too hot to touch. I look at its shield, the sheet of metal that rises vertically and covers the cannon's bore, protecting troops near the gun breech. On the metal of the shield, facing the back side, the words "Praise Allah" have been painted over and over in Arabic.

To the left of the jeep, thousands of Russian T-72 tanks are lined in rows. Beyond them, there are also thousands of ar-

mored personnel carriers and supply trucks—all now blackened and shattered. After a few minutes of inspecting the artillery pieces, Hine and I cross in front of the jeep and begin
nosing around the tanks. Each T-72 weighs more than forty-five
tons, yet here in the vehicle dump they've been tossed around
and stacked like children's toys. Their tracks are broken and
drooping; their turrets half-blown away. They have been destroyed one of three ways. The majority of the tanks are burned
and melted to black; which means they were stopped by HEAT
rounds fired from America's M1A1 "Abrams" tanks: sixty-seven-
ton monsters that can move at sixty miles an hour and have two
feet of front-facing armor. The HEAT rounds, which slammed
into the T-72s from as far away as a mile, drove a 3,000° jet of
flaming gas into the tank's interior, charring the crew, the cockpit, and, ultimately, its engines and weapons. Other tanks seem
relatively unscathed except for a round, golf ball–sized hole in
their armors. These holes were made by DU—or depleted uranium—rounds: yard-long darts tipped with spent uranium that
are capable of cutting through a tank's thick steel like a hot
knife through butter. Once inside the tanks, the uranium darts
rattled around, killing the crews and battering apart the cabin.
Finally, there are the tanks eaten by Aardvarks: Vietnam-
vintage F-111 fighter/bombers equipped with GBU-12 laser-
guided bombs and heat-sensitive infrared targeting systems.
Going out at night, the Aardvarks searched the desert for T-72s
either still running or that had absorbed enough sunshine during the day to leave visible "heat pulse" signatures on the infrared system. Once identified as targets in the cold, black
desert night, the Iraqi tanks stood naked as beer cans teed up

on a farmer's fence post. The Aardvarks employing laser-sighted bombs were to blast dozens of them to bits each night.

I climb on one of the tanks and examine the hole in a turret where a DU round bored its way inside. The turret is made of foot-thick steel, yet the hole cut through is clean and smooth, the steel having been melted back in a circular, wavelike pattern. I stick my finger inside the hole and feel the perfect flatness of the dart's entry path. Inside the T-72, the cabin is small and on two levels; there is barely enough room on each level for two soldiers seated side by side. Now a layer of sand covers everything, and beneath the sand the tank's interior has been shattered. The radioman's electrical equipment has been blasted apart, and wires, transponders, and bits of control switchboard hang in the cockpit's air like the exposed guts of a quartered animal. The crew's seats are gnarled and twisted, too, and the walls are dented and broken. The DU round has, literally, torn everything to pieces.

Hine is standing alongside the tank on the ground. "Those uranium rounds really bust up a machine, don't they?" He shakes his head. "They travel fast enough to cut through the armor, and inside the tank they slow down just a little—so they can't get back out. They ricochet all over and then shatter. It's like shrapnel inside a tank."

The dead inside these tanks, Hine says, were extracted by Kuwait's national Graves and Memorials workers, but just as with all cleanup contractors in Kuwait, it remained CMS's responsibility to evacuate the tanks to this central collection depot, which they did by loading them on "low boy" tractor-trailer trucks. "Before we could move them, though," Hine says, "we had to clear them of existing weapons and drain them of gas, oil, and lubricants, so they wouldn't leak all over the place."

IN THE DESERT of Kuwait, at 10:06 A.M., the mercury in Rocky Rockwell's ground thermometer inches to 55° Celsius, and Rockwell pulls a walkie-talkie from his belt. "That's it for today, boys," he says, radioing to the sweeping teams inside the mine field. "Let's pull out. *Now.*"

Despite the end of active demining for the day, CMS's chores are far from finished. Over the next few hours, secondary squads of mine sweepers will enter the cleared zone of the mine field and carry away the defuzed, sideways-lying mines. They'll count and inventory them all, pile them in tight, squarish stacks a dozen mines tall, and prepare to blow them up.

A half-mile south of where Rockwell stands, four stacks of mines—those retrieved over the past few days—are ready for destruction. Each stack is the size of a family van, and by employing a technique called a daisy chain, the top layer of each pile has been ringed with detonators and attached to four-minute fuzes. The fuzes have been lit at one-minute intervals, and now, as the detonation teams get into their jeeps and drive to a safe, half-mile distance away, a short wait is all that remains before the detonators on each stack blow, setting off the mines beneath them.

As Rockwell stares across the sand, watching the piles of mines through his binoculars, he's talking elliptically about his future. Like all CMS employees and subcontractors, Rockwell's waiting to hear whether the company has been awarded the UN's $34 million contract to clear roads in Mozambique: Blagden's first stab at getting the United Nations involved in mine clearance. If CMS isn't awarded that deal, there will doubtlessly be other assignments. As Rockwell leans against his jeep and stares at the horizon, waiting for the first stack of mines to blow, he says: "I think of the number of mines already in the ground, and I know there'll always be work for me. CMS has been talking to governments in Southeast Asia and Africa. There are mine fields to clear in El Salvador and Somalia and Cambodia. The mines in the former Yugoslavia . . . they'll all have to be pulled up someday. If I want, I'll be able to work until I'm an old, old man."

Rockwell gazes back into his binoculars, then says, "Here we go." With that, the first stack of mines explodes: a roiling, black and orange fireball a quarter-mile across rises into the sky. A second later, a raging *crack* shudders the desert's thin, dry air, sending rumbles deep inside everyone's chest. Then, as quickly as the flame climbed from earth, it's gone, replaced by a slim, mile-high plume of gray-brown smoke.

EPILOGUE

The Furnace

END OF THE CENTURY

TO GET HERE, you've had to brush against a wasteland.

As you travel west from the glassed skyscrapers of Salt Lake City and its vertically majestic Wasatch Mountains, the earth begins to go barren and you enter the Great Salt Lake Desert, an endless-seeming plane of salt left by the receding waters of the Great Salt Lake itself. Barely 10 miles out of town, a layer of white sodium begins to tuft fence posts and sprigs of sagebrush; by 20 miles out, salt is so prevalent in the soil that even sage has difficulty growing along the shoreline. By 40 miles, patches of ground themselves are a pale, salty white, and the now dry lake bed spreads toward the curve of the earth from beneath your feet. Here, where there is no plant life at all—and birds pound across the desert's skies in a hurry to reach the mountains on the far horizon—the desert stays blindingly white all the way to the Nevada border, 130 miles distant. Standing in the center of the salt flat, you see only unvegetated soil and craggy peaks for a thousand square miles, a lifeless rind of land half as large as the State of Connecticut.

Most of the Salt Lake Desert lies inside an almost unpopulated place called Tooele (pronounced "too-*will*-a") County, Utah. For the 29,000 people who live along the desert's outskirts, it is acknowledged that the salt flat at the county's center is perhaps America's most useless place. The earth there supports little vegetation, and ground water is so thick with dissolved salts and minerals that it has been deemed poison by the U.S. government. Not everyone dislikes the place, of course. The Morton Salt Company, for example, finds the lake's saline riches perfect to package as an ice-melter for roads. And the world's rocket-car enthusiasts think it attractive as well: they gather on it twice a year, to chase the land speed record along a ten-mile strip of salt flat called the Bonneville Speedway, perhaps the most obstacle-free spot on the planet. Still, few have found value in the emptiness more than the U.S. Army. In 1941 and 1942, it scooped up 2,100 square miles of desert south of the salt flats and set it off limits forever. During the 1940s, 1950s, and 1960s, at a sage-dotted place called the Tooele Depot, the U.S. Army chose to manufacture and store 44.5 percent of our nation's toxic weapons stockpile. Now, at that same installation, a handful of miles upwind of Salt Lake City, the Department of Defense plans to burn all of it.

WHEN YOU ARRIVE at the Tooele Army Depot for a tour, you are issued a green canvas bag containing the Army's standard

M19 gas mask and three small Mark 1 injector kits. The kits are tubes the size of magic markers, and if the depot's air-monitoring sirens begin to shriek, you are to jam them force-fully against your thigh, releasing their nerve-gas antidote— atropine—along the Mark 1's retractable syringe needles and into your body. After viewing an instructional videotape on how to use the mask and injectors, you are asked to tug your mask into place so that a technician in an incense-scented room can hook an air monitor to a fitting on the mask. Then you are told to turn your head from side to side, nod up and down, roll your jaw in a circle, and, finally, jog in place. While you do this, the monitor checks to make sure no incense seeps in around the mask's seal. After three or four minutes of this— provided you pass—you are free to remove the mask, always keeping it packed in its little green bag and close at hand.

"You'll have to return that when the tour's over, of course," Craig Campbell says, pointing to my green bag as we leave the visitors' center and head toward the incinerator, two miles away. "But you can give it to me, I'll make sure it gets back safe."

Campbell, a large, shamble-walking forty-two-year-old with graying brown hair and a steel-trap mind, is the public affairs officer for what is officially called the Tooele Army Depot Chemical Demilitarization Facility (or TOCDF). As we walk to his car through the wind of a cold October afternoon, he tells me he is not part of the Army but a former high-tech writer and analyst from private industry. He was hired in 1992, and was given his current post in 1994, when, as he puts it, "Some troubles regarding the incinerator's public perception

began to crop up." As I arrive at the car, with Campbell un-
locking the passenger-side door for me, he says: "You've got to
remember the reason for this facility. It has roots in World War
II, a time when no one cared about cleaning up after the Army.
Back then, everyone was concerned with national security."

A minute later, we're rolling down an empty road, toward a
neat subdivision of house-sized bunkers on the horizon,
"igloos," made of poured concrete and covered with layers of
soil and grass. According to the Army, there are 208 igloos at
the Tooele Depot, and their arrangement stretches for more
than a square mile. Taken together, they house the depot's
chemical weapons stockpile: more than 1.2 million rockets,
bombs, shells, and land mines, carrying an estimated 27 million pounds of chemical agent, enough poison, Campbell and
the Department of Defense aver, to kill everything on earth. A
single tablespoon of one variety, called VX, would be enough
to extinguish all 600 workers currently employed at TOCDF.

During the past half-century of creating a chemical weapons
stockpile, the U.S. Army has produced two types and six subva-
rieties of toxic compounds, all of which are referred to as
"agents." Stored at the Tooele Depot are four different varieties
of mustard gas, initially used in World War 1. Called "blister
agents," all four mustard gasses kill the same way: by blistering
the eyes, skin, and mucous membrances of the lungs so completely that the tissues burst. End-stage damage from blistering
ultimately occurs in the lungs, which fill with fluid, drowning
the victim. Also stored at the depot are the other two substances, called "nerve agents." These—GB (or Sarin) and
VX—do not blister flesh, but instead attack the human nervous

system, short-circuiting nerve cell receptors and instructing a body's muscles, including its heart, to clench tightly and never release, making exposure to even trace amounts deadly unless the antidote is readily available. The difference between VX and GB is simple. VX, which was concocted by the U.S. Army in the late 1950s, is a thick, honeylike jelly that settles to the ground after being disbursed by a weapon's explosion. Once "broadcast," it can remain lethal for as long as a month, killing victims not only through inhalation but also by the tiniest brush or physical contact. Because of its long-lasting danger, VX is known as a "persistent agent." GB, on the other hand, was discovered by German insecticide studies in 1936 and turns gaseous at explosion, drifting dangerously on the air and dissipating within an hour or two. Thanks to its relatively short-term killing power, GB is called a "nonpersistent agent." In any case, a few breaths of either GB or VX—or a drop smaller than a pinhead on your skin—initiates a deadly string of symptoms that begins with sweating and drooling, then proceeds to a running nose, uncontrollable muscular twitching, nausea, vomiting, incontinence, coma, respiratory failure, and, finally, death.

Still, despite America's bounty of chemical weapons, the Department of Defense did not believe it had the program it wanted. So in 1985, after years of debate, the U.S. Congress agreed to fund a new generation of chemical arsenal, provided the more than 3.6 million shells and 70,000 tons of existing chemical agents were destroyed by January 1, 2000. Americans have never been alone in keeping these weapons, of course. Ever since the gaseous horrors of World War 1, and despite outlawing under the Geneva Protocol of 1925, at least 148 of the world's nations have maintained deterrent toxic and chemical stockpiles, just in case. (The Russian cache, for instance, is estimated at 40,000 tons of chemical and biological weapons.) And although a Chemical Weapons Convention has been drafted — mandating destruction of all agent within ten years of ratification — the convention has languished for years. To date, 160 states have agreed to the CWC in principle, but only 45 of the 65 nations required for its ratification have committed, the United States not being one of them for reasons having more to do with bipartisan congressional bickering than anything else. In 1990, the United States also agreed to a Bilateral Destruction Agreement with the former Soviet Union, but its original "total destruction" deadline of 1997 has slipped to the year 2004 — and Russia is now maintaining its stockpile as it watches the United States test different furnace technologies. So instead of noble aims, it has been the slow, leaky degradation of the existing weapons, the constantly ballooning cost of a stockpile destruction plan (up from $1.7 billion to $12 billion in a decade), and the overweening desire for a new batch of neurotoxin arms that has recently hurried the United States toward destruction of its current chemical weapons stores. Given that 44.5 percent of its stockpile now rests at the Tooele Depot, with the remainder spread across eight other depots nationwide, Tooele was selected for cleanup first.

"So far, the project here has cost $450 million," Campbell says as he steers the car near the bunkers, slowing and allowing me to examine the igloo buildings separated by gravel paths. "And that cost is only for the incinerator itself. The Army has other funds allocated for regular care and monitoring of the stockpile and bunkers — to make sure no agent is leaking."

According to the Army, there are 1,221 leaking artillery shells stored at the Tooele base right now. The majority are M55 rockets, weapons manufactured during the 1960s whose payloads of nerve agent have been corroding relentlessly through their aluminum skins. "The M55s are safe, though," Campbell says. "We've gotten them secured in air-tight storage. Obviously, we understand the seriousness of the situation."

Campbell pauses for a moment. "If we do get a leaker," he says, "we put it in an emergency overpack container. One of those." He points back, over his shoulder, toward a dented steel canister the size of a large hot tub. This emergency overpack, he explains, was not used for its usual purposes. It was drop-tested. A few years ago, Army engineers filled it with a weight similar to the weapons it would contain and sealed its lid. Then they lifted it high into the air and dropped it on vertical steel poles to find out how much damage it could sustain before springing a leak. "It never broke," Campbell says.

We continue down the road, making another turn and cresting a low hill. Ahead of us, rising like a boxy city, is the Tooele Chemical Disposal Facility. Surrounded by rectangular lab buildings, the incinerator—a plume of white steam lifting from its main smokestack—sits on a 22-acre concrete footing. Atop that footing rest 5 kilns, 33 miles of pipe, 16,000 valves and instruments, 840 miles of electrical wire, and more than 2,000 robotic tools. The Pentagon hopes that sometime in 1996, after two years of delays, the structure will be fully assembled and will have passed eighteen months of "test-burning": dry-running the furnaces with simulated chemical weapons, to make sure they are capable of destroying the stockpile without incident. Then, if all tests have been passed without question, and if the Department of Defense, the Environmental Protection Agency, and the Utah Department of Environmental Control have signed off, the incinerator will run twenty-four hours a day for the next eight years, systematically destroying the arsenal weapons-type by weapons-type in a series of dismantlings, drainings, burnings, meltings, filtrations, and reburnings. Finally, when all the chemical agents and weapons have been burned, TOCDF claims it will destroy the facility, incinerating the labs and outbuildings—even the concrete footing itself. When the job is over, the Army maintains, only water vapor, carbon dioxide smoke, and some grainy ashes will remain. The water and smoke will be free to go, the ash repackaged and buried in hazardous waste landfills.

"It's quite a project," Campbell says. "Like the pyramids or something."

UP CLOSE—AND with my gas mask and antidote injectors hooked on a belt around my waist—the Tooele Disposal Facility looks like any large-scale factory. After Campbell and I collect hard hats and safety glasses from his office, he points out the guard shack at the fence's gate. "Anyone coming or going will have to show I.D.," he says, pointing to a turnstyle behind a bulletproof glass wall. "For obvious reasons, security has to be high." We walk past, and Campbell pauses to explain a prefabricated fiberglass and steel outbuilding. "This is the treaty compliance facility," he says. "It's got a lab and some beds. When the plant is running, Russian inspectors will stay here in accordance with the bilateral agreement. They'll do sampling and analysis."

Campbell shows me TODCF's small, on-site medical center and the pair of diesel generators that exist as backup: "That way, if there's a power outage, we can bring the plant down under control." The eight stainless steel banks of the plant's air filtration system—each stands fifty feet wide and twenty feet tall—are on its far side. For safety, the facility's ventilation system exists as something called "negative air pressure." Inside the plant, giant fans pull fresh air from zones without nerve agent to areas where nerve agent will be present. Once through the agent "containment areas," the air is drawn into this filter system, where it is scoured, leached, and cleaned before being monitored for agent and released.

"There are only two ways air gets out of the plant," Campbell says. "Through the smoke stacks, where it's been burned in kilns and scrubbed by the pollution abatement system before being checked and released—or through these." Inside each filter bank, there is a prefilter, a high-efficiency filter, six charcoal filters, and another high-efficiency filter. There are also three air-monitoring sensors along each bank's airpath, so if one of the filters is compromised they can know which layer of filtration went sour. "We run six banks at a time," Campbell says, pointing. "We always have one on backup and one standing by at all times. If, somehow, agent gets detected along an airpath, we can trap and reroute it to a new, start-up bank."

He points to an inward-opening steel door ahead of us. "It won't happen with this one," he says, pointing to the entrance of the Container Handling Building, "because it's not a negative air zone. But when we get inside the actual incinerator facility, I'll show you why the doors open inward. There's 112,000 cubic feet of air moving through those filters every minute, and if you tried to open a door that swings outside, you wouldn't be strong enough to push it shut. The doors open inward because as soon as they're cracked open a wind will come tearing inside at forty miles an hour. The door will smack you as you open it, so we've installed activators and pushers on the interior walls to close the doors. That's how strong the negative air pressure is."

The Container Handling Building will be the first stop for every toxic weapon entering the Tooele incinerator. As we walk inside the enormous, aircraft hangar–sized building, I can see the floor is covered by wide tracks of stainless steel rollers. "This will be the staging area," Campbell says, "a buffer-storage warehouse that's not negative air pressure. At this point, the weapons will be inside sealed transport overpacks, so there'll be no danger of leakage." Federal and state environmental laws say transport of chemical weapons is only allowed inside sealed overpack containers—and only in daylight and during good weather. "That's why this place is here," he adds, "so we'll have a stock of them inside the building, in case a storm system comes in and prohibits any more movement of agent."

Campbell walks me to one of the containers, which has been left open to show visitors. Each one of these, he says, weighs 10,000 pounds and is made of double-walled stainless steel with a double-sealed lid. The container's interior has been configured to fit the arms of TOCDF's pneumatic lifts, so pallets of weapons can be transported from the igloos to the "chem-demil" incinerator pathway without excessive handling. "Just like inside the igloos," Campbell says, "we'll monitor the air inside each container before reopening it. If a weapon has started to leak during transit, it'll be immediately removed to a negative air-pressure area, where workers in sealed suits will make the necessary security arrangements."

Following Campbell through another door, I find we're back outside, standing in the cold Utah afternoon. Campbell points to a catwalk overhead that links the Container Handling Building to the incinerator. "That's how containers move across," he says. "It's automated, so there's some distance between the storage and live-agent areas."

"Now we're headed into a contained area," he says. "With negative air pressure and, when we get approval, the incineration of 'hot' agent." He pushes against a door handle. There's a slight pause, then a mechanical *whooosh*. Exactly as predicted, the door flies open and a newborn wind screams inside, sucked in by the air filtration system's huge fans. "That's something, huh?" Campbell says, pushing the door's activator to shut it after we have entered.

I look around the room, which Campbell calls the unpack area; it's the size of a high school gym. At one end is the sealed doorway, where the automated catwalk from the handling building enters the containment zone: a door whose size ensures a mammoth incoming gale each time it opens. There are also briefcase-sized steel boxes—air monitors—and closed-circuit video cameras across the room's floors, walls, and ceilings. "We have sixty closed-circuit cameras and sixty air monitors in this area," Campbell says. "Their alarm sounds any time agent is detected at one-fifth the time-weighted average set by the federal government." He pauses for a minute and regards the room and its soaring three-story ceiling, which is hung with yet another TV camera. "How sensitive are these monitors?" he asks. "Well, we like to say that if you filled this area with white golf balls and hid three orange ones in the pile, the monitors would detect it."

Once a load of chemical weapons enters the containment zone, its remaining time on earth is short. When the catwalk door connecting the staging and incinerator buildings has been shut, workers wearing rubber aprons, long rubber gloves, and color-coded oxygen masks attached to umbilical hoses will open the container, lift out the weapons using pneumatic tools, and move them across the floor to conveyors leading through explosion-proof, sealed doorways into the deactivation room: "The real hot zone," Campbell calls it. We walk to one of the conveyor belts. Waist high and armored, its stainless steel rollers, which are deeply grooved to cradle rockets and mortars, will carry each weapon inside the deactivation room with soundless, almost frictionless smoothness. "At this spot, human workers will use cranes to lift the munitions onto conveyor carry-ins," he says. "That's it. Once on this track, the munitions will go through there"—he points to a thick steel door—"and that's the last time they're handled or lifted. The rest is automated. Done by machines and robots."

Campbell steps behind the track, pointing out a two-foot-thick wall of steel-reinforced concrete that is shielded by more steel. It functions as a blast-impervious barrier between the unpack area where we stand and the explosive containment room, a chemical weapons factory in reverse just past the wall. Once inside, a series of machines will dismantle the weapons and siphon off their chemical agents; whole munitions will go in, only to come out as constitutent parts. "Taken together,"

Campbell says, "they're capable of handling any shape or kind of agent container or projectile in existence." The weapons drained and destroyed inside this room, he points out, were never meant to be dismantled—they were intended to be used—so today's Army, the Department of Defense, and its civilian engineers and contractors have spent an extraordinary amount of time thinking for both today's Army, which wants to destroy these things, and the Ike-era Army that invented them fifty years ago.

From tiny land mines to enormous airplane bombs to mortars to bulk storage tanks, the machined steel and vascular pipes inside of the containment room stand ready to take it all and make it safe. As tracks of conveyor rollers enter this room, they split like rail lines in a train yard, leading to a number of different devices: each built to handle its own style of weapon. When a toxic shell or bomb enters the explosive containment room, Campbell says, it goes through five "demilitarization" or "de-mil" steps. The first occurs just inside the final air lock. There, workers using remote-control arms remove the weapon's nose cones or protective sheaths. After that, sitting upright and moving along the conveyor, the projectile or tank continues down the track to a large table that looks something like a guillotine standing above a Lazy Susan turntable. "Currently, the machine is set up for the demilitarization of 105-millimeter mortars," Campbell says. "The projectile will enter here and go through a series of four more de-mil steps."

Once on the table, another remote-control arm will remove the explosive fuze from the projectile. Then, at step three, the small explosive charges beneath the fuze, called "boosters," which set off a vaporizing "burster" charge running the length of the toxic payload, are mechanically removed. These are sent by trap door to a 2,500° Fahrenheit "deactivation furnace" beneath the floor, where they are burned without explosion. Step four removes the burster itself, which is then sent to another machine for "shearing" into bits before also being dropped into the deactivation furnace. Once the explosive danger has been removed, the remaining projectile and its payload of poison is robotically lifted and placed in a stable box back on the conveyor belt. The projectile then rolls down the conveyor to another room, the munitions processing bay, where its chemical payload is siphoned off and pumped into a two-story incinerator while the projectile is sheared up and sent to a scrap iron furnace. Using aerosol nozzles to convert the syrupy chemicals into a mist of droplets, the toxic agents enter the furnace, which burns at 2,700° Fahrenheit, breaking the compounds into less toxic materials like sulfur dioxide and hydrochloric acid. After that, the smoky residue passes through a series of afterburn kilns and filters, which further break down the poison by-products until all that is left is carbon dioxide, nitrogen, nitrous oxide, and water vapor, which can then be returned to the environment through the facility's five smokestacks, each of which is topped by air monitors—for last-ditch protection.

THE TOOELE INCINERATOR is not the first toxic weapons furnace the Army has ever built. In 1985, the Department of Defense and its civilian contractor Raytheon built a prototype for Tooele on a remote South Pacific atoll called the Johnston Islands, 800 miles southwest of Hawaii. That facility, called

JACADS—for Johnston Atoll Chemical Agent Disposal System—has been testing different incineration processes with the
small on-island stockpile since 1991, and its record remains far
from spectacular. In January 1993, for instance, a fire broke out
in the JACADS explosive containment room, and although no
toxic gas was released into the atmosphere, the blaze burned
out of control for hours due to an insufficient sprinkler system.
As the fire continued to rage, managers at JACADS had to
switch off the air filtration system because its suction kept
flames fanned. After that, because ventilation was off line, the
incinerator building became so choked with smoke that closed-
circuit cameras inside could not see that a stock of partially dismantled weapons nearby was threatened. Ultimately, two
JACADS workers in sealed suits had to go into the containment room and douse the fire by hand. Three years later, the
Army still speculates on what started the blaze.

There have been other problems as well. The JACADS project manager's logs, in fact, must read more like the lab reports
of a failing chemistry student than a $250 million federal pro-
ject. There have been clogged pipes and broken meters, faulty
circuit breakers, and a recurring inability to get the agent furnace to burn at a constant 2,700°. There have also been
episodes where blobs of contaminated shell casings—melted to
sticky steel dollops inside the scrap iron furnace—have clung
to conveyor bents, cooled to hardness, and fallen from the line,
blocking other passages. When a bit of burster charge exploded
unexpectedly, blowing a fist-sized hole in a deactivation furnace wall, the Army merely installed a thicker furnace rather
than re-examining the entire process. By the Army's own admission, there have also been at least three cases when live

agent has been released into the atmosphere. On an isolated, Pacific Ocean atoll, the vast, unpeopled sea is an insurance buffer that few humans will die. At the Tooele site, forty miles upwind of Salt Lake City and 1.5 million souls, no such margin of error exists.

FORTY MILES EAST of the Tooele Depot, behind a desk at his secondhand appliance store in the town of Lehi, Steve Jones knows all about the problems at JACADS and TODCF. A former inspector general for the Army and the fired safety director at the Tooele Depot, the sturdy, black-haired Jones can only shake his head when the design flaws in both incinerators are mentioned. "You know what it's going to take to shut TODCF down?" he says. "People are going to have to die. By then the Department of Defense will have spent close to a billion dollars for an incinerator it can't use. That's how screwed up the Tooele Facility is."

Jones's story is a complex one. A former chief nuclear and chemical weapons inspector for the Army's Inspector General, he had a spotless record and was twice awarded the Army's highest safety medal, the only man ever to be so honored. Then, in 1994, he was lured from his job to Tooele. Jones and the Tooele facility seemed a perfect match, since he had been the person inspecting the Johnston Atoll facility. "They wowed me with a good salary and told me everything at Tooele was squared away and on track," he says. "They'd been telling the Pentagon the same thing: all was proceeding to plan."

He began making enemies his first day at Tooele. On June 27, he shut down a storage building because workers without safety masks and proper equipment were renovating its inside, breathing airborne asbestos. The following day, during a routine inspection of a lab, he closed it after finding technicians were not wearing protective gear when handling 1,500 test tubes of diluted nerve agent—and that they were venting the opened tubes directly into the atmosphere.

Then, anticipating an inspector general's visit in mid-August, Jones conducted his own audit of the incinerator. "I couldn't believe it," he says. "By the time it was over, I had a 300-page report. I could cite 119 specific safety violations and more than 2,000 engineering and operating problems, like valves not working, flanges not working, unmarked hydrogen and electrical lines next to each other. There were hundreds of accidents waiting to happen. Hell, I spotted 200 to 300 OSHA violations *alone*." He submitted his report to supervisors, who have since left the facility, and was told: "Never put anything negative about the plant in writing again."

By then, Jones knew his job was on the line. Especially after the inspector general's visit—and an unadmitted tour by a private engineering consultant, MITRE, in May 1994—confirmed Jones's findings and identified even more problems. "The MITRE report listed 3,019 design deficiencies," Jones says, "and more than 150 of them were identified as 'imminent and catastrophic.' I couldn't believe it. Either the Army and the Pentagon hadn't been told what was going on, or the Department of Defense was going to ram this project through, regardless of safety concerns."

With three different reports now listing thousands of design flaws, EG&G, the government contractor that built TODCF, demanded that Jones sign a document stating the problems cited in the MITRE study and elsewhere posed an "acceptable risk" and that no corrective steps were necessary. "That was when I knew I was gone," he says. "I did a check on the MITRE report's findings, and I realized that fixing all the broken valves and flanges and things would take at least a year, so I said: I'm in a lose-lose situation. No, I won't sign. I was fired the next day."

At the center of Jones's decision was the concept of "acceptable risk," which Jones says is a fact of life in the U.S. military. "It means they accept the idea there'll be fatalities," he says. "Their line of thinking is: when you charge a hill in combat there will be casualties; soldiers are going to die. But it seemed to me you can't translate acceptable risk to civilian populations. The people of Lehi and the Salt Lake valley aren't soldiers, they're private citizens. And thousands of them could die because the Army wants to turn a policy for soldiers onto the population. I wouldn't have any part of it. Think about it. By acknowledging acceptable risk, the Army is *admitting* people will probably die."

"For the three days after I was fired," he says, "I made phone calls, trying to get my claims heard along the proper channels. I called the Pentagon, the Army, the Department of Defense's Office of Chem De-mil, OSHA, the EPA . . . I called everybody." He pauses, stands from the desk, and strolls across his office to the shop's soda machine, extracting two orange soft drinks. As he returns to the desk, he says, "By the second day, I knew I was really hot. My calls to the Army were being routed directly to security. I was going to get nowhere. They had Tooele on the tracks, and it was going to roll."

Jones went to the newspapers and television stations, laying out the situation and stating his case. Like most people who understand the situation, he said, he agreed that the chemical weapons had to be destroyed—that wasn't the issue. "It was the *way* they'd chosen to destroy the weapons that remains the problem," Jones says. Then came the threatening telephone calls. "We changed our phone number," he says, "but I still feared that so-called accidental car wreck the callers kept referring to. I stayed pretty close to home." Before long, the Lehi police had decided Jones was under terrorist threat, possibly from his own government, and they patrolled his house twenty-four hours a day. Slowly, the media attention went away. Jones filed a wrongful termination suit, which has been repeatedly stalled in court by EG&G. ("They'll make it up to me—but not until after the incinerator goes hot, if that ever happens," he says.)

In early 1995, Jones and his wife, Diana, purchased the appliance store they now run, and he says he plans to stay in the area. "This is a nice, middle-class town," he says. "The people are honest. They're Mormons, so they're raising big families. They pay in cash."

When asked why he stays, he smiles. "I don't think TODCF will ever run hot," he says. "I think somebody will die first. I just hope it's only one or two workers—and that the accident takes place inside a containment area."

And if it doesn't? What if, as it appears increasingly probable, the Army and EG&G will get the plant certified and running?

"You want a worst-case?" Jones asks, tossing his empty soda can into the trash. "The Army loves to talk about downwind hazards from accidental releases of GB—you know, Sarin. It's nonpersistent, like water. It evaporates quickly. But what about thick, oily VX? What if there's an explosion at the plant? What if a bunker fire takes out some bulk containers? What if incompletely burned VX goes up the stack? Well, the downwind hazard is forty miles. And once that VX is in the air, it's like an oil mist—it has to come down. And it won't only hit people. It'll land on roads and houses and cars and farms and the Great Salt Lake itself. Even rescue workers will have to be dressed against it. We're talking deaths of *biblical* proportions. And all because an incinerator is behind schedule and over budget."

A FEW DAYS later, Craig Campbell hosts me once again at the incinerator. This time, I've been ushered into the incinerator's control room, an eerily quiet place full of computer monitors and closed-circuit TVs. From here, we'll watch a test burn of simulant rockets in the explosive containment room. All told, it's a pretty rinky-dink affair. Because there are no test projectiles shaped like the rockets, technicians stand inside the containment room, sliding burlap sacks of the chemical weapons simulants hexachloroethane and monochlorobenzine down chutes into the double-airlock doors and the deactivation furnace beyond, where the chemicals are burned and the exhaust air monitored.

As in the unpack area, there are TV cameras trained through view ports into the kilns. As each simulated rocket falls into the flame, for a split-second, the burlap and chemicals flare like Fourth of July fireworks. Then they are gone, immolated by the furnace's 1,100° heat. Roughly twenty-four minutes later, the ash from the burlap will roll out of the incinerator and into a cooling area, just as shell casings may do sometime in the near (or not so near) future, the Army one step closer to its new generation of chemical weapons.

"*Overzealous.* That's the word most often used about Steve Jones," Campbell says as we stand in the darkened command center and watch fiery blasts on TV monitors.

From behind us, an alarm sounds. Turning around, I see a technician at a bank of computer keyboards and color readouts that track happenings inside the furnace. He hits a few keystrokes. "It was nothing," he says. "The oxygen level inside the kiln dropped a little. Not enough to affect the burn. There wouldn't have been a stack release."

I turn back to the TV, and the alarm sounds again. The technician silences it by tapping a few more buttons. The warning sounds again, and as the technician hits a few more buttons, I turn back to look at the control room's main console, where a virtual-reality image of the incinerator's exterior shows on a large video screen. At the top of the screen, a computer-generated plume of white smoke drifts on the breeze. An on-screen gauge says the wind is blowing at eleven miles per hour to the northeast, toward Salt Lake City and more than a million people.

Behind me, the alarm sounds once more.

ACKNOWLEDGMENTS

FIRST I NEED to thank my children, James and Anna, whose births in 1993 and 1994 got me thinking about the intersections of past and present and the inseparable relationship they maintain, even when we're not watching.

Also, I need to thank my wife, Janet. For her love, bravery, and countless acts of kindness, I've dedicated this book to her.

And there are the support teams. Magazine editors, friends, neighbors, and family members who deserve a thank you. A few standouts: Mark Bryant at *Outside* magazine and Charles McGrath, Robert Gottlieb, and James Albrecht at *The New Yorker*. And John P. Wiley, Jr., Don Moser, and Alison McLean at *Smithsonian*. Plus Alan Burdick at *The New York Times Magazine* and, finally, David Zinczenko, Steve Perrine, and all the folks at *Men's Health*. I'd also be remiss if I didn't thank Marshall Sella and Will Dana, both of whom helped with patient and precise listenings to whole passages from this text. Also thanks to Ed and Suzanne Chitwood, Grice and Ellie White-ley, and Tom and Cheelie Payne for their support, advice, and friendship to me and my family. Finally, a thanks larger than can be accurately expressed goes to my parents, James and Joan Webster in Chicago, and Janet's folks, Roger and Jean Chisholm in Little Rock. My father especially added to the fac-tual shaping of the final product.

FOR ALFRED NOBEL information, I need to thank Bryan Di Salvatore, whose "Vehement Fire" story in *The New Yorker* (April 27, 1987) served as a source, as did the book *Alfred No-bel: Dynamite King—Architect of Peace*, by Hertha E. Pauli (L. B. Fisher, 1942).

Concerning my chapter about World War I, I need to specif-ically thank the *démineurs*, plus Lisa Chase, whose exquisite French speaking helped decode the French Interior Ministry's intentions to keep me out. In Paris, my gratitude goes to Eric Merle and Larry Bond, as well as Lionel Le Clei and Phillipe LeClerc at the Interior Ministry. I need to say a big thank you, also, to Major Shaw and all the military history professors and instructors at the Army College at West Point, New York. Four books proved especially useful during research: *A History of the Great War* by C.R.M.F. Cruttwell (Academy, 1992); *The Face of Battle* by John Keegan (Viking, 1976); *War* by Ludwig Renn (A. L. Burt/Dodd Mead, 1929); and *Portraits of France* by Robert Daley (Little, Brown, 1991).

For my Russia chapter, thanks go to Lydia Heiden at Rahim (Intourist) Tours, plus, of course, Victor Stepanov, Valery Shtrykov, and Margarita Efremenkova in Volgograd. Also to the Children of Stalingrad Organization for wonderful background information, and to Karin Hübner and ZDF television. For this chapter, three sources proved invaluable: *The Second World War* by John Keegan (Viking, 1989); *Entscheidung Stalingrad* by Guido Knopp (Bertlesmann, 1992); and "Stalingrad: Letters from the Dead" by Timothy W. Ryback which appeared in *The New Yorker* (February 1, 1993).

For my chapter on the Nevada Test Site, I must thank Ted Taylor, author/photographer Robert Del Tredici, Carole Gallagher, whose book *American Ground Zero* (MIT Press, 1993) and words of encouragement were of prodigious help, Jim Werner and the DOE, (Preston) Jay Truman and Steve Erickson of the Downwinders, Robert Schaffer of Public Policy Communications and the Tides Foundation, Arjun Makhijani of the Institute for Energy and Environmental Research, Steve Schwartz and the Brookings Institution, Glenn Campbell and the entire Secrecy Oversight Council, Ursula Hull at the University of Virginia, and, of course, Jim Boyer. As background resources, two books other than Carole Gallagher's were especially enlightening: *The Making of the Atomic Bomb* by Richard Rhodes (Simon & Schuster, 1986) and *The Curve of Binding Energy* by John McPhee (Farrar, Straus and Giroux, 1975).

In Vietnam, it's impossible not to thank Vu Binh. Also, Professor Tran Van Dinh, who proofread the chapter and, earlier, made my initial introduction to Do Cong Minh, director of the

Vietnamese Foreign Press Office in Hanoi. I need to thank Rose Kernochen and Lauren Goldstein of *Details* magazine, who helped me get to Southeast Asia and Bobby Muller of the Vietnam Veterans of America Foundation. Also thank yous to Dr. Ho Hen Van; Randy Wayne White; Gary Roush of the Vietnam Helicopter Pilots Association; Khe Sanh Marine Joe Fulgenetti of Fredericksburg, Virginia; Vietnam authority Al Farrell of the Virginia Military Institute; the folks at the Aviation Museum at Fort Rucker, Alabama; and the U.S.-Indochina Reconciliation Project in New York. Especially helpful resources for this chapter were *Vietnam: A History* by Stanley Karnow (Viking, 1983), *The Wars of America*, Volume II, by Robert Leckie (HarperCollins, 1992), and *Dispatches* by Michael Herr (Knopf, 1977).

In Kuwait, a big "Thanks, Dudes" goes out to Rocky Rockwell, Bruce Halstead, Walt McCauley, Earl Hine, Fred DiBella, and all of the CMS crew who made my trip possible. Also thanks to Phillip Archer of Cairo, Egypt; to Bobby Muller (again) and Jody Williams at VVoAF in Washington, to Steve Goose at the Arms Project for Human Rights Watch, Steve Askin in Washington, D.C. (assembler of amazing land-mine data), Senator Patrick Leahy, Tim Rieser of the U.S. Senate Appropriations Committee, Patrick Blagden of the United Nations, humanitarian physician Dr. Kevin Cahill; defense industry expert Greg Fetter, and Eric Nash and Jack Rosenthal at *The New York Times Magazine*. A wonderful resource for this chapter was the book *Crusade* by Rick Atkinson (Houghton Mifflin, 1993).

In Utah, thank you to Tim Thomas and the U.S. Army and

all at the Tooele Depot. Also to Adam Horowitz at *Outside* magazine, whose extra research was a big help. Thanks, too, to Craig Williams at the Chemical Weapons Working Group, Terry Tempest Williams in Salt Lake City, and Scott Carrier and Howard Berkes of National Public Radio, and also to Robert Poole, Jennifer Reek, and Bill Graves at *National Geographic Magazine.*

I must also thank Pat Hass, who brought me into Pantheon's fold and scoured my final manuscript sentence by sentence. Also Julian Bach, a literary agent whose gentlemanly sensibilities understood that my need to write this book was more important than a big-dollar deal (and you owe me a big "I told you so"). I also must thank my attorney, Edward Lewis of Jenner & Block/Chicago.

My biggest thanks must go to this book's editor, Dan Frank, who kept our overall idea always fixed in his mind, regularly stepping in to focus my words into the tightest, best-reading chapters possible. Thanks also to Claudine O'Hearn at Pantheon.